ANXIETY
Third edition

Anxiety is a complex phenomenon and a central feature of many psychological problems. This thoroughly revised third edition of *Anxiety* has been updated to include astonishing developments in the clinical implementation of knowledge about anxiety. In particular, this edition updates the reader with:

- a new chapter on health anxiety;
- a fully updated chapter on obsessive-compulsive disorders, including the concept of mental contamination and the causes of obsessions;
- an account of advances in therapeutic techniques.

Unique in its combination of an introduction to the subject with comprehensive coverage of the latest developments in research and practice, this book provides an excellent breadth and depth of coverage, which all practising and trainee clinical psychologists will find extremely informative.

Stanley Rachman is a clinical researcher, specializing in psychopathology and psychological therapy. He is currently Professor Emeritus at the Institute of Psychiatry, King's College London and the University of British Columbia, Vancouver. His other publications include *The Treatment of Obsessions*, *Fear of Contamination*, *Panic Disorder* (with Padmal de Silva), and *Obsessive–Compulsive Disorder* (with Padmal de Silva).

Anxiety

Third Edition

Stanley Rachman

Psychology Press
Taylor & Francis Group
LONDON AND NEW YORK

Third edition published 2013
by Psychology Press
27 Church Road, Hove, East Sussex BN3 2FA

Simultaneously published in the USA and Canada
by Psychology Press
711 Third Avenue, New York, NY 10017

Psychology Press is an imprint of the Taylor & Francis Group, an informa business

First edition published by Psychology Press 1998
Second edition published by Psychology Press 2004

British Library Cataloguing in Publication Data

A catalogue record for this book is available from the British Library

Library of Congress Cataloging-in-Publication Data
Rachman, Stanley.
Anxiety / Stanley Rachman. – 3rd Edition.
pages cm
1. Anxiety. 2. Anxiety disorders. I. Title.
RC531.R334 2013
616.85'22–dc23
2012042676

ISBN: 978–0–415–69707–1 (hbk)
ISBN: 978–0–415–69708–8 (pbk)
ISBN: 978–0–203–55449–4 (ebk)

Typeset in Palatino
by Keystroke, Station Road, Codsall, Wolverhampton

Printed and bound by CPI Group (UK) Ltd, Croydon, CR0 4YY

Contents

Series preface   vii
Introduction to the third edition   ix
Introduction to the second edition   xi

1   The nature of anxiety   1
2   Fear, anxiety and avoidance   13
3   Influences on anxiety   29
4   Anxiety, attention, perception, memory and emotional
    processing   41
5   Theories of anxiety   61
6   Specific phobias and the conditioning theory of fear   77
7   Panic and anxiety   93
8   Agoraphobia   121
9   Obsessions and compulsions   127
10 Health anxiety disorders   149
11 Social anxiety   171
12 Generalized anxiety disorder   183
13 Post-traumatic stress disorder (PTSD)   191

Some concluding remarks   205
Suggested reading   207
References   209
Index   231

Series preface

Clinical Psychology: A Modular Course was designed to overcome the problems faced by the traditional textbook in conveying what psychological disorders are really like. All the books in the series, written by leading scholars and practitioners in the field, can be read as stand-alone texts, but they will also integrate with the other modules to form a comprehensive resource in clinical psychology. Students of psychology, medicine, nursing and social work, as well as busy practitioners in many professions, often need an accessible but thorough introduction to how people experience anxiety, depression, addiction or other disorders, how common they are, and who is most likely to suffer from them, as well as up-to-date research evidence on the causes and available treatments. The series will appeal to those who want to go deeper into the subject than the traditional textbook will allow, and base their examination answers, research, projects, assignments or practical decisions on a clearer and more rounded appreciation of the clinical and research evidence.

Chris R. Brewin

Other titles in this series:

Depression, Second Edition
Constance Hammen and Edward Watkins

Stress and Trauma
Patricia A. Resick

Childhood Disorders, Second Edition
Philip C. Kendall and Jonathan S. Comer

Schizophrenia
Max Birchwood and Chris Jackson

Eating and Weight Disorders
Carlos M. Grilo

Personality Disorders
Paul M. G. Emmelkamp and Jan Henk Kamphuis

Addictions, Second Edition
Maree Teesson, Wayne Hall, Heather Proudfoot and Louisa Degenhardt

Introduction to the third edition

A number of important developments in the study of anxiety have taken place since the early 2000s, and the findings are being incorporated into clinical practice. The most remarkable – indeed astonishing – application of the new knowledge and techniques was undertaken by the UK government in 2007. Recognizing that the provision of psychological treatment in the National Health Service (NHS) was insufficient and unsatisfactory, with long waiting lists and poor standards, it was decided to adopt the National Institute for Health and Clinical Excellence (NICE) guidelines for treating anxiety disorders and depression. The treatment recommended for anxiety disorders is cognitive behaviour therapy (CBT), but there was a serious shortage of trained therapists and therefore an extraordinarily ambitious training scheme was introduced in 2007. The aim was to reduce the waiting times for a psychological assessment and possible treatment of anxiety and depression from six months to two weeks, and improve the quality of therapy by using the evidence-based treatments recommended by NICE.

A large sum of money was set aside for training 8,000 new therapists, starting with 3,000 in the first three years. An interim report on the progress of the programme, Improving Access to Psychological Therapies (IAPT), was published by a major contributor, Professor David M. Clark, in 2012. Over 3,600 therapists had been trained by the midpoint of the programme and 'more than 300,000 patients are being treated annually ... clinical and employment related outcomes are generally in line with expectation' (Clark 2012).

On the research side, useful progress has been made in enhancing our understanding of anxiety disorders, notably post-traumatic stress disorder (PTSD), social phobia, obsessive compulsive disorders and health anxiety. Accordingly, a new chapter (10), on health anxiety disorders, has been added and Chapter 9 on obsessive-compulsive disorders has been expanded. Interest in a number of topics included in the earlier editions has faded and hence they were truncated or deleted.

Improvements in therapeutic techniques have been deduced from the prevailing cognitive theories of these disorders, numbers of controlled treatment trials have been completed and others are under way. Increased attention is being paid to the dissemination of the new findings and techniques, and there are many attempts to refine and shorten the amount of time and effort needed to carry out the treatment procedures.

The improvements in developing and testing refined treatment techniques and the efforts put into improving dissemination are welcome, but it is hoped that the need for basic research will not be neglected by the current emphasis on clinical applications.

S. Rachman
Vancouver, 2013

Introduction to
the second edition

Advances in the understanding and treatment of anxiety disorders have made it necessary to revise and expand this book. During the past ten years, several new theories of psychopathology have been published and eight of them deal with the anxiety disorders. Some of them are causal theories – unusual in clinical psychology – and all of them incorporate cognitive concepts. The theories are increasingly specific and most provide platforms for the derivation of specific methods of treatment. The evaluation of theories and treatments is an unavoidably lengthy and demanding process, but several provisional conclusions are permissible.

The basic science deals with the psychology of anxiety, but the current emphasis on applied science, on the nature and treatment of disorders of anxiety, overshadows the basic research. The preoccupation with anxiety disorders, and the pressure to master these distressing problems, are understandable, but have tilted the balance from basic to applied research. However, the interplay between basic and applied research is a two-way process that benefits both. Advances in understanding the phenomena and mechanisms of anxiety disorders help to illuminate fundamental psychological processes. The expansion of understanding of the emotion of fear was largely the result of clinical research. An excellent example of the interplay is now taking place in current analyses of the intriguing disturbances of memory that are so conspicuous in post-traumatic stress disorder (PTSD). Intensive studies of the clinical phenomena have expanded our conceptions of memory processes.

S. Rachman
Vancouver, 2003

The nature of anxiety 1

The nature of anxiety is defined and illustrated by case examples. The similarities and differences between anxiety and fear are described. The main types of fear are set out and the concept of anxiety disorders is elucidated.

Since the mid-1960s, research on anxiety has accelerated and the publication of books and journal articles on the subject continues to increase. Specialized clinics for dealing with anxiety disorders have been introduced and self-help groups established in many parts of the world. In England, a momentous expansion of psychotherapy services for people suffering from anxiety disorders was introduced in 2007.

All of this growth is justified because anxiety is one of the most troubling and pervasive emotions, and large numbers of people are distressed by inappropriate or excessive anxiety. In part, the steep increase in interest was prompted by the decision of the American Psychiatric Association (APA) committee responsible for preparing a new diagnostic system in the *Diagnostic and Statistical Manual of Mental Disorders* (DSM) to create a separate category for anxiety disorders, and to introduce clear definitions and criteria for diagnosing these disorders (Barlow 2002; Norton *et al.* 1995). The definitions and criteria are open to some criticism, and hence the manual is revised regularly, but it is disarming that the total number of 'mental disorders' increases with each revision. The DSM is not an exclusively scientific and research enterprise, and is used for insurance purposes as well. For example, in the United States, it is not easy to obtain insurance cover for the treatment of psychological problems that are not included in the manual and/or do not have a DSM coding number.

The introduction of the DSM classification system was a major advance on the chaos that prevailed prior to 1980, but the scheme has shortcomings. It encourages the unfortunate idea that all problems with anxiety are pathological, are indeed *mental disorders*. The full title of the DSM scheme is *The Diagnostic and Statistical Manual of Mental Disorders*.

This book is a description and psychological analysis of the phenomena of anxiety. The therapeutic implications of current knowledge and theorizing are analysed because anxiety is a central feature of many psychological problems, including those that were formerly called 'neuroses'.

Anxiety disorders are distressing, often disabling and costly. Large-scale surveys carried out in the United States in recent years led to the conclusion that 'anxiety disorders represent the single largest mental health problem in the country' (Barlow 2002: 22). If they are left untreated, anxiety disorders can become chronic. Affected people require and use many specialized services, and affected men are four times as likely as non-sufferers to be chronically unemployed (Leon *et al*. 1995). The rates of alcoholism and drug abuse are elevated among sufferers.

The study of anxiety was invigorated by the infusion of cognitive concepts and analyses. One of the earliest and most influential contributions was made by A. T. Beck (Beck 1976, 2005; Beck and Emery 1985), whose writings on depression in the 1970s were timely and very important. Paradoxically, the extension of cognitive ideas into the study of anxiety and its disorders has been even more successful and more quickly successful than the original work on depression. The introduction of the cognitive theory of panic by Clark (1986) and the cognitive analysis of obsessive-compulsive disorders by Salkovskis (1985) spawned a profusion of new ideas and applications. Virtually all contemporary psychological discussions of anxiety incorporate the cognitive view.

Anxiety is an intriguing and complex phenomenon that lends itself to cognitive analyses because it involves the interplay of vigilance, attention, perception, reasoning and memory – the very meat of cognitive processing. Moreover, many of these operations take place at a non-conscious level.

Psychologists have an excellent reason for pursuing their interest in anxiety because it turns out that they are 'good at it', and have developed demonstrably effective techniques for reducing unadaptive, distressing anxiety. It is one of the major achievements of modern clinical psychology.

Advances in understanding anxiety have led to important changes in the larger subject of psychopathology, and have given rise to the development of effective methods of treatment. In all of this, the mighty debate about the relative importance of biological and psychological influences on anxiety rumbles on.

Defining anxiety

Anxiety is a tense unsettling anticipation of a threatening but formless event; a feeling of uneasy suspense. It is a negative affect (feeling) so closely related to fear that in many circumstances the two terms are used interchangeably. Fear also is a combination of tension and unpleasant anticipation, but distinctions can be made between the causes, duration and maintenance of fear and of anxiety. Strictly, the term *fear* is used to describe an emotional reaction to a perceived danger, to a threat that is identifiable, such as a poisonous snake. Most fear reactions are intense and have the quality of an emergency. The person's level of arousal is sharply elevated. However, feelings of anxiety persist for lengthy periods and can nag away 'at the back of one's mind' for days, weeks or months.

Fear has a specific focus. Typically, it is episodic and recedes or ceases when the danger is removed from the person, or the person from the danger. In this sense, fear is determined by perceivable events or stimuli. The perceived source of the danger may be accurately or inaccurately identified; or correctly identified, but wrongly evaluated. The fear may be rational or irrational. Intense but irrational fears are termed *phobias*, as in claustrophobia (intense fear of enclosed spaces), snake phobia, and so on.

When feeling *anxious*, the person has difficulty in identifying the cause of the uneasy tension or the nature of the anticipated event or disaster. The emotion can be puzzling for the person experiencing it. In its purest form, anxiety is diffuse, objectless, unpleasant and persistent. Unlike fear, it is not so obviously determined. Usually it is unpredictable and uncontrollable. The rise and decline of fear tends to be limited in time and in space, whereas anxiety tends to be pervasive and persistent, with uncertain points of onset and offset. It seems to be present, as if in the background, almost all of the time. 'I constantly feel as if something dreadful is going to happen.' Anxiety is a state of heightened vigilance rather than an emergency reaction. Fear and anxiety are marked by elevated arousal – subjective and/or physiological arousal. Fear is more likely to be intense and brief; it is provoked by triggers and is circumscribed. Anxiety tends to be shapeless, grating along at a lower level of intensity; its onset and offset are difficult to time, and it lacks clear borders. Anxiety is not a lesser and pale form of fear; and in many instances, it is more difficult to tolerate than fear. It is unpleasant, unsettling, persistent, pervasive and draining. Intense and prolonged anxiety can be disabling and even destructive.

It is illustrated by these two examples of people suffering from anxiety, and one of a person suffering from a phobia. Anne complained of being tense, edgy and apprehensive. She awoke each morning with a feeling that something awful but elusive was about to happen. This feeling of dread usually persisted into the late morning, accompanied by uncomfortable bodily sensations such as tremors, nausea, fast pulse and shallow breathing. It was unsettling and tiring. In the first weeks of her experience of this anxiety, she spent a lot of time and energy trying to understand why she was feeling so poorly, struggling to identify what was troubling her. The elusive and puzzling quality of her dread was an added source of discomfort.

Anne made a clear distinction between this daily anxiety and the fear she had experienced when encountering a snake in the countryside. Her reaction to the snake was sharp, intense and focused, but quickly subsided when the snake scurried away into the undergrowth. She experienced strong bodily sensations, especially a rapidly racing heart, but recognized the threat and felt no puzzlement.

Brian worried incessantly about his health, constantly scanning his body for external or internal signs of trouble, and frequently sought medical advice. He dreaded the possibility of illness or injury, and often felt that 'something' was seriously wrong. Brian was careful to avoid sources of real or imagined infection, restricted his diet, and lifted or carried objects with deliberate care. He recognized that he had an excellent health record, and was all the more puzzled by this intrusive and disturbing anxiety about his well-being. Brian was unable to dampen or stifle the continuing feelings of dread. He described episodes of fear, such as his intense but circumscribed and brief reactions to near-accidents on the road, and made a clear distinction between these fearful events and his pervasive anxiety about his health.

A young horticulturalist sought help because her intense, circumscribed fear of spiders was interfering with her work. She was so frightened of encountering spiders that she was unable to work alone in the gardens. The fear was so intense and disabling that it qualified for the term *phobia*. She had no other fears, anxiety or psychological problems. The fear had a specific identifiable focus and was episodically evoked by contact with the threatening stimulus.

It is easier to distinguish between fear and anxiety in theory than in practice. Distinctions between fear and anxiety based on the focus of threat can be blurred in clinical conditions. For example, episodes of acute fear, such as panic, tend to be followed by a mixture of the fear and prolonged anxiety. Episodes of panic leave a residue of anxiety. There is no distinct transition from fear to anxiety, and at times it is not possible to distinguish between the two. Although panic is one of the purest expressions of fear, the triggers of episodes of panic are not always immediately discernible. The relationships between fear and anxiety can be complex. Anxiety often follows fear (as in the anxiety that one might panic again and lose control), but repeated experiences of anxiety can in turn generate fears.

Clinicians and patients devote considerable time and effort to unravelling the cause or causes of the person's anxiety, precisely because of the uncertainty or indeterminacy of the sources of the

TABLE 1.1

Similarities between fear and anxiety

- Elevated arousal
- Negative affect
- Accompanied by bodily sensations
- Tense apprehensiveness
- Uneasiness

TABLE 1.2

Differences between fear and anxiety

Fear	Anxiety
- Specific focus of threat	- Source of threat is elusive
- Understandable connection between threat and fear	- Uncertain connection between anxiety and threat
- Usually episodic	- Pervasive uneasiness
- Persistent	- Can be objectless
- Circumscribed tension	- Cues for anxiety can be elusive
- Identifiable threat	- Persistent
- Provoked by threat cues	- Uncertain offset
- Declines with removal of threat	- Without clear borders
- Offset is clear	- Threat seldom imminent
- Circumscribed focus of threat	- Tension, but no sense of emergency
- Imminent threat	- Bodily sensations of vigilance
- Quality of an emergency	- Puzzling qualities
- Bodily sensations of an emergency	
- Rational quality	

threat. It is assumed by both patient and therapist that there are identifiable causes of anxiety to be found and that these causes are likely to be of considerable significance. Insofar as they are successful in identifying the cause of the patient's apprehensiveness, the definition should change from anxiety to fear, from an unknown source to a focused trigger.

Matters are complicated by the fact that fear/anxiety can be caused by external cues of danger or by internal threats, which tend to be particularly elusive. Furthermore, qualifiers are often introduced when describing different types of anxiety, such as generalized anxiety, unconscious anxiety, free-floating anxiety, and so forth. Earlier hopes that fear and anxiety could be teased apart by physiological analyses of the two states have not been fulfilled, and even the types of behaviour associated with fear and with anxiety (especially avoidance) are not easily distinguishable. Fear and anxiety are both accompanied by bodily sensations, notably muscle tightness, pounding heart, and so forth, but there are some differences in the sensations and subjective discomfort experienced in the two states. The bodily sensations most frequently reported in dangerously frightening military contexts are pounding heart, sweating, a dry mouth and trembling; and the sensations frequently reported by patients with anxiety disorders are dizziness, chest pain and faintness (McMillan and Rachman 1988).

The differences between fear and anxiety are most evident in extreme cases. Sharp and brief fearful reactions to a poisonous snake are different from the pervasive and persistent uneasiness experienced as a result of a disturbed personal relationship. Leaving aside extreme illustrations, however, fear and anxiety often blend in everyday language as in clinical practice. For example, the terms *social anxiety* and *social phobia* are used interchangeably to refer to the same psychological problem – intense discomfort when under social scrutiny, and the subsequent avoidance of social gatherings. The term *anxiety* is also used to describe problems such as public speaking anxiety, and sexual anxiety, even though the focus of the concern is identifiable. The use of the terms fear and anxiety is not always consistent with the definitional distinction made between fear, which has a specific focus; and anxiety, in which there is no such focus.

A number of common assumptions made about the distinctions between fear and anxiety repay consideration. Although psychoanalytic and academic writers differ on almost all important aspects of emotion, many of them share the view that useful distinctions can be made between fear and anxiety. An assumption common to many different points of view, but not necessarily correct, is the idea that anxiety is potentially reducible to fear. If the cause of the anxiety is potentially knowable and the focus is identifiable, then by diligent work, therapeutic or not, it should be possible to convert puzzling anxiety into clear-cut fear. Associated with this assumption, and sometimes contingent on it, is the idea that fear is more manageable than anxiety. Hence it is often assumed that reducing a state of anxiety to a state of fear is a progressive step. Also associated with the idea that anxiety is theoretically reducible to fear is the notion that anxiety is not-fear simply by reason of default; that is, we have anxiety when the focus of fear is elusive.

There is no universally accepted definition of 'anxiety' (Barlow 2002) and some dissatisfaction with the way in which the term is used. In addition to the several meanings of anxiety in technical language, the word also has several meanings in common language, ranging from dread to endeavour or eagerness. For example, 'I am anxious to go to the new production of the opera.'

At least two of the commonly recognized features of fear/anxiety, a state of elevated arousal and negative affect, require comment. In most circumstances, these features are indisputably part of a fear reaction, but fear can also have a positive and desirable quality in exceptional instances. People even seek it out, try to provoke it, as they do in dangerous sports, riding on roller coasters, attending frightening movies, and other curious diversions. These exceptions should be noted, but need not obscure the major and common features of fear. Elevated arousal is one such common feature, but some findings suggest that although elevated arousal is typical of fear, it is less evident in anxiety (Brewin 1996; Rapee 1996).

There is a long-standing debate about the precise meaning of the term *angst*, a concept of particular importance in psychoanalysis. This German term is often taken to mean anxiety, but Lewis (1980) argued that this can be misleading. The disagreement about this term among German writers has been compounded by problems of translation, and in the English literature the term anxiety cannot be taken to mean angst.

The term anxiety itself appears to have been derived from the Greek root *angh*, which means tightness or constriction. Related words such as anguish and anger come from the same root, but are rarely confused with anxiety, even though they are often used to describe related psychological states or reactions (see Barlow [2002] for a full discussion of these terms).

In order to avoid confusion, for the remainder of this book, the terms used by the original writers, clinicians and research workers will be retained except in those instances when to do so would introduce confusion.

The nature of fear

Admissions of fear are discouraged in war, and in population surveys tend to be under-reported because admitting to certain fears is felt to be socially undesirable. In clinical settings, patients may be unable to recognize or report even highly significant fears. People rarely have to be told that they are feeling frightened, but feelings of anxiety can be so diffuse and vague that the affected person may fail to recognize the anxiety until someone else draws attention to it.

The social influences that obscure accurate expression of fear complicate the difficulty of recognizing and describing our feelings and experiences with accuracy. Many people who say that they are fearful of a particular situation are later seen to display fearless behaviour when they encounter it. Assessments of the intensity of the fear are limited by the difficulty involved in translating such expressions as 'extremely frightened', 'terrified' and 'slightly anxious' into a quantitative scale with stable properties. For these reasons among others, psychologists have extended the study of fear beyond an exclusive reliance on subjective reports by including indexes of physiological change and measures of observable behaviour.

It is helpful to think of fear as comprising three main components: the subjective experience of dread, associated physiological changes, and behavioural attempts to avoid or escape from the threatening situation. The three components of fear do not always correspond (Lang *et al*. 1983). Some people experience subjective fear, but remain outwardly calm and show none of the expected physiological correlates of fear, such as trembling, palpitations or perspiring; others report subjective fear, but make no attempt to escape from or avoid the threatening situation. The existence of these three components of fear, and the fact that they do not always correspond, makes it helpful to specify which component of the fear one is describing.

In everyday exchanges, we rely on people telling us of their fears and supplement this information with clues provided by their facial and other bodily expressions. Unfortunately, when our assessments are made in the absence of supporting cues from the context in which the observation is made, the interpretations can be misleading. Moreover, the value of observations of facial and other expressions is limited to certain categories of fear, especially the acute fears. The chronic and diffuse fears are less visible, as is also true for most forms of anxiety. For example, we may without difficulty observe signs of fear in passengers during the descent of an aircraft, but fail to recognize fear in a person who is extremely apprehensive about meeting new people. The signs of anxiety are especially difficult to detect because anxiety tends to be relatively formless, pervasive and puzzling, even to the person experiencing this emotion.

In the course of developing effective techniques for reducing fear, some unexpected and complex findings emerged. Perplexing results also emerged in the clinical application of these techniques. Despite the appearance of marked improvements in behaviour – for example, a claustrophobic person acquiring the ability to travel on underground trains – some patients deny that they have benefitted. In other patients, the physiological reactions to the threatening stimulus diminish after treatment, but the person continues to complain of excessive fear. Moreover, the improvements apparent in a patient's behaviour sometimes are followed only weeks later by subjective improvements.

Repeated observations of this type led to the recognition that the three components of fear might show desynchrony – that is, different rates of change – either in response to treatment or spontaneously (Rachman 1990). In general, the order of change in response to therapy is first a decline in physiological reactivity, then improvements in behaviour, and finally subjective improvements. The prevailing treatment, cognitive behaviour therapy (CBT), aims first and mainly at the patient's maladaptive cognitions, and here the subjective improvements can occur early in the chain.

The low correspondence between some measures of fear also led to difficulties in interpreting laboratory findings on fear reduction. It even produced difficulties at the earliest stage of experiments, in the selection of suitably fearful subjects. Many potential subjects who rate themselves as being fearful display little or no fear when exposed to the fearful object in a specially arranged behavioural avoidance test. Many of them walk in, approach the snake (for example), and lift it without hesitation, in spite of having recorded an extreme fear of snakes on the screening questionnaire. There is a strong tendency for people to over-predict their fears, to anticipate that they will be significantly more frightened in specified circumstances than turns out to be the case when they encounter the particular situation.

Discrepancies between different measures of fear have been encountered in different experiments and in clinical settings. For example, in a classical early experiment by Gordon Paul (1966), designed to reduce the circumscribed fear of public speaking among a group of students, their fears were assessed by a number of self-report measures, two physiological measures, external ratings and a behavioural test of public speaking. Paul found a reasonably high correlation between the self-report measures, but little relationship between these and physiological indicators of fear. As mentioned earlier, it is common in clinical practice to find that patients with phobias of public transport and public space, such as supermarkets, make considerable advances in overcoming their avoidance of these places, but continue to complain of fear for several weeks after these achievements.

'Fear is not a hard phenomenal lump'

Peter Lang, who was responsible for much of the research and theorizing on this subject of fear and fear reduction, expressed the revised view of fear extremely well. He stated (1970: 116) that 'fear is not some hard phenomenal lump that lives inside people, that we may palpate more or less successfully' (see also Lang 1977; Lang et al. 1970). He argued convincingly that the components of fear are related to each other, but imperfectly. The three components are loosely coupled and partially independent.

In an investigation of fear in parachute jumpers, Fenz and Epstein (1967) found evidence of correspondence and lack of correspondence between different measures. The three physiological measures steadily increased during the parachute-jumping sequence, but a different pattern was observed in the measure of subjective fear. This component of fear fluctuated at various stages of the sequence, with an early increase in fear followed by a decrease, then a final increment as the jump approached. These observations were made on a group of veteran parachute jumpers and differed from the results subsequently obtained with novice jumpers. Among the inexperienced group, there was a closer correspondence between subjective fear and physiological reactions. Both of these measures showed extreme reactivity which steadily increased and reached a peak shortly before the jump took place. The mean heart rate at the peak point reached 145 beats per minute. Both sets of measures, physiological and subjective, subsided soon after the landing. The veterans experienced only minimal increases in heart rate, subjective fear and other measures, whereas the novices displayed extremely strong reactions. These observations support the idea that the correspondence between measures increases at very high levels of fear and correspondence is also close at the opposite extreme; that is, the measures are concordant during states of calm. The lack of correspondence between the different components of fear is most evident during moderate levels of emotional arousal.

In view of the loose coupling between the components of fear, what is the best way to describe and predict fear? Following Lang, it is best to avoid relying on a single measure. Self-report measures provide a useful, if crude, basis for the prediction of fear and have some practical advantages over the more elaborate techniques of assessment. The inclusion of a behavioural-approach test is highly desirable in most circumstances and provides information that is not attainable by indirect means. The ratings of fear made by external judges can be useful, but are not free of problems. Some of the physiological measures – that of heart rate, in particular – can provide important data. Heart rate acceleration occurs in response to fear stimuli and at high levels of intensity tends to increase in unison with increases in subjective fear.

The main reason for attempting to measure more than one component of fear, whenever possible, is that a total reliance on the main measure – self-report – can lead us to overestimate the person's fear and significantly underestimate the degree of courage. Total reliance on observed behaviour in a fear test, on the other hand, can lead one to underestimate the degree of a person's fear.

Fear and courage

Incidentally, the view of fear as a complex of imperfectly coupled response systems led to some novel ideas on the nature of courage. A person may be willing to approach a frightening object or situation despite experiencing a high degree of subjective bodily fear and unpleasant bodily reactions. This persistence in the face of subjective and physical sensations of fear leads to a definition of courage that rests on the person's ability to persist despite their subjective fear. This type of courageous behaviour is an example of uncoupling of components, in which the person's behaviour advances beyond subjective discomfort (Rachman 1990).

Few would disagree with the claim that Lang's three components of fear represent an advance; and in particular, the recognition that fear consists of more than one component and is not a unitary phenomenon is enlightening. However, the revised conception may not have escaped the original problem entirely. The three components are loosely coupled and any one of them can predominate as circumstances change. The absence of a physiological response does not prevent us from concluding that the person is frightened. Nor does the absence of avoidance or escape behaviour preclude this conclusion. The experience of fear does not require the presence of all three components, but the presence of a physiological response, or of escape or avoidance behaviour, or even their combination, is not sufficient to justify the term *fear*. A person might display avoidance behaviour and an elevated heart rate as components of the experience of rage or repugnance. However, in the absence of the appropriate verbal report of fear, the meaning of the avoidance behaviour and the physiological response is uncertain. The behavioural and the physiological components of fear usually are prominent, but fear may occur without them. The verbal report is definitional and essential. In this way, the problem that prompted the introduction of the three-component analysis lingers on in a muted form.

Fear, anxiety and avoidance 2

'Fear is a decisive causal factor in avoidance behaviour', according to Mowrer (1960: 97). Ever since its introduction in 1939, Mowrer's two-stage theory of anxiety has had a major influence on the way in which psychologists view fear and anxiety (Mowrer used the terms fear and anxiety interchangeably). The relations between fear, anxiety and avoidance are analysed.

In the original statement of his theory, Mowrer (1939) critically examined the contrasting theories of Freud, Pavlov and Watson and concluded that anxiety is best construed as a conditioned pain reaction. He argued that anxiety is not merely a reaction to painful stimuli or associations, but that it can also energize behaviour. The motivating quality of anxiety is of central importance, and Mowrer added that any behaviour which leads to a reduction of anxiety is stamped in – the reduction of anxiety acts as a reinforcement. The final part of the theory is the proposition that the behaviour motivated by anxiety is avoidant and that when it is successful, it leads to a reduction of anxiety and thereby to the strengthening of the avoidance behaviour itself. 'Fear ... motivates and reinforces behaviour that tends to avoid or prevent the recurrence of the pain producing (unconditioned) stimulus' (Mowrer 1939: 554). In an elaboration, Mowrer shifted the emphasis from the cause of fear to its motivating qualities. He claimed that 'two causal steps are necessary ... fear in the case of both active and passive avoidance behaviour is an essential intermediate "cause" or "vari-able"' (Mowrer 1960: 48–49).

Abundant empirical support for these ideas was obtained and the findings were successfully incorporated into the two-stage theory. For a considerable period, Mowrer's theory had a dominating influence on the way in which experimental psychologists and clinicians viewed the connection between fear and avoidance, and it was an important component of the rationale that was presented in support of a novel form of therapy called *behaviour therapy*.

Excessive and injudicious avoidance behaviour is a common consequence of fear, and investigations of panic disorders provide examples of a causal connection between episodes of intense fear (panic) and the emergence of excessive avoidance behaviour. Panic and avoidance are correlated; most patients attribute their avoidance to the episodes of panic, and the temporal relations between panic and avoidance are all indicative of a strong connection.

However, exceptions do occur and panics are not necessarily followed by avoidance. On the other side, avoidance behaviour is not always a product of fear. Furthermore, there are instances in which fears give rise to approach rather than avoidance behaviour. What then is the connection between fear and avoidance?

There is a great deal of laboratory evidence demonstrating a direct connection between fear and avoidance in animals. If they are shocked in an experimental chamber that allows them to avoid further shocks or avoid exposure to stimuli that predict such shocks, then strong and persisting avoidance is quickly established. The evidence is clear and abundant, and it is easy to reproduce the phenomenon. It is not surprising that theorists attached importance to such a consolidated set of data.

The persistence of avoidance

In due course, however, problems began to emerge. The first difficulty arose from the observation that laboratory animals continue to engage in avoidance behaviour for hundreds of trials even after the unpleasant stimulus is withdrawn. The remarkable persistence of acquired avoidance behaviour presents a problem because in the absence of repeated unpleasant experiences, active avoidance behaviour should gradually weaken until extinguished. The second problem is that the theory incorporates two assumptions that are no longer defensible. It assumes that all fears are acquired by a process of conditioning (see Chapter 6) and that neutral stimuli are all equally prone to be turned into fear signals. As will be seen presently, the conditioning theory of fear can accommodate a large amount of information, but suffers from major weaknesses. The assumptions that all stimuli are potential fear signals, and that their potential is equal, are dubious. The two-stage theory was correctly criticized by Harlow (1954) on the grounds that it exaggerates the motivating role of fear in human behaviour: 'The greater part of our energies are motivated by positive goals, not escape from fear and threat' (Harlow 1954: 37).

The importance of positive goals, and the frequent dominance of 'internal representations of possible future events' over *past* events, are convincingly argued by Seligman *et al.* (2012). Actions are determined in part by past events, but also by aims and thoughts about the future. In attempting to explain behaviour, the neglect of possible futures is regarded as a 'crucial missing piece'. In common with most theories of behaviour, from psychoanalysis to learning theory, Mowrer's construal of fear is 'driven by the past'. The *prospection* perspective of Seligman *et al.* (2012) addresses a question that has widespread implications – 'Drawn into the future or driven by the past?'.

Mowrer's claim that fear is an *essential* causal stage in the development of avoidance behaviour is not correct. A wide range of avoidance responses arise, wax and wane even in the absence of fear. One can provoke, maintain or modify avoidance behaviour without evoking fear at any stage (e.g. avoiding a noisy party, a muddy pathway, an irritating acquaintance, etc.). All of these examples are, of course, future-oriented.

In addition, there are important examples of significant fears that are not followed by persistent avoidance behaviour. For example, Craske *et al.* (1987: 153) concluded from their analysis of 57 patients with panic disorder that 'panic frequency is not the major determinant of avoidance behaviour'. Furthermore, they observed that a long history of repeated panics is not necessarily associated with extensive avoidance. Rather, it appears that the *anticipation of a panic* emerged as the strongest predictor of this type of avoidance, and Telch (1988) argued that cognitive factors played the most important role in its genesis. Other examples of fears that are not followed by avoidance behaviour are abundant in the literature on military psychology.

Weaknesses in Mowrer's theory were identified by Seligman and Johnston (1973). They drew attention to the undue and indeed unpredicted persistence of avoidance behaviour, the absence of associated fear during the avoidance behaviour, and what they refer to as the elusiveness of the conditioned stimulus. It can be difficult to specify precisely what stimulus the person is supposed to be avoiding.

The golden rule

Acting on the foundation of the two-stage theory, clinicians advised and encouraged patients to refrain from avoiding fearful situations, especially during treatment. It was customary to warn patients that they risked *increasing* both fear and avoidance if they fled from the fear-provoking situation. They were told that although temporary relief might be obtained, it would be purchased at the cost of later difficulties. The reduction of fear that is achieved by fleeing serves to increase the avoidance behaviour. For a long period, many therapists urged patients to remain in the fearful situation until the fear begins to subside. This advice was embodied in the so-called golden rule – 'Try never to leave a situation until the fear is going down' (Mathews *et al.* 1981). In many circumstances, clinical and non-clinical, this is a useful rule to follow, even if it is not gold-plated. There are good reasons for agreeing that the reduction of fear can increase avoidance behaviour in many circumstances, but it is unlikely that this behaviour is maintained solely by escape from fear.

In an attempt to find out if the presumed connection between fear and avoidance is inflexible and unvarying, a preliminary study was carried out with eight patients suffering from fear of public places and transport (de Silva and Rachman 1984). Half of the patients were advised to follow the golden rule and avoid leaving the frightening situation until their fear began to subside. The other patients were told to escape as soon as their fear began climbing. Fear and avoidance were assessed by the patients' verbal reports and by their behaviour before, during and after the experimental treatment. The patients in both groups made slight progress, and despite encouragement of an escape strategy for the members of one group, neither their fears nor their avoidance behaviour increased significantly, contrary to predictions that flow from the two-stage theory. The study was replicated on a larger sample consisting of two fresh groups of patients, with a similar outcome (Rachman *et al.* 1986). It was observed that patients tended to overestimate the dangerousness of the treatment excursions, especially in the early stages of the programme, and it is likely that this was a manifestation of the tendency to over-predict the intensity of expected fear (see the next sub-section). It is striking that the patients' fear and avoidance declined regardless of the occurrence or non-occurrence of escape behaviour.

In an attempt to understand and anticipate the occurrence and persistence of avoidance behaviour, new explanations were sought. It was recognized that other factors such as motivation, the expected level of unpleasantness, the availability of safety and other factors all play a part in determining avoidance behaviour. It also appears that the probability of a person engaging in fearful avoidance is determined mainly by his or her expectation that contact with the object or situation will provoke fear. In other words, fearful avoidance behaviour is mainly the product of predicted fear.

It follows that maladaptive avoidance behaviour of potentially fearful situations arises when people over-predict how much fear they will experience in that situation.The gradual correction of these over-predictions are followed by a decline in the avoidance behaviour.

Safety signals also play a part in the determination of avoidance behaviour. The essence of a safety signal is that it indicates a period of freedom from fear, pain or aversive threat. In the presence of such a signal, the person feels safe and therefore can act with greater freedom. Carter *et al.* (1995) showed that patients with panic disorder had a significantly muted response to a laboratory provocation test when they were accompanied by a safe person. In cases of agoraphobic avoidance, the introduction of a measure of safety, such as the presence of a trusted companion, enables the affected person to travel more widely. The anticipated presence of a safety signal can modify one's predictions of fear and thereby weaken the fearful avoidance behaviour. However, the withdrawal of an anticipated safety signal will be followed by a prediction of increased fear and hence by stronger avoidance. This is sometimes seen in the surge of anxiety which people with agoraphobic problems experience when they find themselves without the tranquilizing medication which they feel they require in order to cope.

The over-prediction of fear

Fearful people have a strong tendency to overestimate how frightened they will be when they encounter the object of their fear (Craske and Pontillo 2001; Rachman and Bichard 1988). It is possible that the tendency to over-predict fear is part of a general phenomenon in which we are inclined to overestimate the subjective impact of aversive events of many types, including anticipation of pain. As mentioned previously, the over-prediction of fear (and of pain or other aversive events) is linked to avoidance behaviour. We avoid those events which we predict will be frightening or aversive.

The extensive avoidance behaviour displayed by patients with agoraphobia becomes more intelligible in these terms. Given that patients show the same tendency as people with other types of fear to over-predict fear, their avoidance behaviour might be a product of these very over-predictions. It is not unusual for such patients to report severe and extensive avoidance and then to be somewhat surprised to find that, when it is put to the test, they can move about more widely and with less fear than they had anticipated. They discover that they have been over-predicting the magnitude and intensity of their fear.

When people over-predict their fears, certain consequences follow. If their predictions of fear are repeatedly disconfirmed, they make corrections in the predictions of future experiences – they learn to predict that they will have less and less fear. Sequences of repeated disconfirmation of expected fear are accompanied by steadily decreasing *reports* of fear.

In the analysis of over-predictions of fear, it is necessary to make place for two other types of prediction. On some occasions, people under-predict their fear; that is, the reported fear exceeds their expectations. Of course, people can correct the predictions of their fears, and when they do, the prediction and the report of the fear ultimately coincide.

A military example of over-prediction was observed in a study of the fear experienced by recruits undergoing a course in parachuting. They were asked to anticipate how much fear they would experience during the most difficult final jump of the training course and then report how much fear they actually experienced. It was found that they over-predicted their fear by roughly 10 per cent. Interestingly, their estimates of the dangerousness of jumping remained unchanged (McMillan and Rachman 1988).

The effects of underestimating one's fear tend to be immediate and large. Under-predictions are more disruptive than over-predictions. The effects of overestimating one's fear are slower to emerge, and repeated disconfirmations of erroneous predictions of fear are needed before large and stable corrections are made. There is an asymmetry in the effects of over-predictions and under-predictions.

The evidence can be summarized. Fearful subjects tend to over-predict how much fear they will experience. Their predictions of fear tend to decrease after they make numbers of over-predictions, but increase rapidly if they under-predict their fear reactions. After correct predictions are made, subsequent predictions remain unaltered. The reports of fear tend to decrease with repeated exposure to the fearful stimulus, regardless of the accuracy of earlier predictions. With practice, people can learn to predict their fear with increasing accuracy.

These patterns of prediction, and their consequences, have also been observed in research on panic. Predictions of panic tend to decrease after overestimations and tend to increase after underestimations. Predictions of future panic tend to remain unchanged after a person has made a correct prediction of panic – or a correct prediction of no-panic. It is the erroneous predictions of panic, whether they are overestimations or underestimations, that are followed by changes. The under-prediction of panic, equivalent to an unexpected panic, is particularly disruptive. Expected panics can be distressing, but are unlikely to be unduly disruptive or to produce major changes. It is partly for this reason, no doubt, that the first one or two panics appear to be the most damaging.

The most common consequences of errors of prediction are as follows. After an over-prediction, there is a tendency to report reduced fear and a reduction in predictions of future fear. However, the most common consequences of *under-predictions* are reductions in fear, but increases in prediction of future fear.

Over-predictions of fear can be quickly established, especially after the person has experienced an unexpected panic or an intensely fearful event, but they are rather slow to decline. Several disconfirmations appear to be required before the over-prediction of fear declines. But a single under-predicted fear or panic may be all that is needed to produce a large increment in prediction of subsequent fear. This asymmetry is an example of the tendency to overlook experiences that are uneventful, that produce little or no fear, and to give excessive weight to episodes of intense emotion.

The over-prediction of fear and of other aversive experiences can be functional. On occasions it serves to prevent distress because the over-predictions promote avoidance of potentially aversive situations. In many clinical cases, the prevention of fear is achieved at some cost because avoidance behaviour can become excessive and produce unadaptive limitations on mobility. If the over-predictions of fear promote excessive avoidance behaviour, the opportunities for disconfirming the person's maladaptive expectations are minimized. The fear is preserved.

Over-predictions might be functional in the short term, but dysfunctional in the long term. The same analysis is applicable to problems of chronic pain (Philips and Rachman 1996).

The strong tendency to over-predict fear can even influence social policy. Before the outbreak of World War II, it was anticipated that the British population would experience mass panic during the anticipated bomber attacks, and special clinics were set up to deal with the psychological casualties (Rachman 1990). Speaking in the House of Commons, Winston Churchill warned of mass casualties. The dangers of the effects of continuous air attacks, he said, were material,

> but no less formidable than those material effects are the reactions which will be produced upon the mind of the civilian population. We expect that . . . at least 3 million or 4 million people would be driven out into the open country around the metropolis.
>
> (Jenkins 2002: 476)

But the special clinics were little used and closed as unnecessary.

Varieties of fear

Fear is an emotional reaction to a perceived threat. Generally, there is a strong relationship between the threat encountered and the degree of fear experienced, but fear is not determined solely by objective danger. Numerous studies of combat experiences confirm the relationship between perceived danger and fear, but important exceptions occur.

For example, Stouffer *et al.* (1949) noted that some soldiers experienced considerable fear in the presence of minimal danger and others had little fear, even under the most threatening conditions. At certain periods during World War II, fighter pilots of the Royal Air Force (RAF) had an extremely high casualty rate, but consistently reported less fear than other air crew who, at the times in question, were in less danger (Rachman 1990).

Fear is such a common emotion – indeed, universally experienced – that various attempts have been made to ascertain the range, frequency and severity of human fears. In an attempt to assess the types and degrees of fear prevailing in a normal population, Agras and his colleagues (1969) interviewed 325 randomly chosen adults in a small town in Vermont in the United States. They classified the fear responses into four categories: mild, intense, phobias, and clinical phobias. The most commonly reported was a fear of snakes, with no less than one in four people expressing intense fear of this reptile. Of the total sample, 39 per cent reported at least a mild fear of snakes. The second most common fear was that of heights. Among the severe fears, the fear and avoidance of public places and transport (often called agoraphobia) was the most common, with the fear of injury or illness a close second.

The majority of the fears reached a peak incidence in early adulthood and declined in the following years. Fears of the dark and of animals are examples of this pattern. The second, but less common, pattern was that of a gradual increase of fear, reaching a peak in middle adulthood (e.g. fears of illness, injury). In a large-scale questionnaire study carried out by Kirkpatrick (1984), these patterns were broadly confirmed, and it was also found that with the approach of old age, people begin to show an increased fear of heights and of water. With decreasing visual acuity and physical strength, it is not surprising that elderly people begin to fear heights.

The results of a community study of fear carried out by Costello (1982) in Canada produced results comparable to those found in Vermont. He reported a high prevalence of mild fears (244 per 1,000 of the population) and of phobias (190 per 100,000) in a sample of 449 women. Animal fears were the most common; followed by fears of heights, tunnels and enclosed spaces; then social fears, fears of injury and fears of separation.

These findings on the types and distributions of fear, accumulated by interviewing community samples, have been supplemented by numerous questionnaire studies of fear. One of the largest of these studies of self-reported fears was conducted by an international group which compared the fears of American, British and Dutch university students (Arrindell *et al.* 1995). Well over 1,000 students were asked to fill in a version of the Fear Survey Schedule, originally constructed by Wolpe and Lang in 1964. They were asked to state whether they experienced any of the 75 fears listed in the schedule and if so, to state the degree of fear on a 1 to 5 scale, in which 5 is the most extreme fear score. Consistent with earlier research on this scale, five clusters of fear emerged: social fears, agoraphobic fears, fears of injury or illness, fears of sexual and aggressive scenes, and fears of harmless animals. There were some minor differences between the students in three different countries, but the overall pattern was consistent across the three samples. The most commonly and strongly endorsed cluster was social fears; followed by fears of injury or illness; then agoraphobic fears; and last, fears of sexual/aggressive scenes and fears of harmless animals. Some of these common fears, such as a fear of injury or illness, have a rational basis. However, it is repeatedly found that large numbers of people report that they feel frightened by the sight of small, harmless animals or insects such as spiders. Many of these fears are irrationally disproportionate to the objects that provoke them.

At the other extreme, many people are extraordinarily resilient in the face of great danger. Remarkable examples of this type occurred during World War II. Repeated exposures to aerial bombing raids produced far less fear than anticipated (Lewis 1942) and the pre-war expectations of widespread panic were not confirmed. Some of the most common fears are irrational, in the sense that the object or situation feared is neither dangerous nor even thought to be dangerous; these fears appear to have no biological value or significance. On the other hand, certain rational fears of things which may indeed threaten survival are surprisingly uncommon. Given the great danger of driving at speed, surprisingly few people are frightened to do so. It is highly probable that more people are frightened of small, harmless spiders than of driving at speed.

One of the most evident features of the distribution of human fears is that it is *not* random; some fears are very common and others are extremely rare. The non-random distribution of fears requires an explanation.

Another puzzling feature of the distribution of different types of fear is the occurrence of fears in circumstances where they would not be expected. A remarkable example of this kind is seen in the numbers of people who live in areas that contain few snakes – for example, Hawaii – but nevertheless report that they are frightened of snakes. A weaker, but still relevant, example is provided by the results of Kirkpatrick's survey mentioned earlier. Nearly three quarters of his respondents reported that they were frightened of snakes, even though snakes are too rare in Northern Indiana to account for this fact. This raises the question of whether it is possible to be frightened of an object or situation that one has never encountered. No satisfactory theory of human fear can succeed unless it accommodates the expected and the unexpected distributions of fear, including the fact that the distribution is not random.

The frequent accounts of the fear of insects and harmless animals represent an interesting anomaly. Even harmless snakes and spiders are extremely common objects of fear, and many people who are frightened of them acknowledge that their fear is senseless. They may be embarrassed that their fears are so irrational. These irrational fears can be remarkably intense, and as mentioned above, can occur even in areas that are virtually free of the insects or reptiles that the locals fear.

People can develop fears, even intense and persisting fears, of animals or insects that have never harmed them. They can develop fears of animals that are incapable of harming them, and even of animals which they recognize as being incapable of harming them. To add to the puzzle, people can develop lasting fears of insects or animals which they have never encountered. As mentioned above, people who have never left the virtually snake-free island of Hawaii express a fear of snakes, even harmless snakes. Elderly inhabitants of this island say that a fear of snakes was common even before the introduction of television and movies. Naturally this gives rise to the possibility that people might be inherently predisposed to fear certain objects, and if this is so, then snakes and spiders are likely candidates for the 'release' of these inherent and deeply rooted tendencies (see the discussion of 'Prepared fears', in Chapter 4, 'Anxiety and memory').

In the case of a fear of snakes, it is possible that people start with an inherent tendency to respond fearfully, but learn by various means, especially from harmless encounters, that snakes do not harm them. If so, people who live in areas that allow for many opportunities of this harmless kind should show a lower incidence of snake fears than people who live in areas where there are few or no snakes. The fearful people who live in snake-free areas have fewer opportunities to learn fearlessness by direct encounters.

There is a rational element in some of these fears, in that some spiders and snakes are indeed dangerous. The second rational component is that people who are frightened of snakes or spiders, even the harmless ones, learn to dislike and perhaps even fear their own reactions to the appearance of these creatures. These reactions, which may include trembling and sweating, can be unpleasant in their own right and are consistently provoked by the object in question. It is therefore rational for people to expect and dislike these unpleasant reactions to the appearance of snakes or spiders, but this should not distract attention from the irrationality of the original response.

The boundaries of fear

Fears of snakes and of spiders are so surprisingly common, and many people report that they are frightened of both snakes and spiders, that one is bound to wonder whether we might be dealing with two manifestations of the same fear, rather than two distinct fears. Attempts have been made to tease out one fear from another, to determine whether the fears are discrete or interconnected. If two fears, say the fear of snakes and of spiders, are discrete, then a deliberate change induced in one of these fears should leave the second fear unaltered. On the other hand, if the fears are connected, or perhaps are even a common manifestation of some deeper fear, then a change in one fear should be followed by a comparable change in the second fear. It is argued that if a person responds fearfully to two distinct physical stimuli, when the fear response to one of these stimuli is deliberately reduced, the person's subsequent reaction to the 'untreated' fear should provide a measure of the extent to which the two fears are related.

This approach is illustrated by a study in which 28 volunteers who were frightened of both snakes and spiders were recruited (Rachman and Lopatka 1986). In some instances, the deliberate reduction of the first fear was followed by a comparable reduction in the second fear; but in other instances, a deliberate change in one fear left the second fear unaltered. Contrary to expectations, the connections or absence of connections that emerged after the experimental 'treatment' did not match the subject's self-estimated judgements of the similarity of their fears. Prior to the deliberate change in one of their fears, each participant was asked to rate the extent to which their fears of spiders and snakes were similar or even identical – this was to provide a self-estimated judgement of the similarity of the two fears. As stated, there was no relationship between their estimations of similarity and the responses of their two fears to experimental manipulation, as measured by behavioural expressions of fear in the presence of the real stimulus (behaviour tests of fear).

Research into the relationship between various types of fear has also included investigations of the effects of encountering more than one fear stimulus at a time. Do fears summate, and is a person who has two fears more frightened than a person who has a single fear? If Stimulus A (snake) produces fear and Stimulus B (spider) also provokes fear, what happens when they are presented simultaneously? In the main, it appears that fears can summate. Summation occurs regardless of whether the two stimuli are presented simultaneously or in succession. If summation takes place, the sheer order of presentation, snake first or spider first, plays no part in the result. There was, however, an interesting variation on the general pattern. If the first stimulus (e.g. snake) produced a stronger fear than the second stimulus (e.g. spider), the simultaneous presentation of both the spider and the snake resulted in a subtraction rather than a summation. The fear reported in the presence of both of the stimuli was weaker than the fear provoked by the first stimulus acting alone. However, if the first stimulus produced a weak fear and the second one a strong fear, summation did occur.

The occurrence of summation probably means that the two fears share important attributes, and therefore when the two are presented simultaneously, the quantity of these attributes increases, as when we add apples to apples. On the other hand, summation might also mean that the two fears differ on some important attribute – what is being added? If the two fears are very similar, then their simultaneous provocation should produce little or no additional fear. The occurrence of subtraction can be explained in a similar way. If the two fears are highly similar and therefore Fear A (say snakes) fully predicts Fear B (spiders), then their simultaneous presentation should produce no summation because the 'full fear' has already been produced.

The concept of anxiety disorders

Excessive anxiety is the central feature of many psychological disorders. In the DSM classificatory system for psychological and psychiatric disorders, several types of anxiety disorder are included (see Table 2.1). An eighth type, health anxiety disorders, is described here because of its importance (see Chapter 10).

Panic disorder is the term used to describe repeated episodes of intense fear of rapid onset (panics); at least some of these episodes are unexpected, they appear to come out of the blue. Panic disorder with agoraphobia, a common association, refers to panics that are followed by pervasive avoidance behaviour, especially of public transport and public places. In a small number of instances, the agoraphobic avoidance behaviour is not preceded by panics.

The term *agoraphobia* strictly means 'fear of the marketplace', but is now used to refer to a fear of being in public places from which an escape may be difficult, or even a fear of coming to harm when alone in one's own home. Depending on the person's particular fears, the avoidance of 'unsafe' situations may be focused on one or a few places; or in severe cases, the person is housebound. In these severe cases, the person is unable to travel anywhere alone, and even when accompanied by a trusted adult, can travel only for short distances, using specific routes at specific times.

TABLE 2.1

The anxiety disorders

- Panic disorder, with or without agoraphobia
- Agoraphobia without a history of panics
- Social phobia
- Specific phobia
- Generalized anxiety disorder
- Obsessive-compulsive disorder
- Post-traumatic stress disorder (and acute stress disorder)
- Health anxiety disorders

A diagnosis of *social phobia* is appropriate if the person complains of intense and persistent anxiety about social situations, especially if there is a possibility of being exposed to scrutiny. In *specific phobias,* the central feature is an extremely intense, circumscribed fear of a specific object or place, such as an extreme fear of spiders, or of heights.

Obsessive-compulsive disorder consists of repetitive, intentional, stereotyped acts, such as compulsive handwashing, and / or recurring, unwanted, intrusive thoughts of an unacceptable / repugnant quality, which the affected person resists.

Post-traumatic stress disorder (PTSD) consists of many symptoms, including anxiety, disturbances of memory, elevated arousal, avoidance, and fear or horror, that persist for prolonged periods after an unusually distressing experience, such as a natural disaster, an accident or a violent attack. Many of these traumas are life-threatening, but PTSD can also develop after major life-altering events such as degradation, grievous loss or betrayal. Fears associated with the disorder tend to be accompanied by high levels of arousal, an involuntary tendency to recall or re-experience the event during dreams or at other times, and by strong tendencies to avoid people or places that are associated with the original stress. A full account of PTSD is provided in another volume in this series, *Stress and Trauma* by Patricia A. Resick.

Generalized anxiety disorder is characterized by persistent, excessive, unrealistic anxiety about possible misfortunes, such as financial losses, ill-health, the welfare of one's children, or combinations of these misfortunes.

Health anxiety disorders consist of intense, pervasive preoccupation and anxiety about one's present and / or future health and well-being, and / or a preoccupation with the health and well-being of family and friends.

As mentioned in Chapter 1, the DSM classification was a great improvement on the diagnostic anarchy that prevailed until the 1970s. It is clearly set out, based on defined criteria and useable. However, the limitations should not be overlooked. The scheme implies that a wide variety of unusual experiences and behaviour are signs of mental illness: the entire system is over-inclusive. The despairingly long list of 'mental disorders' (well over 400) increases with each new edition.

All of the anxiety disorders have a common feature – excessive anxiety. Not infrequently, anxiety is associated with other psychological problems, notably depression. In obsessional disorders, the anxiety may even be overshadowed by the presence of unyielding depression. Most of the anxiety disorders are justifiably grouped together by the dominance of intense fear or anxiety. The rationale for the DSM is given in the introductory section of the DSM-IV and in numerous publications (Frances *et al.* 1995; Spitzer 1991). Critical commentaries were given by Wakefield (1992), Eysenck *et al.* (1983), and others (Burstow 2005; Follette 1996; Follette and Houts 1996; Harvey and Bryant 2002; Kirk and Kutchins 1992; Zimmerman 2011).

Summary

Anxiety is a common and pervasive emotion. It is a feeling of uneasy suspense, the tense anticipation of a threatening but obscure event. Fear and anxiety share some common features, but fears tend to have a specific, usually identifiable, focus, and to be more intense and episodic. Anxiety is more pervasive and persistent.

Fear can be construed as consisting of three loosely coupled components: the subjective sense of dread, associated physiological changes and behavioural attempts to escape. Fear is both a reaction and a motivating force, usually giving rise to attempts to escape or avoid. Avoidance is promoted by expectations of threat, and fearful people tend to over-predict how frightened they will be if they encounter the object of their fear.

Fears of animals are the most common, followed by fears of injury / illness, heights, enclosed spaces, and social fears. The most intense and irrational fears are classified as phobias or anxiety disorders, of which there are eight types: panic disorder, agoraphobia, social phobia, specific phobia, generalized anxiety disorder, obsessive-compulsive disorder, post-traumatic stress disorder, health anxiety disorders.

Influences on anxiety 3

In this chapter, a model of anxiety is set out and the factors that influence anxiety are described. There are many components involved in the activation and the experience of anxiety. It is a process, rather than a categorical event that occurs or does not occur. In an attempt to simplify some of these complexities, a didactic model, which has gaps and at times skirts around the complexities, is set out (see Figure 3.1). Hypervigilance, cues and cognitions that evoke anxiety, and vulnerability to anxiety are discussed.

Hypervigilance

People vary in their proneness to experience anxiety, and the vulnerable ones become hypervigilant when entering a novel or potentially intimidating situation. Their hypervigilance promotes rapid and global scanning, followed by an intense narrow focus if a threat is detected. The transition from the global scanning stage to narrowly focused attention can be illustrated by the idea of tuning a radio. Initially one scans fairly rapidly across a wide band until a signal is picked up. Then we turn to fine tuning and raise the volume. So the anxious patient entering a potentially threatening situation carries out broad global scanning until a threat signal is detected. The person's attention then focuses narrowly and intensely on the potential threat, with enhanced perceptual sensitivity and even distortion.

Threatening objects appear to be clearer, sharper, even larger. The detection of a threat triggers an inhibition of ongoing behaviour, perhaps seen in the form of attentive stillness and high arousal. The perceived information, whether from an external or internal source, is

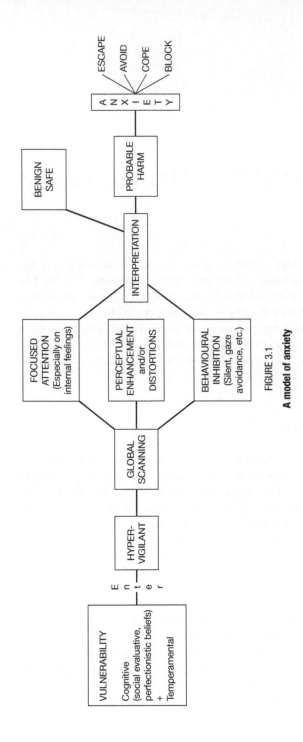

FIGURE 3.1

A model of anxiety

then interpreted as signifying danger or safety. According to Beck and Emery (1985: 56), 'when a threat is perceived the relevant cognitive schemas are activated; these are used to evaluate and assign a meaning to the event'. If safe, the person can then resume the ongoing behaviour, but if there is danger of harm, anxiety arises, and may be followed by escape or avoidance or coping.

The early detection of threat is of survival value, and appropriate apprehensive anxiety has obvious functional significance. It follows that there should be a selective attentional bias favouring the detection of threats, especially when one is entering circumstances that are unfamiliar or that have a history of threat and danger.

Psychological analyses of the nature of attention have produced evidence of important processes of which the person remains unaware. These include pre-attentive processes (Eysenck 1992; Eysenck *et al.* 2007), which can include the phenomena of perceptual defence, implicit memory, and unaware detection of auditory or visual stimuli. These processes are studied by the use of tasks such as dichotic listening and tachistoscope presentations. In potentially threatening situations, as in other situations, people attend to some cues in a non-conscious fashion. They do so without awareness.

Vulnerability

The idea that people vary in the degree to which they are vulnerable to experiencing anxiety (e.g. Brewin 1988, 2003) gains support from the clinical and experimental evidence of widespread individual differences in the detection of threat. To begin with, there is evidence of experiential and biological determinants of proneness to anxiety, much of it assembled and presented in the theories of H. J. Eysenck (1957, 1967) and in clinical theories such as those proposed by Beck and Emery (1985), D. M. Clark (1988) and D. A. Clark and Beck (2010). In addition to these temperamental vulnerabilities, there is growing evidence of a vulnerability that is largely cognitive in nature – see, for example, M. Eysenck (1992, 2007) and D. M. Clark (1988, 1996). People are *primed* to detect threat cues by their past experiences and present beliefs. They are prepared, even before entering the potentially threatening situation, by memories of past misfortunes and anxiety which combine with their current beliefs about the sources of danger that can threaten them.

People who have a temperamental vulnerability obtain high scores on measures of introversion and neuroticism. The cognitive vulnerability appears to include differences in vigilance, the collection and use of information, perceptual processes, variations in attentional processes, and judgemental biases, among other variables. Numerous instruments have been introduced in an attempt to measure vulnerability to anxiety, including the well-used scales designed to measure state and trait anxiety and the Anxiety Sensitivity Inventory (Reiss and McNally 1985; Taylor 1995). As will be seen presently, this self-report scale includes some temperamental factors, some items dealing with interpretation and misinterpretation, and others dealing with levels of arousal.

One of the keenest proponents of the need to distinguish between *state anxiety* and *trait anxiety* was Spielberger (1966, 1983) who employed a down-to-earth approach, emphasizing the practical implications of the concept of anxiety proneness in developing psychometric instruments for measuring anxiety. Anxiety *states* are said to be transitory; they recur when evoked by perceived threats and endure for a limited period after the disappearance of the threat. The *trait* of anxiety, on the other hand, refers to an enduring difference between people in the way in which they perceive the world and respond to it. People with elevated trait anxiety have a low threshold for reacting anxiously and are inclined to react and behave with predictable regularity to perceived threats. It follows that the stronger the trait of anxiety, the more probable it is that the person will experience anxiety in a range of situations, with comparatively minimal provocation, and to experience more intense levels of anxiety than would people who are low in this trait.

Flowing from his distinction between state and trait anxiety, Spielberger constructed an inventory (the State–Trait Anxiety Inventory [STAI]) to measure the two forms of anxiety. The STAI is a self-report inventory of 20 items designed to measure increasing levels of intensity of anxiety, with low scores indicating states of calmness and serenity . . . and high scores reflecting states of intense apprehension and fearfulness that approach panic. The items include statements such as, 'I lack self-confidence', and the respondent is asked to endorse one of four degrees of agreement ranging from 'Almost never' which scores one, to 'Almost always' which scores four. The anxiety state scale also consists of 20 items, similarly ranked from one ('Not at all') to four ('Very much so'). These items are divided between feelings of tension, nervousness, worry and apprehension on the one hand; and ten items expressing feelings of calmness and contentment. Respondents are asked to state how they feel at the very moment of completing the questionnaire. The maximum score on the state anxiety scale is 80.

The STAI is subject to all of the limitations of self-report inventories, but it is widely used because of its ease of administration and flexibility. It provides an approximate measure of prevailing anxiety and can be used on repeated occasions during investigations in which the fluctuations of anxiety are an important element. It is also useful for assessing the anxiety-provoking effects of particular interventions or experimental manipulations. It has been widely used in investigations of anxiety that arises during medical and surgical investigations or procedures, and is the most common method for tracking changes in anxiety during processes such as preparation for surgery and adjustments during the post-operative period (e.g. Johnston 1980; Kincey *et al.* 1991; Weller and Hener 1993).

It has been observed, and therefore the objection has been made, that trait anxiety and state anxiety are too highly correlated. In some circumstances, this limits the use of these scales and concepts. However, the correlation between the two concepts is unavoidable and if it did not exist would give rise to suspicion about the psychometric validity of the scales, because the occurrence and intensity of episodes of state anxiety are bound to be influenced by the person's pre-existing proneness to anxiety.

Most of these developments in theory and in psychometric research took place before the widespread infusion of cognitive concepts and techniques into clinical psychology generally (Brewin 1988, 2003; Clark 1999), and into the field of anxiety disorders in particular. There is no doubt about the importance of cognitive appraisal in anxiety and therefore there is a need to study and measure anxiety cognitions. The need for refined measurements of these cognitions is clear in the successful and influential theory of panic disorder, in which 'catastrophic cognitions' play a central role (see Chapter 7), and in the assessment of health anxiety disorders (Chapter 10).

Although it was not introduced for this particular purpose, the concept of anxiety sensitivity has found a useful place in cognitive approaches to anxiety (Reiss *et al.* 1986; Reiss 1987, 1991; Taylor 1995). Anxiety sensitivity is a fear of bodily sensations that are interpreted as having potentially harmful physical or psychological consequences, and hence give rise to significant anxiety. The Anxiety Sensitivity Index (ASI) (Peterson and Reiss 1987) is a self-report questionnaire that measures the subject's beliefs about the perceived threat of these bodily sensations, and the associated fear of these very sensations. It includes items such as feeling frightened by one's rapidly beating heart, experiencing alarm when short of breath, etc. The ASI results show that anxiety sensitivity is elevated across all anxiety disorders, especially

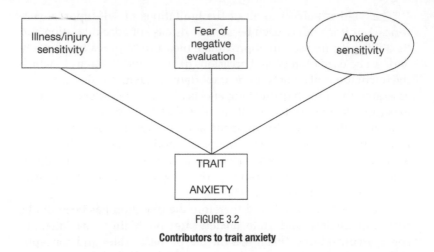

FIGURE 3.2

Contributors to trait anxiety

in panic disorder. The anxiety sensitivity scores of people who have circumscribed phobias are not significantly greater than those that occur in a non-clinical population (Taylor 1995).

It has been said that the notion of anxiety sensitivity is little more than a new version of the concept of trait anxiety, but McNally (1995) has argued that anxiety sensitivity is a specific tendency to respond fearfully to one's own sensations, whereas trait anxiety is a broader tendency to respond fearfully to an extensive range of potential threats. After reviewing the psychometric data, Taylor (1995) concluded that anxiety sensitivity is one of three major factors that contribute to trait anxiety. The three factors – anxiety sensitivity, illness/injury sensitivity, and fear of negative evaluation – all contribute to the general trait of anxiety proneness, and are illustrated in Figure 3.2.

The concept of cognitive vulnerability is important to the cognitive theory of anxiety and if disconfirmed would leave a gap in the explanation. In the absence of cognitive vulnerability, the negative cognitions reported by anxious people might better be regarded as parallel effects of anxiety or even the results of anxiety, and it would be difficult to press the view that negative cognitions play a causal role in the generation of anxiety.

'To a man who is afraid everything rustles' (Sophocles)

A particularly clear account of the nature of anxious hypervigilance is given by Michael Eysenck (1992), who regards the phenomenon as both a reaction to potential threat and as a component of cognitive vulnerability to anxiety. According to Eysenck, people who are predisposed to anxiety manifest hypervigilance in these ways. They engage in a

> high rate of environmental scanning which involves numerous rapid eye movements throughout the visual field . . . a propensity to attend selectively to threat-related rather than neutral stimuli; a broadening of attention prior to the detection of such stimuli, and a narrowing of attention when a salient stimulus is being processed.
>
> (Eysenck 1992: 43)

Eysenck argues that hypervigilance is a vulnerability factor for anxiety disorders, and is evident in patients, and in non-patient groups, who are high in trait anxiety. Hypervigilance is especially obvious under stressful conditions. However, as it is not found in patients who have overcome their anxiety disorders, he concludes that hypervigilance is best regarded as a vulnerability factor. In clinical practice with patients suffering from anxiety disorders, the occurrence of hypervigilance and selective attention is an obvious and daily occurrence.

In extreme cases, the attentional processes are so distorted that the patients engage in rapid visual scanning in virtually all new or ambiguous situations. For example, a 38-year-old accountant who was suffering from a severe obsessive-compulsive disorder which centred on his fear of disease contamination, and in particular of AIDS, engaged in rapid broad visual scanning whenever he left his home. The scanning was particularly intense and agitated whenever he went into situations in which he thought that the risk of encountering AIDS-contaminated material was increased. During one treatment session that took place in the grounds of a large hospital, he carried out vigorous visual scanning of the parking lot, searching for any signs of discarded hypodermics, or other medical materials, which he regarded as presenting a serious threat to his health. It was extraordinarily difficult to persuade him to stop scanning the ground around him and instead to look upwards at the buildings ahead of him. Whenever he observed a suspicious object, and this included an astonishingly wide range of perfectly neutral stimuli, he rapidly concentrated his full attention on the suspect object. Where he could risk it, he would then approach very gingerly to make a precise determination of what the object was and whether or not it might constitute a danger. If he was able to satisfy himself that it was indeed a harmless object, he would then return to his broad general scanning. On those occasions, however, when his narrow intense focusing of attention on the object led him to conclude that it might be some contaminated medical material, he rapidly escaped and was disinclined to go anywhere near that part of the hospital approach for the remainder of the treatment session. Many months later he was able to recall in detail all of the threatening items he had observed during his therapeutic walk through the hospital grounds.

Another patient with obsessive-compulsive problems who had a severe fear of diseases, including AIDS, was particularly frightened by the prospect of encountering other people's blood; he felt this would constitute a serious threat to his health, even if it was the smallest trace of dried blood, and even if he approached no closer than three or four feet from the spot of dried blood. His interpretation of the threat emanating from other people's blood, including people who were wearing the smallest piece of plaster to cover a minor nick, was a gross – indeed catastrophic – misinterpretation of the probability of harm coming to him and an overestimation of the seriousness of any contact. Nevertheless, his fear of other people's blood was so intense that whenever he went into a public place, he would rapidly scan the physical environment and also the people he encountered, constantly looking for evidence of blood, cuts, bandages, adhesive tape, and so forth. He had trained himself so well that he could indeed pick up traces of red spots at a considerable distance and was usually accurate. However, his perception of red spots was grossly in error in over-perceiving the occurrence of red spots of blood. He tended to mis-perceive as blood a wide range of spots of different colours along the colour continuum, so that spots of almost any dark hue were mistaken as evidence of blood (e.g. spots of mud, or small pieces of waste paper, etc.). He was able to recall in detail the innumerable blood or blood-related items that he had encountered in the previous 12 years.

Context and attention

It is assumed that people who are vulnerable to anxiety enter most situations that are novel and/or intimidating with well-formed expectations. They become hypervigilant and carry out global searching scans of the external and also internal environments. They are selectively tuned to attend to stimuli that might be threatening; that is, they display selective attention. If their attentive processes pick up a potential threat signal, then the focus narrows. This narrowing of attention is accompanied by elevations of arousal and increased effort. Given that attentional processes are of limited capacity (e.g. Kahneman and Treisman 1983; Kahneman *et al.* 1983), the narrowed focus of attention, directed at the perceived threat, is accompanied by a relative neglect of other stimuli. In people who suffer from excessively high or persistent levels of anxiety, this can appear as inattentiveness to other people, and the appearance – or more than the appearance – of excessive preoccupation with oneself. In addition, the effort involved in the narrowing of the attentional focus 'drains away' attention from other tasks, and leads affected people to experience and complain of an inability to concentrate on their jobs or other matters. Beck and Emery (1985) reported that 86 per cent of their cases of patients with anxiety disorder complained of impaired concentration.

The liberating effects of reducing hypervigilance are observed during the treatment of patients with obsessive-compulsive disorders. A tactic called the 'off-duty/on-duty contrast' is often used to good effect. The patients are taught how to instruct themselves to go on-duty or off-duty at will. When they are off-duty, they are no longer required to scan and collect threat-related information. As they become skilled at using this self-induced contrast, their vigilance is reduced and becomes more specific and controlled. The off-duty periods are a relief, and even more important, they learn that the burdensome hypervigilance is not a permanent fact of life, but an aspect of their daily functioning that is modifiable and reasonably controllable (Rachman 2003).

Of course when people enter novel or potentially threatening situations, they do not always become anxious. Even in those circumstances when they enter a novel or potentially threatening situation with high expectations of encountering danger, they might instead find evidence of safety rather than danger. If the search for safety is successful, minimal anxiety arises – for example, if a patient suffering from a panic disorder anticipates experiencing palpitations and laboured breathing, which might be symptoms of an impending heart attack, but then notices that he is outside a reputable hospital or clinic, this can be taken as a sign of safety and the anticipated panic does not occur.

The signs of anxiety can also be aborted later in the process. If on entering the situation, the person becomes hypervigilant, carries out a global scan of the situation, appears to perceive a potential threat, but then after giving it her selective attention, finds evidence of dependable safety, the anxiety will diminish.

Interpretation and misinterpretation

In a novel or potentially threatening situation, the information that the person collects as a result of selective attention and focusing is open to interpretation. If the information is given a benign interpretation – for example, the person interprets his palpitations and laboured breathing as normal expressions of the fact that he has been running – this benign interpretation will be followed by a decline in whatever anxiety had been generated up to this point. If, however, the person misinterprets these bodily sensations as indicators of an impending heart attack, high levels of anxiety, even of panic, can be expected (Clark 1986).

Important misinterpretations tend to have two elements. They can be misinterpretations in which the probability of an aversive event occurring is exaggerated, or the misinterpretation can be an overestimation of the seriousness of the anticipated event (or of course, a combination of high probability and high seriousness). We already know that people who suffer from excessive levels of anxiety or of depression are inclined to overestimate the probability and the seriousness of unfortunate events (Beck and Emery 1985; D. M. Clark 1986, 1988, 1996; D. A. Clark and Beck 2010; Ehlers 1992).

In addition to the two by-products of anxiety already mentioned – inattentiveness to other people or stimuli, and the impairment of desired concentration – we have to add feelings of fatigue. Much to the puzzlement of friends and relatives, people who suffer from excessive levels of anxiety can complain of being extremely tired, even though they have spent the entire day housebound and physically inactive. In fact, the hypervigilance, selective attention and concentrated attempts to deal with anxiety all require considerable effort, and it is not surprising that people who experience persistent anxiety so often report feeling drained.

Consequences

Anxiety is unpleasant and most people engage in attempts to reduce this aversive state. The methods which they employ depend on their previous experiences with anxiety and the success or failure of the methods which they have adopted in the past. One of the most common reactions to anxiety is to escape from an unpleasant situation and, wherever possible, avoid coming into contact with it. For example, people who experience excessive anxiety when shopping in a supermarket experience overpowering urges to escape from the situation as soon as possible. After one or two unpleasant experiences in the supermarket, they quickly adopt a pattern of avoidance, in which they encourage other people to do the shopping for them; or make their own shopping expeditions contingent on being accompanied by a trusted person who can care for them if things go wrong; or confine their shopping to very quiet periods when an escape can be made quickly and without impediment should it be necessary. Escape and avoidance behaviour are successful in the short term. For the most part they are followed by reductions in anxiety which provide temporary relief, but in the long term strengthen the escape and avoidance behaviour (Mowrer 1960; Rachman 1990).

Anxiety, attention, perception, memory and emotional processing 4

Interactions between attention, perception, memory and anxiety are described and analysed. The concept of emotional processing, with respect to anxiety, is discussed. Manifestations of test anxiety, social anxiety and sexual anxiety are described.

Health anxiety arises from a threat to one's own health or a threat to the health of others, and is nowhere more evident than in parental anxiety regarding their children's safety and well-being. For this reason, Parkinson and Rachman (1980) collected evidence of attentional selectivity from a group of anxious mothers during the course of a study of the effects of an uncontrived stress on emotional reactions. The reactions of 25 mothers whose children were being admitted to hospital for surgery were compared to those of 25 control-group mothers whose children were of the same age, but were not receiving medical treatment at the time of the study. One of the four tasks given to these mothers consisted of a signal detection task. The rationale for this technique was that during periods of anxiety, threat-related stimuli will be detected more sensitively than neutral stimuli.

Accordingly, the test determined the level of volume at which threat-related or neutral words could be detected by the mothers while they were listening to music that was played at an audible level. The detection rate was assessed by counting the number of correct recognitions of the key words at each of five increasing levels of volume. After setting the volume at a comfortable level chosen by the participant, music was presented binaurally throughout the task. At random points during the presentation of the musical tape, 30 words were inserted. Of these, ten were threat-related trigger words (e.g. injection, bleeding, operation, etc.); ten were words with a different meaning, but a similar sound; and ten were neutral words. The mothers were asked to repeat each word as they heard it. Five trials were given. On the first trial, the words were presented at a very low level of volume, on the second trial at a slightly higher level, on the third trial even louder, and so on until the five trials had been completed. The volume of the music was kept constant across all trials. In this way, it was possible to determine the level at which the subjects recognized each of the three categories of words.

Evidence of attentional selectivity was obtained. At the lowest volume during trial 1, the mothers in the experimental group reported six times more threat-related words than did the mothers in the control group. On the second trial, the mothers reported twice as many trigger words as did the control groups. By trials 4 and 5, however, the difference between the groups disappeared. Across all trials there was a significant improvement in the detection rate of the participants of both groups, reflecting a combination of practice effects and the ease of recognition at increasing levels of volume.

Medical and surgical procedures are among the most anxiety-provoking experiences that people encounter throughout their lives, and it is regrettable that this large fact is not more widely appreciated and acted upon in clinics and hospitals. People experience intense anxiety while waiting for the results of X-rays, scans, MRIs, biopsies and other potentially threatening medical tests. Some of the highest scores on anxiety scales have been reported in medical circumstances (e.g. Kincey *et al.* 1991; Weller and Hener 1993).

A prime example of selective attention occurs when new parents bring their baby home. They tend to start off by listening for the baby's every breath, and the slightest baby noise can arouse them from sleep. Other examples of selective attention are provided by Michael Eysenck (1992). The attentional bias that occurs when people get anxious is evident in people who are suffering from panic disorder, when there are threats to one's health, fears of social embarrassment, threats of unpleasant mental events, and so forth (Ehlers *et al.* 1988).

Attentional selectivity increases in the presence of potential danger, but we are dealing with a complex concept. There are different types and levels of attention. Attention can be directed towards external stimuli or, as is important in cases of panic disorder, to internal sensations. Attention can be passive or it can be active, it can be conscious or non-conscious, and so forth. The subject is a full and rather complicated one, but there are a number of excellent analyses of the phenomenon including Barlow (2002), D. A. Clark and Beck (2010), Craske (2001), Eysenck (1992), Eysenck *et al.* (2007), McNally (1994, 1995) among others.

Self-focused attention

The narrowing of attention that occurs in response to a threat can be directed externally or internally. Attention directed towards internal events – physical sensations such as heartbeat, images, thoughts, feelings – is of course a normal process, but if it becomes excessive, can cause serious difficulties. Self-focused attention can be intense, constricting and preoccupying. Excessive self-attention is believed to be the basis for certain kinds of abnormal experience and behaviour. The cognitive theory of panic disorder, described in Chapter 7, attributes the cause of episodes of panic to a catastrophic misinterpretation of certain bodily sensations, such as chest pain, sweating, a pounding heart, dizziness (Clark 1986). In vulnerable people, excessive monitoring of one's bodily sensations increases the opportunities for panic. The same is true for other internal events such as memories and images. In cases of obsessive-compulsive disorder (OCD), it has been argued, serious misinterpretations of one's unwanted intrusive thoughts can generate persisting obsessions (Chapter 9). In many instances, the person's hypervigilant monitoring of the acceptability of their thoughts is the root of the trouble.

Excessive self-focused attention is thought to play a significant part in several of the anxiety disorders. There is evidence of a heightened degree of self-focused attention in social anxiety, in test anxiety, sexual anxiety, OCD, health anxiety and panic disorder. Barlow regards the differences in self-evaluative attention as one of the major distinctions between normal and unadaptive anxiety: 'In view of the enormously important role this component [self-evaluative internal focus] seems to play . . . it seems that targeting self-focused attention is essential during therapy' (Barlow 1988: 316). Clinical illustrations are described by D. A. Clark and Beck (2010: 356–358).

Some of the earliest and most convincing evidence of heightened self-focusing was collected by Sarason (1980) and his colleagues in their protracted research into the nature and causes of test anxiety (discussed later in this chapter; see p. 49). One of their major conclusions was that a preoccupation with one's self and one's sensations in the test situation is a major cause of the discomfort and impairment that is observed in affected people. In a classic study by Deffenbacher (1978), subjects worked on anagram problems under high- or low-stress conditions. Measures were obtained of the amount of time that they spent thinking about the task itself, thinking about intrusive ideas that were not relevant to the task, and directing attention towards their bodily sensations. The people who were predisposed to anxiety showed a significant reduction in task-relevant thoughts during the stressful condition relative to the comparison participants. The affected participants also reported more anxiety, more thought interference, and more thoughts that were directed at monitoring their sensations and thinking about the consequences of their test performance. Broadly speaking, the association between self-focused attention and anxiety that is observed in test situations is a multiple of predisposition to anxiety, initial level of arousal, the nature and significance of the particular task, and the degree of stress produced by the task itself. The more complex and demanding the task, and the more significant the outcome, the greater is the likelihood of heightened self-focused attention and consequent anxiety.

Heightened self-focusing occurs among people who experience anxiety in social situations, and indeed the occurrence of this phenomenon is believed to play a major part in producing and maintaining social phobias (see Chapter 11):

> The evidence regarding social and generalized anxiety is also generally supportive of a relation between increased self-focused attention and anxious affect. In individuals with clinical levels of social anxiety, self-focusing does appear to be heightened and related to [the] generalized level of anxiety.
>
> (Ingram 1990: 161)

People who have a chronically high level of self-focused attention are at risk for various psychological difficulties (Ingram 1990: 162). In keeping with the importance attached to self-focused attention, significant reductions in this unadaptive attention are reported after successful treatment (Barlow 2002). In passing, it is interesting to notice that alcohol appears to inhibit self-focusing, and presumably this is why some people use drink to reduce their anxiety in social or other intimidating situations.

There remain a number of problems about the nature of self-focused attention and these include a lack of clarity about the exact differences between excessive self-focused attention and normal self-focused attention. All of this bears on the nature of attentional processes themselves, and it is assumed in all of the theorizing about the role of self-focusing attention that people have a limited attentional capacity, and that an excessive concern with self-focused attention will detract from the attention that might or should be paid to external matters. The concept of limited attentional capacity has been subjected to criticism, but the general idea is as plausible as its opposite – unlimited attentional capacity – is implausible. It is true, however, that the concept of attention is a complex one and we have to take account of the fact that it varies within the same person throughout the day, and can also vary over longer periods, so that one's level of attention may appear to be high for several weeks and then decline in the weeks that follow. We also attend to stimuli that are being perceived by different modalities, as we watch and listen and smell and taste all at the same time. The way in which these attentional resources are allocated, and how the information coming through these different channels is integrated, are fascinating questions. For present purposes, however, the observed association between heightened self-focusing and anxiety, and its probable contribution to anxiety disorders, have useful explanatory value (Clark and Wells 1995). It should be noted, however, that the association between self-focused attention and anxiety is not an exclusive one; there is equally good evidence of a relationship between heightened self-focused attention and depression (Ingram 1990).

The main barrier to elucidating the nature and role of self-focused attention is its elusiveness. Progress is hampered by technical obstacles to measuring self-focused attention. In most circumstances, we are obliged to depend on the person's (usually retrospective) report of what happened. There is also the awkward problem that the act of observing and later reporting one's self-focused attention is bound to affect the very process under examination. There is no shortage of methodological challenges.

Perceptual factors

In addition to selective attention, there is evidence of selective perception and indeed of distortions of perception. Clinical observations indicate that perceptual distortions can take place during episodes of fear, and that the distortions decline after a reduction of the pertinent fear. A patient who experienced increasing apprehension about his ability to control his car experienced acute fear as he approached bridges. As he drove towards a bridge, it appeared to be sloping at a potentially dangerous angle and also seemed to be extremely long. This perceptual distortion occurred only when he was the driver of the vehicle. When the therapist took the wheel, the patient perceived the bridge accurately.

In a second case of driving phobia, the patient had a fear of losing control of the vehicle and reported that when she was frightened, the road appeared to tilt sharply to the right, seemingly dragging the car with it. In response, she tended to over-correct and turn the steering wheel towards the centre of the road, sometimes carrying out this action abruptly. During episodes of intense fear, the surface of the road appeared to deteriorate, and objectively smooth road surfaces were perceived as being corrugated. As in the previous case, she experienced no perceptual distortions whatsoever when the therapist was driving.

A third patient avoided walking over bridges because he feared he might lose control and either run into the oncoming traffic or jump off the bridge. Whenever he felt extremely fearful, the bridges appeared to be longer and far higher than he knew them to be when he was feeling calm. A fourth patient, who suffered from frequent episodes of panic, dating back to a traumatic incident when she experienced a noxious reaction after taking an illicit drug, reported disturbing distortions of perception during periods of extreme anxiety. During these periods, she was inclined to perceive people as being unnaturally thin and tall, just as she had done during the three days following her unfortunate experience with the stimulant drug. She experienced these perceptual distortions only when she was extremely anxious.

The occurrence of fearful distortions was confirmed in an experiment carried out on 60 snake-phobic or spider-phobic volunteer participants (Rachman and Cuk 1992). They were asked to describe their perceptions of the feared object during episodes of fear, and then again after their fears had been reduced. The snake-phobic and spider-phobic subjects showed evidence of some perceptual distortions in the activity of the pertinent feared object, but no distortions of size. After reduction of the relevant fear, the participants reported a significant decline in the perceived activity of the fear-provoking creature. The spider-phobic participants were inclined to perceive the spider as jumping, and the snake-phobic participants perceived more tongue movements in the snake than did the non-fearful comparison participants.

It is probable that there is a connection between frightening distortions and the narrowing of attention that is observed during fear. Both of these biases appear to serve the same psychological function, namely to select and enhance possible sources of threat, all the better to perceive and deal with them. During periods of apprehensive hypervigilance, people concentrate their attention on a narrow focus and probably experience a perceptual enhancement of potential sources of threat.

Anxiety and sexual functioning

Disorders of sexual functioning can arise from biological causes, psychological causes or a combination of both. Erectile dysfunctions, one of the most commonly reported sexual problems, can occur as a result of biological factors or from psychological causes. Similarly, the most commonly reported female sexual problem, low sexual desire, can have a biological or psychological basis (Bancroft 1989).

Barlow (2002) commented on the similarities between sexual anxiety, social anxiety and test anxiety. In all three phenomena, the level of autonomic arousal is only loosely related to the person's performance. Instead, the amount of irrelevant cognitive activity (especially regarding how one is being evaluated and the possibility of failure) is a more reliable predictor of poor performance. Students who are suffering from test anxiety do worse when they focus their attention on self-evaluation than do those students who concentrate on the requirements of the task. In sexual contexts, the perception that one has to perform up to an expected standard, 'elicits negative affective responding, including perceptions of lack of control or inability to obtain desired results . . . at this point a critical shift of attention occurs from external focus (on erotic material in this instance) to a more internal self-evaluative focus' (Barlow 1988: 247). According to Barlow, self-focused attention becomes bound up with 'negative affect' and this in turn increases the intensity of the self-focused attention. These processes cause disruptions in concentration and often will lead to impaired performance. The impaired performance is interpreted as an indication of impending or actual failure, with a consequent increment in anxiety.Although it was widely asserted by clinicians that anxiety is a major contributor to psycho-sexual dysfunctioning (e.g. Wolpe 1958; Barlow 1988; Bancroft 1989), the evidence collected in laboratory studies is not always consistent with this view. The assumption that anxiety impedes sexual performance influenced the considerable efforts made by therapists to reduce their patients' anxiety by techniques such as systematic desensitization (Wolpe 1958), behavioural rehearsals (Masters and Johnson 1970), and so on. Masters and Johnson described anxiety as a major obstacle to normal sexual functioning, and it was believed to be largely responsible for psychological interferences with sexual arousal, particularly in difficulties that men might experience in gaining or maintaining erections. The results of psychological treatment of these difficulties, particularly the difficulties in sexual arousal experienced by men, were modest, but not inconsistent with the beliefs about the connection between anxiety and sexual dysfunction. In keeping with the emphasis placed on self-focused attention and maladaptive cognitions in the related disorders of test anxiety, health anxiety and social anxiety, there has been a shift from anxiety-reducing techniques to the modification of cognitions (Sbrocco and Barlow 1996).

There is an association between anxiety and sexual disorders, but anxiety might not play a causal role; it may be a consequence of some underlying sexual dysfunction or a parallel co-effect (Bancroft 1989). He listed some of the types of anxiety encountered by therapists dealing with sexual problems: a fear of failure, a fear of humiliation, a fear of pain or discomfort, anxiety about satisfying one's partner, a fear of loss of control. To this list we must add the fear of contracting AIDS. Bancroft described the potential for feeling vulnerable in sexual encounters and the need for both partners to have a degree of trust in each other. In the absence of such trust, vulnerability is increased.

For many years it was assumed that anxiety almost always impairs sexual functioning, and might well be the major cause of psychosexual problems. There are, however, exceptions in which anxiety may facilitate rather than decrease sexual arousal and performance (Barlow 2002; Palace and Gorzalka 1990). As mentioned, the results of psychological treatment of erectile difficulties are modest, whereas medications such as Viagra are effective, thereby undermining earlier beliefs about the crucial role of psychological factors. However, the assumption that anxiety plays a significant causal role in most psychosexual disorders remains embedded in contemporary clinical practice.

In the course of studying the relation between anxiety and sexual arousal, it was found that men who appear to have no sexual problems report and show a decrease in sexual arousal under conditions of distraction. On the other hand, men with sexual problems are surprisingly unaffected by the introduction of distractions (Edelmann 1992; Sbrocco and Barlow 1996). There are conditions in which anxiety facilitates rather than inhibits sexual arousal in women, but a comprehensive explanation remains to be set out. A complicating factor is that sexually dysfunctional women report elevated self-focused attention, but are poor at 'reading' the signs of their physiological/sexual arousal, tending to underrate it. They are inclined to be over-attentive but inaccurate.

The earlier view that anxiety is sexually inhibiting is not wholly correct, and an explanation is needed for the facilitatory effects of anxiety on arousal. Clinically, the successful modification of erectile problems by medications, but the modest effects of psychological treatment, have to be taken into account.

Test anxiety

People who experience intense anxiety when carrying out formal tests or other tasks on which they are to be evaluated are said to suffer from *test anxiety*. One of the most influential explanations of test anxiety, promoted by Sarason (1980) and others, is that test-anxious people are negatively self-preoccupied and that during the task, their attention is inappropriately focused on their bodily feelings, expectations of failure, and so on – to the detriment of their test performance. They experience more irrelevant thoughts during the test than do people who are relatively free of anxiety in the test conditions.

> Highly test-anxious individuals typically perform more poorly on cognitive tasks than less anxious individuals, especially if the tasks are difficult and are given under situational conditions of evaluative stress ... the test-anxious individual dividing attention between self-preoccupied worry and task cues and the less anxious person focusing more fully on task-relevant variables.
>
> (Wine 1971)

Although exceptions to these generalizations have been recorded, the overall thrust of the evidence indicates that test-anxious people do approach their evaluative tasks with negative cognitions and also devote a good deal of their attentional efforts to task-irrelevant topics during the test (Sarason 1980). There is also consistent evidence that test-anxious people are more highly aroused in the test situation than are people who are free of anxiety. This difference in level of arousal was taken as a starting point for a number of attempts to treat test anxiety using fear-reducing techniques, such as relaxation and systematic desensitization.

The comparative success of these techniques is consistent with the evidence of increased arousal during test taking, but does little to explain the causal connection between elevated arousal and misdirection of attention. It is probable that arousal and the misdirected attention are interactive. Cognitions can influence the level of arousal, just as the level of arousal can promote an increase in negative cognitions.

The comparative success of the theory introduced to explain test anxiety, and the moderate efficacy of treatment techniques derived from this explanation, are welcome, but should not obscure the fact that in some circumstances, mild to moderate increases in anxiety can facilitate rather than impair performance and achievement (Sarason 1980).

As with all cognitive explanations of anxiety phenomena, there are methodological obstacles to the definition and measurement of the relevant cognitions – which are of course at the core of all of these explanations. Most investigatory procedures require people to assess their own attention, and this affects the very subject under study – attention. Leaving aside questions of the accuracy of self-assessment and self-report, here we have a curious situation in which we ask people to pay attention to their own attention – a potentially muddling regression.

Anxiety and memory

It seems inevitable that we should remember those places, people and events that are threatening, but the evidence is inconsistent. Williams *et al.* (1988: 96) concluded that there is an 'absence of a negative bias in explicit memory for patients with generalized anxiety disorder . . . and it is all the more surprising because there is substantial evidence for the existence of such a bias in depressed patients' (depressed people easily recall upsetting events –an explicit memory bias – but people who are troubled by general anxiety do not show a comparable memory bias for upsetting events). However, it is possible that anxious people do have an *implicit* memory bias regarding negative events. 'Anxious patients definitely do not have a negative memory bias in explicit memory, but there are indications that they may possess a negative implicit memory bias' (Eysenck 1992: 96). That is, they might be influenced by negative memories without being fully aware of the memory and/or its effects on them.

Although there is ample evidence of attentional biases in anxious people, for many years there was only weak and contradictory evidence of *memory* biases in these people. The studies showing conclusive evidence of memory biases in depressed subjects were difficult to replicate in people with anxiety.

> It appears that different emotions may be more specific in their effects on cognitive processing than was originally thought. One possible interpretation of the data . . . is that anxious subjects, but not depressed subjects, orient their attention towards threat. Depressed subjects (but not generally anxious subjects) may selectively remember negative material.
>
> (Williams *et al.* 1988: 168)

The evidence on memory biases is not consistent (Coles and Heimberg 2002; Edelmann 1992; Eysenck 1992; Williams *et al.* 1988). There is evidence of memory bias in one anxiety disorder, but not in another. The distinction between implicit and explicit memory is sometimes lost, and results from recall and recognition tasks can differ. Memory bias is particularly difficult to demonstrate in broad, non-focused disorders of anxiety such as generalized anxiety disorder (GAD), but easier to find in focused disorders such as panic disorder and OCD. Memory biases are so prominent in post-traumatic stress disorders (PTSD) that they are a diagnostic sign.

Cloitre *et al.* (1992) found evidence of a memory advantage for threat-related material among patients with panic disorder, but no evidence of a comparable bias among social phobic patients. A similar failure was reported by Rapee *et al.* (1992) and by Chambless and Hope (1996). Dalgleish (1994) also failed to find a relationship between anxiety and memory bias.

On the other hand, McNally *et al.* (1995) found memory disorders in patients suffering from post-traumatic stress disorder, and Sher *et al.* (1984) reported that normal respondents who scored highly on a questionnaire of obsessive-compulsiveness had poorer memory for prior actions than did control participants who returned merely average scores on the questionnaire. In contrast, Constans *et al.* (1995) found that patients with obsessional problems showed recall of recent actions that was, if anything, superior to that of controls. Comparable findings were obtained by Radomsky and Rachman (1999) and by Ceschi *et al.* (2003).

The memory for threatening stimuli was studied in a group of people with OCD who had fears of contamination. They were shown

25 clean and 25 contaminated items (Radomsky and Rachman 1999) and then completed a standard test of memory, after which they were asked to recall the original 50 items. They showed a superior recall of the contaminated items, unlike the participants in the two comparison groups. There were no differences between the groups on a standard test of memory. In a replication of this study, Ceschi *et al.* (2003) found superior recognition, but not recall, of the contaminated items.

Bradley *et al.* (1995) produced evidence of explicit and implicit memory biases in depressed patients, but found no evidence of these biases in anxious patients. These results were consistent with their view that

> depressives show memory biases in explicit memory tasks
> ... such as free recall or recognition ... there is little
> evidence that they are biased in early attentional processes.
> By contrast anxiety is associated with early attentional
> mood-congruent biases but there is little consistent evi-
> dence of such biases in explicit memory tasks.
>
> (Bradley *et al.* 1995: 755)

These results and conclusions were consistent with the evidence available at the time, but there are reasons to expect that these cognitive biases in attention and memory will be found to operate in depression and in anxiety.

For elaborate reasons, Williams *et al.* (1988) and Mathews *et al.* (1989) argued that clinically anxious people should display a negative bias in implicit memory, but not in explicit memory. Williams *et al.* (1988: 167) reported that 'repeated attempts to demonstrate a relation between anxiety and recall have failed'.

These failures speak to the elusiveness of the phenomenon, rather than its non-existence. The failures were ironic because one of the earliest and prized examples of implicit memory, confirming the operation of non-conscious processes in memory, was provided by Claparède (1911) in a clinical situation in which anxiety may well have been operative.

Claparède carried out a series of investigations into the memorial functioning of a 47-year-old woman residing at the Bel-Air asylum. Her memory for distant events was intact, but she did not know where she was, or even that she had been in the asylum for five years. She did not recognize the physicians whom she saw every day, nor her nurse who had been with her every day for six months. She forgot from one moment to the next what she had been told, and knew neither the day nor month, even though she was repeatedly given this information. Interestingly, she remembered the position of the toilets, the times for meals, etc., even though she was unable to recognize the asylum or her presence in it.

In a famous demonstration, Claparède pricked her hand with a pin held between his fingers. The pain was as quickly forgotten as all other new information, and seconds after being pricked, she could remember nothing of the event. However, when he brought his hand close to hers a second time, she pulled back her hand without knowing why. When asked why she pulled back, she responded: 'Well, don't I have the right to pull my hand away?', 'Maybe there is a pin hidden in your hand?' When asked why she thought about the pin, she replied, 'It's just an idea which crossed my mind.' She never recognized the idea of being 'pricked' as a memory. Her avoidance behaviour indicates that she was responding to the threat of repeated pain, even though she could not recall the reason for her fear.

Given that anxiety arises from the detection of a signal of threat, it is inconceivable that dependable and even enhanced memory does not play a major part in this process of detection. The alternative, a threat detection system without a memory, seems inconceivable. We would enter every potentially threatening situation fresh and unarmed, as if each situation was novel. Of course we are not so unprepared. There is abundant evidence of the occurrence of acquired anxiety, including the much studied conditioned form of anxiety, which was for many years the foundation on which the entire theory of anxiety was based (Eysenck and Rachman 1965; Mowrer 1939, 1960; Wolpe 1958). Learned anxiety, including conditioned anxiety, is readily re-evoked or recalled. We have memories of fear and anxiety, and many of these are so accessible that they can be recalled with relative ease.

In cases of PTSD, however, some important events are relatively inaccessible to the verbal memory system. Brewin (2001, 2011) makes a critical distinction between verbally accessible memories and 'situational' memories in PTSD (see Chapter 13). The inaccessible memories tend to be vivid and intense (e.g. flashbacks) and are negatively biased for the most part. However, some can be readily evoked by trauma-related cues, and in this sense are positively biased. A patient who had been traumatized by a serious accident was unable to recall the details of the event, but the sound of a collision instantly triggered a full, vivid recall of the crash.

For therapeutic purposes, as in the first and best established of the modern techniques for reducing fear, desensitization (Wolpe 1958), past fears are deliberately re-evoked. Non-clinical participants and patients are easily capable of recalling the content and qualities of past episodes of anxiety; and in most instances, can re-experience anxiety that resembles past episodes of anxiety if they wish to do so for therapeutic or other reasons. Recent findings on the power of intrusive aversive images (often of past events or associations with such events) reveal them to be intense, evocative, vivid and unchanging. There is a large memorial component in many of the images. Given the emotional impact and personal significance of aversive images – for example, in cases of PTSD – the operation of a memorial bias seems certain.

Given the role of memory in anxiety, and the evidence of significant memory biases in disorders such as depression, it is highly probable that biases of memory are at play in anxiety. Otherwise, we are left to assume that memory in anxiety is uniquely unbiased and peculiarly accurate.

If memories of past episodes of anxiety are essential for the efficient operation of the threat detection system, and if we can easily recall past anxiety, it is certain that we are also influenced by memories of which we are not always aware (e.g. as in conditioned fears and in PTSD). Just as non-conscious factors influence the selective attentional processes involved in anxiety, so it is highly probable that non-conscious memorial processes, such as those involved in implicit memory, influence anxiety. The nature and operations of the non-conscious memorial processes involved in anxiety remain to be elucidated. No doubt they too will be found to be subject to bias and also to be of considerable importance.

It is likely that mood-congruent recall occurs in anxious moods. It is certainly the case that the relations between mood and memory, particularly as set out by Bower (1981), are more complex and elusive than was originally thought, and the occurrence of mood-congruent recall associated with depressive mood is well established (Suedfeld and Eich 1995). The vivid case histories described by Grinker and Spiegel (1945) provide powerful, if inconclusive, evidence of anxious-mood-congruent recall of traumatic experiences.

Memories can be enhanced or impaired by anxiety. In some circumstances, anxiety decreases the accessibility of a memory rather than increasing it. For example, McNally et al. (1995) found impaired accessibility of autobiographical memories in PTSD sufferers.

The very selectivity of selective attention implies the operation of memorial influences. Certainly some signals of threat have intrinsically alarming characteristics (e.g. Gray 1971, 1982) and the entire concept of prepared fears (Seligman 1971) rests on a similar assumption, but the leading theorists on the subject of 'intrinsic' fear signals, namely Gray and Seligman, also attach considerable importance to the influence of learned signals of threat or danger. These learned signals of threat can be evoked or recalled and are bound to influence the selectivity and focus of one's attention when entering a potentially threatening situation. The selectivity of attention in a threatening situation is likely to be influenced by memories of previous encounters with the particular situation and encounters with other comparable situations. Again, it seems probable that these influential memories are subject to bias. Given the evidence of memory biases in depression, it seems inevitable that attentional processes in anxiety are also biased.

The patients with obsessive-compulsive disorder whose attention was intensely focused on signs of blood or other threatening stimuli, described in Chapter 3 ('Vulnerability'), were attending to these particular stimuli because of their biased recall of threatening information regarding diseases such as AIDS, and because of their past encounters with blood spots and traces. The selectivity of their anxious attention was determined in large part by their particular memories, some of which were definitely skewed. Their memories were more disturbed (and disturbing) than the original events which were the subject of their recall. Comparatively mild events had become transformed into remembered catastrophes. But not all of these memories are errors of negative bias. Some of the memories are enhanced; that is, positively biased.

It is evident to clinicians that many patients with OCD have well-developed memorial abilities and can recall precise details of situations and experiences that were disturbing or threatening in the past (Radomsky and Rachman 1999). As described in Chapter 3, a patient who was intensely frightened of disease-related contaminants, could recall in detail the types of blood stain or other threatening material that he had encountered in particular places as far back as 12 years ago. The same patient also had a milder fear of making errors, and as a result, engaged in a certain amount of checking behaviour, especially to ensure the stove had been switched off. As is common in compulsive checking, he frequently had difficulty remembering whether or not he had correctly turned off the stove, and on numerous occasions felt compelled to return to the kitchen to check his memory. So we have a not uncommon example in this type of disorder of a curious combination of excellent and precisely accurate memory relating to some threats, but a weak and infirm recollection of other activities. Incidentally, this kind of intra-person inconsistency in memorial ability and performance is not easily compatible with assumptions of a biological causation of significant memory and other cognitive impairments in the anxiety disorders (e.g. memory impairments in OCD).

In some disorders, notably PTSD, disturbances of memory are of central importance and for this reason, as well as general scientific interest, the relation between anxiety and memory is of considerable interest.

Emotional processing

In the face of a potential threat, anxiety is appropriate. However, there are many instances in which the anxiety is disproportionately intense or persists long after the removal of the threat. The model of emotional processing was introduced primarily to tackle the phenomenon of the persistence of unabsorbed emotional experiences, such as excessively persistent anxiety, nightmares, obsessions, and so forth. It is assumed that there is a natural tendency for people to absorb emotionally disruptive experiences, including anxiety, and that the failure to do so is an indication of unsatisfactory emotional processing. It is inviting to think of successful emotional processing as a manifestation of the psychological immune system.

Satisfactory emotional processing is evident when the anxiety declines, agitated behaviour decreases, concentration improves and the person returns to 'routine' behaviour and thoughts. The person can talk about, see, listen to or be reminded of emotional events without experiencing stress or disruptions. Failures of emotional processing (nightmares, disturbing intrusive images and memories, unrelenting anxiety) can be seen as failures of the psychological immune system (Rachman 2001).

Satisfactory emotional processing is promoted by graded exposures to the threatening situation, calm rehearsals, catharsis, relaxation, and correction of misinterpretations of threat. Variables that impede emotional processing include excessive avoidance behaviour, unpredicted re-exposures, uncontrollable re-exposure, fatigue and persisting misinterpretations of the nature and consequences of the perceived threat. Discussions of the nature of emotional processing are provided by Lang (1977, 1985) and Rachman (1980, 1990, 2001).

Affect and cognition

Many accounts of the connections between affect and cognition assume that the cognitions which influence affective experience are essentially conscious and easily accessible. This view has been criticized on many grounds, and the assumption that reasoning always precedes emotional reactions has been challenged by Zajonc (1980). He asserted that 'preferences need no inferences', and although he overstated his argument, Zajonc provided examples of writings on the subject of cognition and affect that fail to take into account the influence of non-conscious factors on emotional experiences and manifestations. There is evidence that some of the cognitive processes involved in emotional experiences are outside of easy awareness, and function at an automatic level.

Thoughts and feelings – concepts that have been expanded and renamed cognition and affect – commonly combine, but it is their opposing pulls that evoke greatest interest. They are so finely intertwined that the task of unravelling them can seem futile. People often need to exert a great deal of effort in attempting to control their fear and anxiety by cognitive means, because these emotions can be so aversive and dominating. Anxiety disorders are examples of such domination. Patients who are persistently anxious about dying of a heart attack, even though they accept medical advice that they are in sound health, can be said to suffer from an imbalance between cognition and affect, to suffer from an imbalance between thoughts and feelings. Patients suffering from obsessive-compulsive disorders can also be said to be suffering from a domination of affect. They are well aware that their intense fears of disease contagion are excessive and even groundless, and that washing their hands repetitively is futile. Their anxiety is so dominating, however, that it overrules their rational appraisal.

The concept of irrational behaviour – illustrated by obsessive-compulsive disorders, for example – incorporates the idea of a clash between affect and cognition. In addition to conflicts of this character, there are other inconsistencies between cognition and affect. It is common to feel extreme apprehension without a satisfactory explanation of the cause or source of the dread, a disconnection that is embedded in most definitions of anxiety. For example, one might have a conditioned anxiety reaction to stimuli of which one is unaware. It is also possible to attribute one's extreme apprehension to an incorrect cause or source – such misinterpretations are regarded by cognitive behaviour therapists as the very basis of anxiety disorders (D. A. Clark and Beck 2010; D. M. Clark 1986, 1997; Salkovskis 1996a).

Zajonc argued that affective judgements

> may be fairly independent of and precede in time the sorts of perceptual and cognitive operations commonly assumed to be the basis of these affective judgments ... affective reactions can occur without extensive perceptual and cognitive encoding, are made with greater confidence than cognitive judgments and can be made sooner ... it is concluded that affect and cognition are under the control of separate and partially independent systems...
>
> (Zajonc 1980: 151)

He laid great stress on the claim that affect is often, even usually, pre-cognitive. According to Zajonc, the features of a stimulus or set of stimuli that determine affective reactions 'might be gross, vague and global ... thus they might be insufficient as a basis for cognitive judgments...' (1980: 159). He contrasted affective responses with 'cold cognitions' and described affective responses as 'effortless, inescapable, irrevocable, holistic, more difficult to verbalize, yet easy to communicate and understand' (1980: 169). He also described affective responses as instantaneous, dominant, primary, pre-cognitive and automatic. For example, we might experience an 'instant' liking for a person on first meeting, and a troubling 'instant' dislike of a new person, even though we recognize the absurdity and injustice of our reactions.

Most of Zajonc's supportive evidence was drawn from research in social psychology, with an emphasis on the development of affective preferences, but some of his observations have been extended to clinical phenomena. Evidence for non-conscious cognitive processing comes from various sources, including subliminal perceptions (e.g. Dixon 1981), selective attention (e.g. Broadbent 1958, 1971; Treisman 1960), implicit memory (e.g. Tulving 1983; Teasdale and Barnard 1993), verbal reports of cognitive operations (Nisbett and Wilson 1977), the phenomena of automatic cognitive processing (e.g. McNally 1995). Reviews of non-conscious processes involved in anxiety are provided by Michael Eysenck (1992), Eysenck *et al.* (2007) .

The attentional processes that play so important a part in anxiety are not always in the forefront of awareness (see McNally 1995). On a broader level, the implicational meaning of the cognitions that may well contribute to anxiety are not readily accessible (Teasdale and

Barnard 1993). As Michael Eysenck (1992) noted in his analysis of the biological value of anxiety, a system that is 'specially adapted for the purpose of threat detection' must include 'sensors' that facilitate rapid, early, accurate detection. He suggests that, 'Almost certainly, pre-attentive and/or attentional processes are centrally involved' (1992: 5). Given that the rapid detection of early warning signs of danger is of value for survival, any warning system that depended on a careful, rational appraisal of each threat would forfeit refinement for failure.

Summary

People become highly vigilant when entering a potentially intimidating situation; they scan broadly, then focus narrowly on any perceived threat. Attention and sensitivity are enhanced and ongoing behaviour is inhibited. If the potential threat is interpreted as dangerous, then anxiety arises and is followed by escape, avoidance or coping behaviour. The narrowing of attention can be directed externally or internally (self-focused attention). Excessive self-focused attention is implicated in various forms of anxiety, notably test anxiety, health anxiety, social anxiety and sexual anxiety.

People vary in their vulnerability to anxiety, with the most anxiety-prone people inclined to be overly vigilant and to scan rapidly. They are also inclined to misperceive or misinterpret events and/or exaggerate their seriousness.

Anxiety and memory interact and influence the processing of emotional events or materials. Emotional processing is impeded by excessive arousal, avoidance, fatigue, misperceptions and misinterpretations. The relations between affect (feelings), such as anxiety, and cognition are complex and contain important non-conscious elements.

Theories of anxiety 5

The four main approaches to anxiety are learning theory accounts (including the conditioning theory), cognitive explanations, psycho-analytic theory and biological explanations.

Anxiety as the product of learning

The idea that fear and anxiety are acquired by a process of learning, most particularly by conditioning, has a long and fruitful history. It originated from Pavlov's discovery of conditioning processes and its application to the acquisition of emotional responses. The idea was revised and developed by Watson and Rayner (1920) and Jones (1924) and subsequently elevated to a formal theory by Mowrer (1939) in his classic paper entitled, 'A stimulus-response theory of anxiety'. Some of the key ideas were subjected to experimental analyses and later applied to clinical problems by Wolpe (1958), and incorporated into his general theory of personality by H. J. Eysenck (1957, 1967). Eysenck's successor as Professor of Psychology at the Institute of Psychiatry, Gray (1971, 1982, 1987) later developed an essentially psycho-physiological extension of these ideas, and introduced many novel ones. In keeping with the increasing influence of cognitive analyses in psychology in general, the learning theory analysis of anxiety has now been expanded to include important cognitive components. In particular, the writings of Beck and Emery (1985), Beck and D. A. Clark (1997), D. A. Clark and Beck (2010), D. M. Clark (1986, 1999), Salkovskis (1985, 1996a), Salkovskis *et al.* (1998) and Barlow (1988, 2002) have strongly influenced the way that anxiety is construed (Rachman 1996, 2009).

The essence of the learning theory approach is that fears are acquired by conditioning or other learning processes and in turn generate escape and/or avoidance behaviour. The fear-generated behaviour persists because it is at least partly successful – escape or avoidance typically is followed by a significant reduction in fear or anxiety, thereby reinforcing the successful behaviour itself. In one of the earliest statements of the learning theory of fear, it was assumed that any neutral stimulus is potentially capable of being converted through a process of conditioning into a stimulus.

'Phobias are regarded as conditioned anxiety (fear) reactions. Any "neutral" stimulus, simple or complex, that happens to impact on an individual at about the time that a fear reaction is evoked acquires the ability to evoke fear subsequently' (Wolpe and Rachman 1960: 145). As will be seen, this statement of the theory underwent significant revisions.

Eysenck's theory

Eysenck's theory (1957, 1967) and that of Wolpe (1958) had important implications for the psychology of anxiety. Both of them set their theories of neuroses in a learning theory framework, emphasizing the role of conditioning processes. Eysenck was most interested in neuroses and the personality factors that predispose people to develop these disorders. He argued that emotionally unstable introverts are at high risk for acquiring conditioned anxiety responses, whereas unstable extroverts are at risk for developing conduct disorders, personality problems or hysteria. Wolpe's aim was to explain the genesis of neuroses with a view to developing effective methods of treatment. Wolpe was a clinician-researcher, Eysenck a personality theorist who drew clinical implications from his main theory.

Eysenck's (1957) original work on the anxiety neuroses was based on his two-dimensional model of personality. The two dimensions, which can be plotted at right angles to each other are emotional instability (neuroticism) and introversion/extraversion.

> In our general system introverts are postulated to condition more easily and therefore, to acquire the conditioned anxieties and fears characteristic of the dysthymic more easily than other people, whereas psychopaths and prisoners generally are people who condition poorly and who,

therefore, fail to acquire the conditioned responses characterizing the socialization process.

(Eysenck and Rachman 1965: 24)

Conditioned anxiety responses are the result of a single traumatic event or a series of sub-traumatic events, involving strong nervous system reactions. It was assumed that a previously neutral stimulus becomes connected through association with an unconditioned stimulus that evoked traumatic emotional reactions.

From now on it will be found that the conditioned stimulus, as well as the unconditioned stimulus, produces the original maladaptive emotional behaviour. This, it seems to us, is the essential learning process which takes place in the development of a neurosis.

(Eysenck and Rachman 1965: 4)

Those conditioned responses which are not reinforced begin to be extinguished. This extinction process occurs in conditioned anxiety responses, as it does in all other conditioned responses, and gives rise to the clinical phenomenon of 'spontaneous remission'.

Eysenck relied on Mowrer's (1939, 1960) theory to explain the persistence of anxiety and the associated avoidance behaviour. In brief,

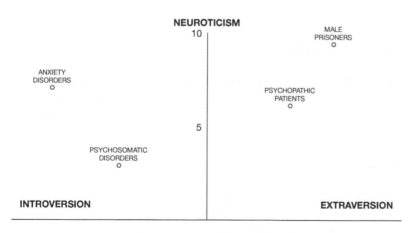

FIGURE 5.1

Eysenck's two-dimensional model of neurosis

Adapted from Eysenck and Rachman (1965: 21)

anxiety reactions also take on motivating properties. In an attempt to reduce their anxiety, people engage in escape or avoidance behaviour. To the extent that the escape or avoidance is indeed followed by a reduction in anxiety, this behaviour becomes strengthened, and the anxiety reactions are preserved from extinction. The personality theory was supported by a great deal of psychometric and experimental data and the clinical implications were drawn out (Eysenck 1957, 1967).

Wolpe's theory (1958) of the neuroses was similarly based on the assumption that the anxiety, a major feature of neuroses, arises through a process of conditioning. His explanation for the maintenance of the conditioned anxiety and other neurotic reactions similarly relied on Mowrer's ideas of reinforcement through the reduction of anxiety. Wolpe (1958) then went on to develop laboratory techniques for inhibiting the conditioned anxiety reactions, ultimately transferring these to clinical practice (Wolpe 1958). The best established of the fear-reducing techniques which he introduced, systematic desensitization, was assumed to operate through a process of reciprocal inhibition. The deliberate and repeated superimposition of an incompatible response on the anxiety reaction steadily gives rise to the development of inhibitory processes that will eventually lead to the elimination of the anxiety pattern. The technique was investigated intensively in the laboratory and widely adopted in clinical practice, laying the foundation for one of the two major streams of what became known as behaviour therapy (Lang 1970; Lang et al. 1970; Rachman 1996, 2009).

Gray's theory

Gray (1971, 1982, 1987) agreed with several components of Eysenck's theory, including the dimensional approach to the analysis of personality predispositions to anxiety, recognition of the biological contributions to the main dimensions of personality, the role of conditioning, and so forth. However, Gray's elaboration of the theory was primarily psycho-physiological and was based on a formidable assembly of psychopharmacological data and countless experiments on learning in animals. He suggested a rotation of Eysenck's dimensions of introversion and emotional stability to emphasize the importance of impulsivity (Gray 1987: 350). Gray claimed that, contrary to Eysenck's suggestion, extroverts have difficulty in acquiring fear reactions, but are not slow at developing conditioned responses in general. According to Gray, neuroticism indicates heightened sensitivity to reinforcing events, and introversion represents increasing sensitivity to signals of punishment rather than to signals of reward.

Gray collected convincing evidence that the behavioural effects of punishment and of non-reward are similar and probably mediated by common processes. There is also evidence suggesting a similarity between reward and non-punishment. Signals of punishment or of non-reward trigger the behavioural inhibition system, a psycho-physiological system that causes an inhibition of ongoing behaviour. This behavioural inhibition system can also be triggered by novel stimuli or by stimuli that are innately fear-producing. Anxiety is 'a central state that mediates behavioural responses to stimuli that signal either punishment or non-reward' (Gray 1986: 220).

This analysis led Gray to reconsider the nature of avoidance conditioning, and in particular, to propose some improvements to the Mowrer theory. This, it will be recalled, states that stimuli which are followed by punishment come to elicit conditioned fear reactions. Behaviour that produces a reduction in this fear is reinforced. Seligman and Johnston (1973) argued that Mowrer's theory has difficulty in accounting for the persistence of the avoidance behaviour, among other problems. Gray made extensive use of the concept of *safety signals* in his reinterpretation of this persistence. These signals are promoted when an anticipated punishment fails to occur. Safety signals are rewards and elicit approach behaviour. They also signal a period and a place of safety, a period and place in which the person or animal can expect freedom from punishment. 'Safety signals reduce fear and provide secondary reward for the avoidance response; but at the same time they preserve fear from complete extinction and so ensure their own continued potency.' (Gray 1987: 227). As will be seen presently, this elegant analysis of safety signals, the details of which are not necessary for present purposes, is relevant for understanding various aspects of anxiety, including generalized anxiety (see Chapter 12). Gray's inclusion of 'innate fear stimuli' as one of the four triggers of the behavioural inhibition system is consistent with the views of Seligman, Ohman and others. According to Seligman:

[T]he great majority of phobias are about objects of natural importance to the survival of the species . . . The theory does not deny that other phobias are possible, it only claims that they should be less frequent, since they are less prepared.

(Seligman and Hager 1972: 450)

Seligman argued that human phobias are largely restricted to objects that have 'threatened survival, potential predators, unfamiliar places, and the dark' (Seligman and Hager 1972: 465). Like Gray, Seligman argues that certain kinds of fears are readily acquired because of an inherent biological preparedness. According to Seligman, prepared fears are easily acquired, selective, resistant to extinction and probably non-cognitive. The prepared fears can be acquired even by watered-down representations of the actual threat. This idea of selectivity runs contrary to the earlier view of conditioning in which it was assumed that *any* neutral stimulus can be turned into a conditioned signal of fear, and that no differences should be anticipated between stimuli.

Seligman's introduction of the concept of preparedness, constructed within the framework of modern learning theory, provoked a good deal of interest, and results from the pioneering experiments carried out by Ohman and his colleagues (1975) were followed closely. They demonstrated that people respond differently to presentations of prepared stimuli than they do to unprepared neutral stimuli. For example, fear responses to photographs of snakes differed from those evoked by photographs of flowers or mushrooms. By this step, they were able to promote Seligman's ideas and provide a test-bed for further investigations. Regrettably, over the next few years, there was a gradual accumulation of disappointing results and interest in the concept of prepared phobias waned (McNally 1987).

Evidence that the prepared fears generated in the laboratory are easily wiped out by verbal instructions undermined one of the most appealing characteristics of the concept, for these laboratory fears fall far short of the main features of phobias. The laboratory fears are not easily acquired, or stable, or non-cognitive, and show little resemblance to the concept of prepared phobias as set out by Seligman.

It has been suggested that these disappointing results are attributable to a weak methodology, and that more powerful stimuli and more appropriate measures of fear are needed before the theory can be subjected to rigorous testing. The prepared phobias which are the subject of the theory are intense, vivid, resistant and persisting fears, and it is on such fears that the theory must be assessed and not on the fragile and fleeting fears that were reproduced in the original laboratory experiments. An excellent research model was provided by Mineka's (1985) outstanding experiments on intense and vivid fears in monkeys. She proved that monkeys are indeed predisposed to fear snakes (but not to 'unprepared' cues), and that their fears can be triggered by observational learning.The broader significance of this research is considered in the section on pathways to fear (see Chapter 10).

Longitudinal studies, exemplified by the Dunedin cohort study described in Chapter 6 ('Fears born and bred'), are another source of information about learned and prepared fears. Information about the genesis of fears provided by experimental analyses and longitudinal research is an essential complement to the common method of interviewing and/or questionnaires because the person's recollections may be elusive, incomplete or incorrect. A total reliance on interviews and questionnaires is unsatisfactory.

Cognitive analyses of anxiety

The infusion of cognitive concepts into abnormal psychology has promoted an expanded and deeper understanding of anxiety (Barlow 2002; Beck and Rush 1985; Brewin 1996, 2003; Rachman 2009). Beck's work has been particularly influential.

> It is hypothesized that a precipitating event (or series of events) elicits or magnifies an underlying attitude of fear. These events may impinge on the patient's specific vulnerabilities to elicit such danger related ideation. Subsequently, the patient is overly vigilant of danger. He scans internal and external stimuli for 'dangerous' properties. When new situations with possibilities of unpleasant outcomes are encountered, they are construed as dangerous. That is, the patient magnifies the possibility and intensity of unpleasant outcomes in his cognition of the situation.
>
> (Beck and Rush 1985: 365)

Beck's approach was elaborated by Salkovskis:

> The fundamental idea is that emotions are experienced as a result of the way in which events are interpreted or appraised. It is the meaning of events that triggers emotions rather than the events themselves. The particular appraisal made will depend on the context in which an event occurs, the mood the person is in at the time it occurs, and the person's past experiences. Particular types of emotions depend upon this specific interpretation. Effectively this means that the same event can evoke a different

emotion in different people, or even different emotions in the same person on different occasions.

(Salkovskis 1996a: 48)

Significant advances have been made in coming to grips with the nature of panic disorder, social phobias, health anxiety, PTSD, obsessions and compulsions. The cognitive analyses of panic set out by Barlow (1988, 2002) and by D. M. Clark (1986, 1988, 1996, 1999) are broadly similar, but were arrived at independently. For purposes of the present account, Clark's theory will be taken as the example. He argued with notable success that panics are caused by catastrophic misinterpretations of bodily sensations. This idea, the evidence for and against, and a critical evaluation are given in Chapter 7 ('The cognitive theory of panic'); but for the present, it suffices to say that it also produced secondary benefits in the form of fresh re-examinations of a host of anxiety phenomena and disorders (Rachman 1996, 2009, 2012).

The theoretical analyses set out by D. M. Clark (1986, 1997, 1999), Barlow (1988, 2002), Salkovskis (1985), Salkovskis *et al.* (1998) and others were strongly influenced by Beck's ideas, and then expanded beyond Beck's theory. The expanded theories are less 'pathological' and regard many problems as understandable errors of normal functioning rather than as signs of deep-rooted abnormalities, be they biological or characterological. Emphasis is placed on the continuities between normal and abnormal anxiety. The theories place great emphasis on the links between cognitions and behaviour. Given their background and training, most of the new theorists moved from a preoccupation with behaviour towards the inclusion of cognitive concepts, whereas Beck began as a 'cognitivist' and gradually increased his attention to the behavioural determinants of anxiety disorders and their treatment. Beck later incorporated information-processing ideas into his construal of anxiety, consistent with the trends in anxiety research generally.

The current cognitive model of anxiety consists of three stages: registration of the threat, 'activation of a primal threat mode', and the subsequent evocation of secondary, elaborative checking (Beck and D. A. Clark 1997: 49; D. A. Clark and Beck 2010). The treatment of anxiety must deactivate the primal threat mode.

The cognitive theories make full allowance for the acquisition of fears by the processes of learning, including conditioning, but place the main emphasis on the affected person's interpretation of the events, regardless of whether they are conditioned or not. Moreover, it is argued that the anxiety reactions persist largely as a result of the persisting maladaptive cognitions and that the most effective and most lasting way to reduce or remove unadaptive anxiety is to modify or remove the responsible cognitions. At the same time, it is recognized that bringing about behavioural changes is a powerful way of modifying maladaptive anxiety-producing cognitions – in addition to inhibiting self-defeating escape and avoidance patterns of behaviour. It is not always the case that the anxious behaviour is driven solely by the cognitions. In many instances, the cognitions appear to be driven and maintained by inappropriate behaviour such as avoidance, physical or mental escape and so forth. Critical evaluations of the progress and standing of the cognitive theory of anxiety have been made by Austin and Richards (2000), Clark (1999), Klein (1987) and McNally (1994).

Psychoanalytic explanations

Freud (1948, 1950) was one of the earliest writers to draw attention to the importance of anxiety. He argued that anxiety is a pervasive and critical component of the neuroses, and distinguished between 'objective anxiety' and 'neurotic anxiety'. By objective anxiety, he meant fear reactions to the perception of an external danger or in expectation of an injury which is foreseen. He cautioned that objective anxiety is rational and expedient in many cases, but there are many instances in which it is inappropriate or excessive and shades over into neurotic anxiety. Neurotic anxiety was regarded as inexpedient and excessive, paralyzing actions and even hindering flight. The main characteristic of neurotic anxiety, according to Freud, is a general apprehensiveness, 'free-floating' anxiety (Freud 1949: 332). People who constantly experience this 'expectant dread' are tormented and always anticipate the worst outcomes. This tendency, to be over-anxious and pessimistic, was regarded as a character trait.

Freud also described another form of anxiety, a more circumscribed type. This category consists of what would today be called phobias, such as intense fears of closed spaces, snakes, crowds, and so forth. These phobias are not inherently irrational, in that the fear is not entirely groundless, but if it is excessive or inappropriate, then it qualifies for the term phobia. In passing, it is interesting to notice that Freud accepted the view expressed by G. Stanley Hall that 'there is a peculiar prepotent quality about some of these fears that suggest such ancient origin . . . [and] their relative intensity fits past conditions far better than it does present ones' (Hall 1897: 245–246). Freud wrote that certain fears are innate in the sense that we are predisposed to develop them very readily – 'the fear of small animals, thunderstorms, etc. might perhaps be accounted for as vestigial traces of the congenital preparedness to meet objective dangers which is so strongly developed in other animals' (Freud 1953: 286). Hall and Freud's writings foreshadowed the concept of 'prepared fears' described in 1971 by Martin Seligman.

The psychoanalytic approach to *anxiety* is in keeping with the general theory of psychoanalysis. Anxiety is said to be largely sexual in origin and for this reason the unacceptable sexual impulses are repressed into the unconscious. These repressed ideas and impulses are then transformed into symbolic representations. According to Freud, 'it remains incontestable that for the average human being anxiety is closely connected with sexual restriction' (Freud 1949; 336). The resultant anxiety is replaced by neurotic symptoms, dream symbols, and so forth. The development of anxiety is said to be the reaction of the ego to danger from the demands of its libido, and in this way an internal danger is converted into an external one (Freud 1949; 338). When a person's sexual drive cannot be satisfied, it is 'discharged through being converted into dread' (Freud 1949: 339).

According to Sperling (1971: 493), a fear of spiders is 'an indication of unresolved separation conflict and a high degree of ambivalence which intensifies bisexuality and the problem of sexual identification'. The development of a fear of spiders, according to Sperling, is a form of defence against more threatening problems or impulses of a sexual kind. Abraham (1927), a close colleague of Freud's, maintained that the fear of spiders is symbolic of an unconscious fear of sexual genitalia – the penis embedded in the female genitals. It should be said, however, that these complex and colourful explanations of the fear of spiders, as in the case of fear of snakes and other fears, are difficult to reconcile with modern experimental analyses of these fears. The fear of spiders – as with a fear of snakes and other circumscribed fears or phobias – is relatively simple and readily reduced, typically within three to six sessions, or with the newest methods, even within a single session (Ost 1989).

The foundation for the psychoanalytic theory of fears was laid by Freud himself in the famous case of a five-year-old boy, little Hans, who feared horses (Freud 1905). This case history was celebrated as a major advance and was thought to provide essential support for some of the important concepts of psychoanalysis including the Oedipus complex, repression, castration anxiety and so forth. In this famous monograph, Freud described and discussed in great detail, covering

140 pages, the events of a few months. The case material on which his analysis was based was collected by the father of the little boy, and he kept Freud informed of the developments by regular written reports on his son. The father had several consultations with Freud about the boy's fear (both parents were lay adherents of psychoanalysis). During the analysis, Freud saw the little boy once.

The essence of the case is that at the age of four, little Hans began to complain of a fear of horses and this generalized towards animals and objects that had some resemblance to a horse's muzzle. During the period when he complained of the fear, Hans was engaged by his father in repeated conversations and interrogations, and the father then communicated his interpretations to Freud. The material on which Freud's extended account is based, and which provided the raw material for a theory of fear, and for other concepts in the general theory of psychoanalysis, was almost entirely third-hand, and the reporter was a central figure emotionally involved in the case.

The little boy's fear of horses was interpreted as a symbol of a more serious latent fear. In him, as in so many others, it was said to be a fear of his father engendered by anticipation of punishment (probably castration) for having experienced sexual desires for his mother. The fear of horses was interpreted as a manifestation of the child's Oedipus complex: little Hans experienced a sexual desire for his mother, followed by a fear of retribution from his father. These thoughts were unacceptable and the fear of his father was transformed into a more acceptable fear – of horses.

The interpretation of this case has been subject to criticism (e.g. Crews 1998; Wolpe and Rachman 1960). Freud conceded that:

> It is true that during the analysis Hans had to be told many things which he could not say himself, that he had to be presented with the thoughts that he had so far showed no signs of possessing and that his attention had to be turned in the direction from which his father was expecting something to come. This detracts from the evidential value of the analysis, but the procedure is the same in every case.
>
> (Freud 1905: 246)

The little boy's explanation of the origin of his phobia was straightforward. He claimed that it started when he witnessed a street accident in which a horse collapsed. His father added that all of this was confirmed by his wife, and by the fact that Hans's fear emerged immediately after the accident.

The fascinating psychoanalytic theory of anxiety is ambitious and not without value, but the entire psychoanalytic enterprise has withered over the years (e.g. Eysenck 1985; Grunbaum 1977), and the psychoanalytic theory of fear has been questioned (Rachman 1990).

The theory of psychoanalysis was constructed on evidence drawn primarily from case histories and suffers from the inevitable deficiencies and limitations of such data (e.g. Eysenck 1985; Wolpe and Rachman 1960). The paucity of reproducible evidence is a major shortcoming of psychoanalysis. The entire enterprise, including the theory of anxiety, is rich in theorizing, but is lacking in methodological rigour, and deficient in facts. The historian Edward Boring (1991) described psychoanalysis as 'pre-scientific'.

On the evidence, bearing in mind the poor methodology, there is little reason to accept Freud's assertion that phobias never occur if the person has a normal sexual adjustment – 'the main point in the problem of phobias seems to me that phobias do not occur at all when the vita sexualis is normal' (Freud 1950: 120). The assertion was never proven and is incorrect. Many people with anxiety and specific phobias have a satisfactory sexual life, and can establish and maintain satisfying sexual relationships. Research collected over the past 30 years has expanded our knowledge of human fears, and modern methods are capable of significantly reducing these fears with little difficulty, contrary to what would be expected from the deep complexities of psychoanalytic theory. Fears can be reduced without undertaking a major analysis of the person's personality, childhood, sexual life, or other topics that are so important in the psychoanalytic theory. It is perfectly possible to approach the fear directly, to describe and measure it directly, and to modify it directly. Phobias can even be treated in a single session, and without paying any attention to the person's sexual life (Ost 1989, 1996).

This does not mean that the psychoanalytic theory is entirely valueless. There is reasonable evidence that some fears have significant symbolic elements in them, and that 'unconscious' factors influence the emergence and continuation of anxiety. Modern research has shown that some cognitive processes of which the person is unaware, such as priming of memory and pre-attentive processes, play a significant part in our responses to signs of potential danger. Although it was not an intrinsic part of Freud's theory of anxiety, and regrettably he did not develop the idea, the notion that we are predisposed to develop fears of certain kinds of situations or objects, is likely to be correct, and it features in the writings of modern theorists such as Gray (1982) and Seligman (1971) and latterly in the work of Poulton and Menzies (2002) who argue the case for non-associative fears such as acrophobia and aquaphobia.

The intense debates for and against psychoanalysis that took place in psychology, and in literary criticism, in the first half of the twentieth century eventually ran out of steam, and the subject became less relevant. Contemporary psychiatry and clinical psychology are based on a comprehensive classificatory and diagnostic system, the *Diagnostic and Statistical Manual of Mental Disorders* (DSM). Psychoanalytic diagnoses, concepts and terms play no part in the DSM arena. They do not appear, and are irrelevant for modern diagnoses, treatment and research. The diagnostic tests that were used in the psychoanalytic scheme, especially the projective tests such as the Rorschach and the Thematic Apperception Test (TAT) – whatever their merits (and considerable weaknesses) – have no bearing on prevailing diagnostic and treatment procedures. They are not relevant. The modern diagnostic system is used in current treatments which are pharmacological and psychological (predominantly cognitive therapy), and are employed separately or in combination. Psychoanalytic therapy is absent from the treatment recommendations set out by the National Institute of Health and Clinical Excellence (NICE) in the UK and by the National Institute of Mental Health (NIMH) in the United States.

Biological theories of anxiety

Despite the common wish for a reconciliation between biological and psychological theories of anxiety, and some progress in this direction, such as Gray's (1971, 1982, 1987), the two approaches tend to proceed independently, occasionally taking time off from their separate pursuits to collide with each other. With few exceptions, the biological theories are explanations for particular disorders rather than broad theories of anxiety. The psycho-biological theories of Eysenck (1967) and Gray (1971, 1987) are broad and exceptional.

Two of the most colourful debates are about the competing explanations for panic disorder and for obsessive-compulsive disorders (Chapter 9). The conflicting explanations for panic are described in Chapter 7. Klein's (1987, 1996) theory is predominantly biological and states that when a physiological suffocation alarm system is triggered by a threat to the supply of useable air, a panic ensues. The leading psychological theory states, to the contrary, that panics are caused by catastrophic misinterpretations of certain bodily sensations (Clark 1986). These competing explanations of panic share some features, but lead to different predictions and different treatments. For example, where the psychological theory asserts that a catastrophic misinterpretation is a necessary condition for panic, the biological theory does not – rather, a specific biological dysfunction is the necessary condition for panic. The psychological theory leads to a specific form of psychological treatment and the biological theory leads specifically to medication.

An influential biological theory of obsessive-compulsive disorders (OCD) suggested that OCD was biochemical in nature, and postulated that OCD results from a deficiency of serotonin or a deficiency in serotonin metabolism. Evidence to support this theory is reviewed by Insel (1991), Insel and Winslow (1992), Hollander and Leibowitz (1990), Jenike et al. (1990), Rapoport (1989) and Zohar et al. (1991) among others.

The main evidence in support of the biochemical explanation comes from the therapeutic effects of medications that interfere with the uptake of serotonin. Several of these medications are indeed capable of reducing, but seldom removing, OCD. 'At their best [the anti-obsessive drugs] provide only a partial remission for OCD. Most studies report a 50% improvement.' (Insel 1991: 15) and many patients derive no benefit. Serotonin dysfunction cannot, even at its best, provide a full explanation of OCD. Proponents of the serotonin theory have emphasized the specificity of the selective serotonin re-uptake inhibitor (SSRI) drugs, arguing that other types of anti-depressants fail to improve OCD. Much of the evidence appears to support this claim, but not all of it does so, and some of the supportive studies are flawed. For example, in the study by Foa et al. (1987, 1992), a standard anti-depressant (imipramine) was used as a comparison with behaviour therapy, but it failed to reduce the patients' depression, which remained well in the clinical range. Hence the study failed to test the hypothesis that anti-depressant medications help with OCD because they reduce depression. Moreover, the poor effect of the imipramine anti-depressant was not in keeping with the results of other studies (e.g. Mavissakalian 1983).

There is no evidence that patients with OCD have more or less serotonin than non-patients, or more or less serotonin than patients with other forms of anxiety disorder. A great deal of research has been carried out in testing aspects of the serotonin theory of OCD and 'the data indicate that the serotonergic system is probably intact in OCD' (Salkovskis 1996b, 1996c: 197). Much of the research involves assessments of cerebro-spinal fluid (CSF) and Pigott et al. (1996: 141) also concluded that 'recent CSF studies have failed to demonstrate significant differences between OCD patients and controls'. There is no convincing evidence of a specific, selective serotonin dysfunction (Insel 1991; Insel and Winslow 1992). Nor is there a correspondence between serotonin levels and response to treatment. Different types of SSRI drugs do not 'add up', or transfer their effects. The most effective drugs for inhibiting serotonin re-uptake are not the best for reducing OCD.

The therapeutic effects of SSRI drugs do not provide an adequate foundation for the biochemical theory, and recall the famous example of the aspirin and the headache. Aspirins can remove a headache, but can we conclude that this proves the headache was caused by an insufficiency of aspirin? The relief of OCD by serotonin re-uptake inhibitors does not inform us about the cause of OCD. Another problem for the biochemical explanation is raised by the repeatedly confirmed therapeutic effects of purely psychological therapy (Barlow 2002; D. A. Clark and Beck 2010). The therapy achieves its effects without drugs, and leaves the biological account wanting. The claim that psychological treatment might inadvertently produce the exact biochemical changes needed to overcome OCD is far-fetched and lacks confirmation. It will not pass unnoticed that the therapeutic efficacy of psychotherapy presents a problem for purely biological theories.

Problems with the serotonin theory, and the increasing use of the new neuro-imaging diagnostic techniques gave rise to a second biological theory, one which attributes OCD to the presence of a structural and/or functional dysfunction in the central nervous system – an abnormality of the CNS, probably in the basal ganglia (Rapoport 1989; Rapoport and Wise 1988; see also Insel 1988; McGuire 1995). Rapoport, in particular, argued for a dysfunction located in the basal ganglia, the repository of innate psychomotor functions. The idea is that hypersensitivity of the basal ganglia generates repetitive motor behaviour, such as the OCD symptom of compulsive handwashing, but the supporting evidence is patchy. In the study reported by Aylward et al. (1996: 577), 'all structural basal ganglia measures failed to exhibit differences between patients with OCD and matched normal control subjects', and this result was consistent with their review of the existing literature.

By concentrating on the repetitive qualities of some symptoms, Rapoport lost the essence of OCD, which includes a sense of subjective compulsion, purposeful directed behaviour, inflated responsibility, guilt, obsessional thoughts, and so on. Repetitiveness is one feature of OCD, but it is neither necessary nor sufficient. Moreover, the repetitive symptoms of OCD are neither mechanical nor automatic. It is highly improbable that psychological treatment inadvertently produces the specific changes in the basal ganglia that reduce OCD.

Recognizing the problems encountered by purely biological explanations, a leading biological theorist concluded that 'the link between OCD and serotonin is not a clear one . . . there is a profound mismatch in the time domains of these two events' (rapid uptake inhibition occurs within hours, but the clinical response requires many weeks, and so on) (Insel 1991: 14). 'The importance of serotonin in the pathophysiology of this disorder remains speculative' (Insel 1991: 15) and it is 'a bit premature to be proposing a neural lesion in OCD' (Insel 1991: 14).

Even though the biochemical and the neurophysiological theories have each attracted some support, they do not sit well together. There is no satisfactory connection between these two biological theories and it is unlikely that both can be correct.

It should be mentioned that just as the therapeutic effects of psychological treatment raise problems for the biological theories, the therapeutic value of anti-depressant medications, such as clomipramine, raises problems for purely psychological explanations of OCD.

Summary

The essence of learning theory accounts of anxiety is that fears are acquired by conditioning or other learning processes, and that these acquired fears in turn generate escape or avoidance behaviour. The explanations put forward by H. J. Eysenck and by Wolpe differed in detail, but both were based on the assumption that anxiety is essentially learned. Gray's psycho-physiological theory expands on these earlier accounts and roots his explanation firmly into physiology.

The psychoanalytic interpretation of anxiety is an important part of Freudian theory, with an emphasis on sexual motivation, the unconscious and symbolism. Anxiety is said to be closely connected to sexual restriction, and anxiety is a symbolic transformation of unacceptable sexual feelings.

The biological theories of anxiety are attempts to explain particular anxiety disorders, notably panic disorder and obsessive-compulsive disorder. They share a common belief in the biological causation of anxiety, but differ widely in the details.

Specific phobias and the conditioning theory of fear 6

The conditioning theory of fear is explained and the positive support-ing evidence assembled. Eight weaknesses of the theory are then set out, and it is concluded that conditioning is one of three pathways to fear.

Conditioned fears

The major postulate of the theory is that fears are acquired, by a process of conditioning. 'Neurotic reactions, like all others, are *learned* reactions and must obey the laws of learning' (Eysenck 1960: 5; original empha-sis). Neutral stimuli that are associated with a pain-producing or fear-producing state of affairs develop fearful qualities; they become conditioned fear stimuli. The strength of the fear is determined by the number of repetitions of the association between the stimulus and pain/fear experienced, and by the intensity of the fear or pain that is experienced. Stimuli resembling the fear-evoking ones acquire fearful properties; they become secondary conditioned stimuli. The likelihood of fear developing is increased by confinement, by exposure to high-intensity pain and/or fear situations, and by frequent repetitions of the association between the new conditioned stimulus and the pain/fear. It was proposed further that once objects or situations acquire fear-provoking qualities, they develop motivating properties. A secondary fear-drive emerges. Behaviour that successfully reduces fear (e.g. avoidance) increases in strength.

Wolpe's (1958) explanation of fear conditioning did not include an account of individual differences in vulnerability, but Eysenck attached considerable importance to such differences. It was postulated that (neurotic) introverts condition easily and hence are prone to develop excessive fears (Eysenck and Rachman 1965).

Evidence for the conditioning theory

Supporting evidence was drawn from six sources:

1 research on the induction of fear in animals;
2 the development of persisting anxiety in combat soldiers;
3 experiments on the induction of fear in a small number of children;
4 clinical observations;
5 incidental findings from the use of aversion therapy; and
6 a few experiments on the effects of traumatic stimulation.

The role of individual vulnerability was supported by evidence of ease of conditioning in introverts, and by psychometric analyses of samples of neurotic patients.

The strongest and most systematic evidence was drawn from a multitude of experiments on laboratory animals. Evidently it is easy to generate fear reactions in animals by exposing them to a conjunction of neutral and aversive stimuli, usually electric shock. The acquired fear reactions (usually inferred from the emergence of avoidance behaviour, physiological disturbances and disruptive behaviour, or by some combination of these three indexes) can be produced readily by employing conventional conditioning procedures. There is little doubt about the facility with which fear reactions can be conditioned, at least in animals that are tested under laboratory constraints.

Flanagan (1948) reported that the overwhelming majority of combat air crew experienced fear during their missions and although these reactions were relatively transient, they sometimes presaged the development of persistent combat fatigue that included strong elements of fear. A minority of air crew developed significant and lasting fears. The form and content of these fears, their tendency to generalize, and the conditions under which they arose are consistent with the conditioning theory.

Observations of the traumatic effects of combat were instrumental in the development of the concept of post-traumatic stress disorders (PTSD). The range of trauma is wide, including natural disasters, abuse, road accidents and assaults. In a majority of instances, the event(s) that triggered the PTSD are known and for the most part, the processes involved are partly or wholly conditioning. The fears that so often are the result of trauma are easily construed as conditioned fears and therefore add to the evidence that conditioning is an important pathway to fear.

The development of conditioned nausea reactions is commonly observed in patients receiving chemotherapy (Burish and Carey 1986; Cella *et al.* 1986). The factors that influence conditioning processes in other circumstances are similarly influential in the emergence of the persisting reactions of nausea. In their review of numerous reports, covering roughly 1,700 adult patients, Burish and Carey (1986) calculated that 32 per cent reported anticipatory nausea. The figures for anticipatory nausea are large (e.g. 80 per cent of 60 patients in the Cella *et al.* study). The nausea/vomiting lasted for more than two years in most of their cases (Cella *et al.* 1986). Bearing in mind the caution that conditioning of nausea or disgust does not necessarily imply that *fear* responses are conditionable, we can turn to the clinical accounts of fear acquisition.

In clinical practice, it is not uncommon for patients to give an account of the development of their fears that can be construed in conditioning terms. Sometimes they can date the onset of the fear to a specific conditioning experience. Every one of 34 cases of dental phobia reported having had a traumatic dental experience, such as fearing suffocation from an anaesthetic mask, on at least one occasion in childhood (Lautch 1971). However, these 34 people were described as generally neurotic and ten comparison subjects who had experienced comparable traumatic incidents with dentists during their childhood showed little sign of dental fear.

In a study of people who are frightened of dogs, di Nardo *et al.* (1988) found that nearly two-thirds had experienced a conditioning event in which a dog featured; and in over half of these instances, the animal had inflicted pain. However, two-thirds of a comparable group of subjects who were not frightened of dogs reported that they too had experienced a potentially conditioning event; and that in half of the instances, the animal had inflicted pain. These reports provide some support for the theory, but also illustrate the fact that conditioning experiences, even those of a painful nature, do not necessarily give rise to fear.

Here, as in other instances, there was less fear than an unqualified conditioning theory would lead us to predict. Presumably those people who experienced conditioning events, even painful ones, but failed to acquire a fear, placed a different interpretation on the event than did those who became frightened. It was noted by di Nardo and his colleagues (1988: n.p.) that all of their fearful subjects 'believed that fear and physical harm were likely consequences of an encounter with a dog, while very few non-fearful subjects had such expectations ... an exaggerated expectation of harm appears to be a factor in the maintenance of the fear.'

The classical demonstration by Watson and Rayner (1920) of the deliberate genesis of fear in a young child had a considerable influence on early theorists, but attempts to reproduce these findings had little success (e.g. Bregman 1934; Valentine 1946). A systematic collection of information on the induction of conditioned fear in humans was carried out by Ohman and his colleagues in Sweden (Ohman 1987). Stimulated by Seligman's (1971) concept of prepared fears, Ohman and his colleagues undertook a lengthy programme of research to discover whether people are 'prepared' to acquire fears in response to particular stimuli. They found that it is possible to produce conditioned fear responses in humans under laboratory conditions, but the responses tend to be weak, transient and incomplete. They are incomplete in the sense that the evidence for conditioning is confined largely to changes in electrodermal activity, and it has not been possible to obtain dependable consistent evidence of conditioned heart-rate responses. (Electrodermal activity can be used to index fear, but heart rate is a preferable measure [Cook et al. 1988; Lang et al. 1970; Ost 1989; Prigatano and Johnson 1974; Sartory et al. 1977; Sartory 1989]). The conditioned responses were of small magnitude and not readily evoked, and with few exceptions, the electrodermal responses were extinguished within a few trials. Also, the conditioned responses were easily altered or abolished by instructions (McNally 1987).

Incidental observations arising out of the use of aversion therapy, a technique explicitly based on the classical conditioning theory, provided some early support for the theory and in recent years has been supplemented by work carried out by Baker et al. (1984). After undergoing repeated associations between alcohol and chemically induced nausea, many patients experience nausea when they taste or even smell alcohol. In a famous case reported by Hammersley (1957), a successfully treated patient subsequently changed his mind and decided that abstinence was not the lesser of two evils. He embarked on a 'de-conditioning' programme and repeatedly drank himself through many episodes of intense nausea until his conditioned reaction to alcohol subsided and finally disappeared.

Another source of support for a conditioning theory of fear acquisition comes from experiments in which subjects were given injections of scoline, which produces a disturbance of breathing (Sanderson *et al.* 1963). Not surprisingly, most of the subjects who underwent this very unpleasant experience developed intense fears of the stimulus encountered in or connected with the experimental setting. The intensity of their fears tended to increase even in the absence of further unpleasant experiences (providing one of the few examples of fear incubation).

The conditioning theory of fear acquisition does not require single-trial or traumatic onsets, but fears that arise in an acute manner are more readily accommodated, partly because our conception of conditioned fear is based largely on laboratory experiments in which the aversive stimulus is often traumatic. However, we also have to account for fears that are produced by experiences of a sub-traumatic or even of a non-traumatic nature.

Fears that emerge in the absence of any identifiable learning experience present difficulties for the theory. Hence, fears that develop gradually (e.g. social fears) and cannot be traced to specific occurrences are a potential embarrassment. Even more troublesome are those fears that arise even in the absence of any direct contact with the fear stimulus (see 'Neo-conditioning', below).

The evidence on individual vulnerability was documented by Eysenck (1967). There is little doubt about the association between introversion and anxiety disorders, but the putative causal connection was not resolved, especially as it proved difficult to confirm that introverts always are more 'conditionable' than extroverts. The existence of individual differences in vulnerability to fear acquisition is evident, and the latest approach to the problem emphasizes differences in sensitivity (the concept of anxiety sensitivity). There are high correlations between anxiety sensitivity and total scores on fear questionnaires (Reiss *et al.* 1986), and there is an overlap between this sensitivity and Eysenck's (1967) concept of 'dysthymia' (high introversion and high neuroticism).

There is sufficient evidence to support the idea that fears can be acquired by a conditioning process. This conclusion is justified even though some of the evidence is subject to contrary interpretations, or is inherently weak. The strongest evidence, both in the sense of its replicability and completeness, comes from the genesis of fear in laboratory animals. This voluminous evidence is supported by some limited findings on the induction of fear reactions in adults, but the stimuli were traumatic. The work on the induction of fear in children is inconsistent, based on very small numbers, and all of the experiments have been criticized for errors of contamination and confounding. Clinical observations provide interesting supporting evidence, but unfortunately the quality of the information is unsatisfactory, comprising as it almost always does a selected set of observations rarely supported by external confirmatory evidence. This is an unsatisfactory basis for building a theory.

The theory is well supported, but is not a satisfactorily comprehensive account of the genesis, or the maintenance, of human fears. The conditioning theory of fear acquisition cannot encompass all of the observed fears. There is more than one pathway to fear.

The conditioning theory: contrary evidence and arguments

There are eight arguments against acceptance of the conditioning theory as a comprehensive explanation (Rachman 1978, 1990, 1991). People fail to acquire fears in what should be fear-conditioning situations, such as air raids. It is difficult to produce stable conditioned fear reactions in human participants, even under controlled laboratory conditions. The conditioning theory rests on the untenable equipotentiality premise. The distribution of fears in normal and neurotic populations is difficult to reconcile with the conditioning theory. A significant number of people with phobias recount histories that cannot be accommodated by the theory. Fears can be acquired indirectly or vicariously. Fears can be acquired even when the causal critical events are temporally separated.

Failures to acquire fear

It would seem that few experiences could be more frightening than undergoing an air raid, but the great majority of people endured air raids extraordinarily well during World War II, contrary to the universal expectation of mass panic (Janis 1951; Rachman 1978, 1990). Exposure to repeated bombing did not produce significant increases in psychiatric disorders. Short-lived fear reactions were common, but surprisingly few persistent phobic reactions developed. Few of the civilians who were injured or wounded developed a significant fear of the situation in which they received the injury (Rachman 1990).

The observations of comparative fearlessness – despite repeated exposures to intense trauma, uncontrollability, uncertainty and even injury – are contrary to the conditioning theory of fear acquisition. People subjected to repeated air raids should acquire multiple intense conditioned fear reactions and these should be strengthened by repeated exposures. Civilian reactions to the warlike conditions in Northern Ireland (Cairns and Wilson 1984) and the Middle East (Saigh 1984, 1988) are consistent with the findings from World War II. These findings run contrary to prediction.

As stated, the phenomenon of PTSD provides convincing evidence of conditioning onsets of fear, but a majority of the people who experience these traumas do *not* develop PTSD (Ehlers and Clark 2000). Lesser examples of the failure to acquire fear include people who fail to develop a fear of dogs, despite having unpleasant experiences with them, and even having been bitten (di Nardo *et al.* 1988; Poulton and Menzies 2002). Dental fears are fairly common, but large numbers of people fail to develop a fear of dental treatment even though they have undergone uncomfortable and even painful experiences while confined in the dentist's chair (e.g. Lautch 1971; Davey 1988).

The absence of a direct relationship between injury and subsequent fear runs contrary to conditioning theory. There should be a direct connection between injury and fear, but there is not (Rachman 1990). Additional evidence of a disconnection between injuries and fear comes from a study of the emergence of fears in early childhood (Poulton and Menzies 2002).

The conditioning of human fears

Deliberate attempts to generate conditioned fears in humans, as in the original attempts to treat alcoholism by establishing a conditioned aversion to alcohol, had little success.

The equipotentiality premise

The theory assumes that any stimulus can be transformed into a fear signal; the choice of stimulus is a matter of indifference. Seligman (1970, 1971) argued convincingly that this premise is untenable, and hence its incorporation in the theory is a weakness.

The distribution of fears

The corollary of the equipotentiality premise is that all stimuli have an equal chance of being transformed into fear signals. However, this is not borne out by surveys of the distribution of fears, either in a general population or in psychiatric samples (Rachman 1990).

Subject only to their prominence in the environment, many objects and situations should have an equal probability of provoking fear.

What we find instead is that some fears are exceedingly common, and certainly far too common for the theory. Other fears are far too rare.

The fear of snakes is common and the fear of lambs is rare; moreover, a genuine fear of snakes is reported by people who have not had contact with the reptiles. Even more surprising is the absence of fear of motor cars, and the small incidence of fears of motor travel, despite the risks involved. The fear of snakes in the absence of direct contact opens four possibilities. The fear of snakes is innate, or it can be transmitted indirectly, or the fear of snakes is 'lurking' and will appear with only slight provocation. The last two of these possibilities are compatible. The fourth possibility, discussed below, is that *contiguity* between a conditioned stimulus and an unconditioned stimulus 'is neither necessary nor sufficient for conditioning' (Papini and Bitterman 1990: 396).

Patient's reports of fear onset

It can be difficult to determine the origin of a patient's phobia, and there are phobias in which there was 'no apparent trauma to initiate the phobia' (Marks 1969: 42; McNally 2003). The absence of a plausible conditioning precipitant in a significant number of phobic patients was demonstrated in the analysis by Ost (1985). Sixty-five per cent of 183 phobic patients acquired the phobia by conditioning; 21 per cent reportedly acquired their phobia indirectly; and the remaining 14 per cent were unable to recall the onset. In an expansion of this study, Ost (1987) found an association between the manner in which the phobia was acquired and the age of onset. The indirectly acquired phobias developed at an earlier age than the phobias with a conditioning origin.

The vicarious acquisition of fear

Advances in our understanding of the processes of observational learning and modelling have made it plain that we acquire much of our behaviour, including emotional responses, by vicarious experiences (Bandura 1969, 1977; Rachman 1978, 1990). Mineka's outstanding research on monkeys (see p. 66) showed conclusively that fears can be acquired by observational learning. Gerull and Rapee (2002) demonstrated the acquisition of a fear of snakes and spiders in 30 toddlers who were shown a rubber spider and snake in alternate pairings with positive, negative or neutral facial expressions of their mothers. They found 'strong observational learning' results, consistent with the view that early fears can be produced vicariously.

Acquisition by transmission of verbal information

Fears can be acquired by absorbing verbal or other forms of information that convey a threat (Rachman 1978). The social transmission of intense fear, even panic, is well illustrated by recurrent epidemics of *koro* in Southeast Asia. *Koro*, derived from the Malay word for 'head of a turtle', is a 'condition of psychiatric panic characterized by complaints of genital shrinkage coupled with fear of impending death' (Tseng *et al.* 1988: 1538). Episodes of this intense fear, involving hundreds or thousands of people, occurred in Singapore (1967), Thailand (1976), Assam (1982) and China (1984/1985 and 1987), and mainly affected isolated, poorly educated people who are strongly influenced by folk beliefs. In a survey of 232 victims of the 1984/1985 epidemic in China, Tseng *et al.* (1988) found that the episodes of *koro* were characterized by panic (intense fear, palpitations, tremor, perspiration, fear of impending death or catastrophe). The Singapore epidemic appears to have been set off by a verbal report that the Viet Cong had poisoned food to produce impotence.

Ollendick and King (1991) found that 89 per cent of children attributed their various fears to negative information, 56 per cent to modelling and 36 per cent to conditioning. These findings have been replicated twice. Moreover, Field *et al.* (2001) showed in a prospective study that the fears of children aged between seven and nine were significantly increased by negative information. Muris *et al.* (2003) reported comparable findings. Negative or positive information about an imaginary doglike beast was given to 285 children, between 4 and 12 years old. The negative information steeply increased their fear of the beast; the fear was not transient and showed some generalization to dogs and predators. The children who received positive information showed a small reduction in fear.

Fears born and bred: non-associative fears

Perhaps people are innately predisposed to acquire specific types of fear. Modern psychologists have devoted a great deal of time and effort to explain the acquisition of fears, and can claim some successes, but in the process, have tended to overlook the possibility that some people are innately predisposed to acquire certain fears. The idea that some 'fears are born not bred' has a long history and was considered by many writers, Darwin, Stanley Hall and Freud among them.

The possibility of predisposed, 'born' fears arises for various reasons, starting with the non-random distribution of fears; for example, a fear of snakes is common (but a fear of lambs is rare) and includes the curious fact that even people who have never actually encountered a snake express a fear of this unpopular reptile. The islands of Hawaii are virtually free of snakes, but the fear of snakes is widely endorsed, and according to elderly inhabitants of the islands, the fear was common even before the introduction of television programmes, thereby ruling out the likelihood that the fear was acquired observationally. An added appeal of the notion that some fears may be innate comes from speculation that they have survival value; a fear of heights is one example, and a fear of immersion in water is another.

If the idea of predisposed fears is accepted, however, the distribution of fears remains problematic. Are a majority, or a minority, of people predisposed to fear heights and immersion in water? There are two possibilities: the predisposition is genetically determined and like other human propensities and characteristics is inherently random; or innate predispositions to a fear can be modified by experiences. People acquire fears, they certainly learn some fears, but they can also unlearn fears and/or learn to overcome their dispositions to fear (Rachman 1978, 1990).

The results of a remarkable longitudinal study of a complete cohort of children carried out in New Zealand provide unique evidence of the occurrence and/or development of fears from early childhood to middle and late childhood. The findings were gathered in a health and development study of all the children born in Dunedin between 1 April 1972 and 31 March 1973, and the mass of data was thoroughly analysed. The children were assessed at regular intervals until the age of 21 and beyond. Many of the fears reported by the children and/or their parents had no learned onset, but apparently were present from early in life, notably the fears of water and heights. There was a relation between early childhood learning experiences of climbing – including falls, errors and injuries – and an *absence* of fears of heights in middle and late childhood (Poulton and Menzies 2002). Children who had minimal early experience of climbing, and of falls, had significantly stronger fears of heights than did the experienced children. Moreover, the children with a fear of heights had experienced *fewer* falls from heights than had the non-fearful children. In another example of a non-associative acquisition of fear, their analyses of water phobias yielded no connections between early conditioning experiences (e.g. water skills, water trauma) and fears/phobias of water in middle and late childhood. The authors did, however, obtain evidence of some

acquired fears, notably a connection between dental caries and subsequent dental fears.

Poulton and Menzies (2002: 140) concluded from their longitudinal
study and a review of the literature that the 'three pathways to fear-
acquisition' model needed to be revised: 'An expansion of the . . . three
pathways of fear acquisition to include a fourth, non-associative
pathway is warranted.'

Conclusion

The weaknesses of the classical theory of conditioning are significant,
but not fatal. One can either search for an entirely new theory to replace
it, or formulate modifications and extensions of the theory. It can
provide a partial explanation for the genesis of some fears. However,
it cannot explain the observed distribution of fears, the uncertain point
of onset of many phobias, the indirect transmission of fears, the ready
acquisition of prepared phobias, and the failure of fears to arise in
circumstances predicted by the theory. Fears acquired without contact
with a fearful stimulus are an added problem for the theory, and the
acquisition of fears when the causal events are temporally separated
was considered to be a serious problem until conditioning theory was
'liberalized' (see p. 65). There is a plausible case for accommodating
fears that emerge very early in life in the apparent absence of conditioning or other learning processes. The innately predisposed fears are
reminiscent of Seligman's concept of prepared fears discussed earlier
(see p. 66), and are a reminder that people do learn certain fears, but
they also learn to *not fear* (e.g. '[what] we learn is how to overcome our
existing predispositions . . . in large part we learn to stop responding
fearfully to predisposed or prepared stimuli' [Rachman 1978: 255]).

A satisfactorily comprehensive theory of fear acquisition must
accommodate all of that information plus the facts that fears can
emerge gradually as well as suddenly, that there are individual differences in susceptibility, and the probable acquisition of fears of objects /
situations which the person has never encountered (Merckelbach *et al.*
1996).

Neo-conditioning

The traditional belief that contiguity of the conditioned stimulus
(CS) and the unconditioned stimulus (US) is necessary for the establishment of a conditioned response is mistaken (Papini and Bitterman

1990). Recognition of the occurrence of non-contiguous conditioning removes some objections to the conditioning theory of fear acquisition. Conditioned responses can develop even when the conditioned stimulus and the unconditioned event are separated in time. The most convincing examples of non-contiguous conditioning come from the literature on food aversions. If animals eat a novel food and are made ill minutes or even hours later, they tend to develop an aversion to the food. A single experience is sufficient to establish a lasting conditioned aversion.

The troublesome fact that many people cannot trace the onset of their fears to particular conditioning episodes can be absorbed by assuming that non-contiguous conditioning may have taken place. The many failures to acquire fear despite contiguous associations (e.g. dog bites not followed by fear) can be accounted for by blocking (see below). Animals, and people, can learn that a stimulus is irrelevant 'as a predictor of anything of significance' (Dickinson 1987: 66).

Rescorla (1988: 154) observed that, 'although conditioning can sometimes be slow, in fact most modern conditioning preparations routinely show rapid learning. One-trial learning is not confined to flavor-aversion'. Moreover, the associative span of animals 'is capable of bridging long temporal intervals' (Mackintosh 1983: 172). However, the learning must be selective, otherwise the animals would collect a 'useless clutter of irrelevant associations' (1983: 172). According to Mackintosh, the 'function of conditioning is to enable organisms to discover probable causes of events of significance' (1983: 172).

Additional evidence that conditioning processes are not bound by contiguity comes from research on the *blocking* effect and on the consequences of *random control*. A stimulus will not become a conditioned signal (CS) even if it is repeatedly presented immediately before an unconditioned stimulus (US) event, unless it is of some value. If the US event is already well predicted by another stimulus, the addition of a second stimulus is of no value and hence no conditioning occurs. The established CS prevents (blocks) the development of a second CS. If the delivery of the electric shock is already well predicted by a tone (CS), then introducing a visual stimulus (CS?) in addition to the tone will be of no predictive value and will fail to develop into a conditioned signal. The second stimulus is redundant, and conditioning will not develop even if the stimulus is repeatedly presented in contiguity with the electric shock (US). The existing conditioned response is sufficient and blocks the development of a redundant new signal.

The revised view of conditioning is not merely an exercise in discrediting the classical explanation. Interesting new phenomena have been discovered, fresh predictions are possible, and new explanations of associative learning have been put forward. Simple contiguity is insufficient; information is the key, and the prevalent view is that conditioning involves learning about the relations between events. Rescorla (1988: 153) argues that 'Pavlovian conditioning is not a stupid process by which the organism willy-nilly forms associations between any two stimuli that happen to co-occur.' Rather, the organism is better seen as 'an information seeker, using logical and perceptual relations among events . . . to form a sophisticated representation of its world' (1988: 154). Conditioning is not merely a transfer of power from one stimulus to another.

Contrary to an assumption of the classical theory, stimuli are not equally likely to develop conditioning properties; some are more easily turned into conditioned signals than others. Pain is more readily associated with auditory and visual stimuli than with gustatory stimuli, and gastric distress is more easily associated with taste than with vision. People, certainly adults, do not come fresh to new stimuli; they already have a history of associations with the available stimuli. These previous associations influence the occurrence or non-occurrence of conditioning. So for example, we all have a history of (benign) associations with dog collars. No one, not even people who have distressing experiences with dogs, ever learns to fear collars, despite the contiguous presence of the dog collar during the unpleasant events. Dog collars do not predict distress, and they do not become conditioned elicitors of fear.

Although many people who have distressing experiences with dogs learn to fear them, comparable numbers of people who have had such experiences fail to acquire the fear (di Nardo *et al.* 1988). Presumably, a previous history of pleasant and friendly experiences with dogs produces conditioned predictions of harmless exchanges, and those predictions are not overturned by one or several unpleasant events. The history of the stimulus influences the conditioning process. Food aversions develop most readily to novel foods (Revusky 1979). Familiar and especially well-liked familiar foods are relatively immune to conditioned food aversions. Presumably, familiar and well-liked people, places and animals are also relatively immune to conditioned fears. A relative fear immunity to familiar stimuli and situations may underlie the success of Neal Miller's (1960) 'toughening up' exercises as a way of preventing the development of fear.

Animals can be conditioned not only to discrete stimuli but also to the relationships between stimuli, in support of Rescorla's (1988: 158) claim that 'conditioning involves the learning of relations among events that are complexly represented'. We have come a long way from classical Pavlovian conditioning, and the flexibility and range of conditioning are far greater than was previously supposed (Davey 1988; Mackintosh 1983; Rescorla 1980, 1988). Conditioning can occur even when the stimuli are separated in time, and in space, and it can occur not only to discrete stimuli but also to abstract relationships between two or more stimuli. Conditioning is a highly flexible and functional process.

The refreshing revival of interest in conditioning clarified some puzzles, but neo-conditioning is not free of problems. Expanding the scope of the concept of conditioning is welcome, but it lacks clear limits. There is little that it disallows. Even the revised theory cannot account for fears that arise without any contact between the feared stimulus and an aversive event, and it also has difficulty accommodating some important examples in which fears fail to develop in circumstances in which the theory would predict them (e.g. being subjected to aerial bombing). Fears can be acquired by conditioning – or by vicarious means or by absorbing verbal information that contains threat. It is highly probable that humans are 'prepared' readily to acquire fears of particular stimuli, such as snakes (Rachman 1990).

Specific phobias

Intense and persistent fear of snakes, even harmless snakes, is a common example of a *specific phobia* – one of the anxiety disorders. The specific phobias tend to fall into one of three clusters: social phobias, animal phobias and phobias of injury/illness (including fear of suffocation). A fear qualifies for the term *phobia* if it is severe, persistent and maladaptive. The borderline between fears and phobias is fuzzy, and most people with intense fears, or even phobias, endure them or circumvent them. Only a small number of people with phobias seek professional help.

For those who do, psychologists are well able to help. Since the mid-1980s, dependably effective and efficient methods of treatment have been developed (Barlow 2002; D. A. Clark and Beck 2010; Marks 1987; Ost 1989, 1997, 2001). The first of the fear-reducing techniques, desensitization, was developed by Wolpe (1958) and consists of repeatedly exposing the phobic person to the fear-evoking stimulus in a graded and gradual manner, while the person is kept in a state of relaxation. These graded, gradual presentations can be exposures to the actual stimulus (so-called *in vivo* exposures) or to imaginal representations of the feared stimulus. The former version, *in vivo* exposure, is more powerful and is the preferred form whenever possible. The supplementary use of 'therapeutic modeling', in which the patient is encouraged gradually to imitate the approach behaviour of the therapist, expedites the exposure treatment (Bandura 1969, 1977).

Improved forms of treating specific phobias are rolling out. A refined and concentrated one-session form of exposure treatment that is completed in between one and three hours, produces substantial and lasting reductions in certain phobias, notably fear of spiders and small animals (e.g. Ost 1989, 2001). The effect sizes are substantial and equal or surpass those achieved by standard exposure treatments. A new form of exposure therapy, easier to tolerate than '*in vivo*' exposures, but equally effective – especially in treating a fear of flying, and fear of heights – involves exposure to 'virtual reality' recreations of life-like scenes and situations by using computer graphics and sensory devices (Emmelkamp *et al.* 2007). It too produces large effect sizes that equal or surpass standard exposure treatments, and the improvements are stable and enduring (Powers and Emmelkamp 2008a; Krijn *et al.* 2004).

These advances in technique are both variations of the well-established exposure method for treating phobias. Most treatments for other anxiety disorders include some exposure, plus other techniques such as cognitive modifications; but at present, repeated exposures to the fear-evoking situation or stimulus are essential for treating specific phobias.

For a considerable period, cognitive therapy had little to offer in the treatment of specific phobias (Last 1987), but some progress is being made. In some cases, purely cognitive interventions can reduce phobias. For example, Booth and Rachman (1992) found that cognitive therapy was as effective as the standard exposure treatment of claustrophobia (fear of enclosed spaces). It has also been shown that abrupt and complete reductions of phobias can occasionally be achieved by pure cognitive therapy (Rachman and Whittal 1989). Drugs have not proven to be useful in treating phobias: 'No psychotropic drug has been demonstrated to be effective in the treatment of simple phobias' (Fyer 1987: 190).

The theories that have been advanced to explain the effects of exposure treatment are: reciprocal inhibition, habituation, extinction (see Rachman 1990). Each explanation has some merit, but none of them provide a comprehensive explanation for the effects of treatment.

Summary

The main postulate of the conditioning theory is that fears are acquired by a process of conditioning. Fears develop motivating properties, and behaviour which successfully reduces fear increases in strength.

Supporting evidence comes from six sources:

1 laboratory research in inducing fear in animals;
2 fears that arise in combat;
3 clinical observations;
4 studies of fear in children;
5 incidental observations from the use of aversion therapy; and
6 the effects of traumatic stimulation.

The contrary evidence includes the failure of people to develop significant fears in situations that should produce conditioned fear; the difficulty in producing fear reactions in human subjects under controlled laboratory conditions; and the clinical reports of people who have phobias, but cannot recall relevant conditioning experiences. In addition, the distribution of fears cannot be accounted for by the classical conditioning theory. The neo-conditioning perspective, especially the demotion of contiguity as a necessary condition for such learning, has made possible a fresh view of the distribution of fears, but it suffers from an absence of limits.

Fears can be acquired directly by learning processes, including conditioning; or indirectly, by vicarious exposures, or by the simple transmission of information. Some fears such as aquaphobia and acrophobia are evident at an early age and appear in the absence of associative learning.

Some of the objections to the original conditioning theory can be overcome by re-analysing them in terms of neo-conditioning theory, according to which the function of conditioning is to enable people or animals to discover the probable causes of significant events. Nevertheless, other objections remain to the belief that conditioning is the single path to fear acquisition . There appear to be three pathways to fear acquisition: conditioning, vicarious acquisition, and by absorbing threatening information.

Specific phobias are intense, lasting fears that have an irrational element and are resistant to change, except when established fear-reducing techniques are applied.

Panic and anxiety 7

The nature of panic and its incidence are described. Recurrent panics are disturbing and impairing. The main explanations for the occurrence of panics are set out and evaluated, and the methods of treatment are described.

A *panic* is an episode of intense fear of sudden onset. The fear, often bordering on terror, is accompanied by disturbing bodily sensations, difficulty in reasoning, and a feeling of imminent catastrophe (Rachman and de Silva 2010). There is a close relationship between panic and anxiety, and at times they interact. Episodes of panic provide a useful basis for analysing the relationship between fear and anxiety.

Elevated anxiety increases the probable occurrence of an episode of panic (Margraf *et al.* 1986), and a panic in turn is usually followed by prolonged anxiety, a residue of anxiety. In addition to this short-term residue of anxiety, Klein *et al.* (1977: 27) observed that 'as a result of these panics, they [patients] develop [longer-term] anticipatory anxiety'.

In all of the various forms of anxiety disorder, including obsessive-compulsive disorders, social phobias, and so on, episodes of panic are common. According to Barlow and Craske (1988: 20), 'panic is an ubiquitous problem among patients with anxiety disorders and at least 83% of patients in any diagnostic category reported at least one panic attack'. (The term *panic episode* is preferable to the more usual *panic attack* which has misleading connotations, especially with heart attacks. However, the terms originally used by the writers are retained throughout this text.)

The occurrence of isolated episodes of panic is common. Approximately 22.7 per cent of people report having experienced a panic (Kessler *et al.* 2006). *Recurrent* episodes – at least some of which are spontaneous ('out of the blue') and are distressing and impairing – are diagnosed as *panic disorders*, a potentially serious anxiety disorder. In a replication of a large-scale US national survey, Kessler *et al.* (2006) calculated a lifetime prevalence of 5.8 per cent for this disorder. Panics and agoraphobia, a fear and avoidance of public places and public transport, are sometimes associated. The 12-month prevalence of panic disorder and agoraphobia is 1.6 per cent, but cases of agoraphobia unaccompanied by panic are not common. These figures reflect a major change in the construal of agoraphobia.

Prior to 1987, agoraphobia was regarded as a major, and common, psychological problem and attracted a great deal of attention from clinicians and researchers. Influential psychologists such as Wolpe (1958) and Eysenck (1957, 1960) used it as an exemplar of neurotic behaviour because it is a form of extreme unadaptive avoidance, and agoraphobia provided a convenient link to the avoidance behaviour that was intensively studied in innumerable experiments on animals. The general idea was to use the laboratory findings to shape methods for treating agoraphobic patients.

The occurrence of episodes of panic was regarded as marginal and of little significance. However, in 1987, Klein brought about a radical change in the construal of panics and their relation to agoraphobia. He argued that the recurrent episodes of panic are the *major* problem, and that agoraphobia is a by-product (see Chapter 8). After experiencing recurrent panics, numbers of patients develop symptoms of agoraphobia.

The experience of panic

The feelings of imminent catastrophe that provoke a panic are described in various ways. Some people report that 'I feel that I am in great danger', or 'something terrible is happening to me', or 'I am about to completely lose control'. The term *panic* is derived from the Greek god Pan whose shrill and unexpected noises frightened people. During a panic, people commonly fear that they might be dying, losing control, going insane or losing consciousness. Some of the panics are unexpected and seem to 'come out of the blue'. However, the majority of isolated episodes are provoked by exposure to identifiable stressors, and therefore can be anticipated (McNally 1994). The threat of a serious motor accident can provoke it, as can an attack by a vicious dog. These predictable panics are distressing and share some features of the unexpected panics, but they are easily understandable. In contrast, episodes of panic that occur unexpectedly can be bewildering and therefore especially troubling. A panic that occurs while at leisure in one's home is difficult to comprehend. In the absence of any apparent psychological stress, it is not surprising that affected people grope for a medical cause of their distress. The panics that occur 'out of the blue', unpredictably and inexplicably, are a central feature of panic disorder. On average, episodes of panic last between 5 and 20 minutes, are distressing and leave the person feeling drained and anxious.

Panics that occur in response to a true threat are appropriate, if at times excessive, and they serve to protect the person from pain, injury or discomfort. In contrast to these true alarms, episodes of panic that arise in response to threats that are minimal, or entirely misconceived, can be regarded as similar to the triggering of a false alarm. Two of the leading theorists on the subject of panic disorder, Barlow (1988, 2002) and Klein (1987 1993), construe abnormal episodes of panic as false alarms, but their explanations of the nature and causes of these alarms differ.

These are some examples of unexpected panics triggered by unusual and even threatening events that were then catastrophically misinterpreted and resulted in the rapid onset of intense fear, i.e. panic. A 23-year-old woman described her first unexpected episode of panic in these words:

> I was at home one week-end and suddenly had trouble with my breathing. My heart was pounding and I began sweating heavily. I thought that my heart had given in and felt that I was about to die. My husband rushed me to the hospital emergency where they tested my heart and assured me that there was no danger. I gradually calmed down and returned home after an hour or so, feeling shaken but no longer terrified.

A physically fit security guard of 32 experienced his first panic while exercising in the gym. During the course of his customary programme of exercises, he suddenly became extremely sensitive to his rapid heartbeats and interpreted them as a sign that he was about to have a heart attack. He became understandably frightened and gasping for air, asked a friend to call for an ambulance. He was rushed to the emergency room of the local hospital, but during the trip felt that he might die before reaching help. At the hospital he was treated as an emergency and immediately wheeled into the examination room. No evidence of any cardiac irregularity or other problem was found and he was assured that he was healthy and could return home. After resting at the hospital for an hour, during which he felt relieved but exhausted, he returned home. Two weeks later he had another unexpected panic while jogging, and again the doctor at the hospital reassured him about his health. A full examination carried out by his family doctor on the following day led to the diagnosis of panic disorder and he was referred for psychological treatment.

In these two examples, unusual or unexplained bodily sensations were catastrophically misinterpreted as signs of an imminent heart attack – a rather typical sequence of events in the onset of panic. Other common catastrophic thoughts involved in episodes of panic are the feeling that one is losing control, the fear of going insane, the fear of losing consciousness, the fear of acting strangely and/or screaming.

A 25-year-old lawyer was walking across a bridge one afternoon when she began to feel extremely dizzy and her heart began to pound. She felt that she might lose consciousness, or worse, lose self-control and run into the road in the face of oncoming traffic. These thoughts terrified her and she fled as fast as she could off the bridge. Thereafter she had a number of repetitions of the episode of panic, and in each case, the major fear was that she would lose control, and act in a bizarre manner or self-destructively. These thoughts in turn led to a further fear that she might go insane and end up in a restrictive ward at a psychiatric hospital. A fourth example is provided by an anxious young accountant with a long history of worries about her health. On one occasion, she nearly choked when a piece of meat was lodged in her throat. She thought that she was about to choke to death and was terrified. Even after the meat was dislodged, she remained frightened and upset for more than an hour, and after this incident she became extremely fearful of choking and therefore limited herself to a very narrow, strict diet of soft and easily swallowed foods. Even so, she occasionally felt that some food had not gone down smoothly and would then feel panicky. Episodes were always provoked by the same easily recognized event and she was able to predict which foods and situations would provoke a panic, and hence avoided them.

The DSM features of a panic disorder are that the person has repeatedly experienced episodes of panic, some of which were unexpected, and at least one of the episodes was followed by persistent worries (one month or more) of having another panic. During the episodes, at least four of the following sensations or feelings are experienced: shortness of breath, dizziness or faintness, increased heart rate, trembling or shaking, choking, sweating, stomach distress or nausea, feeling that one's surroundings or self are not quite real, feelings of numbness, hot flashes or chills, chest pain or discomfort, a fear of dying or losing control or going crazy. In cases of panic disorder, the episodes may occur daily or several times a week. Typically, after the first episode of unexpected and inexplicable panic, medical reassurance is sufficient to provide temporary relief and a state of calm. However, when the second or subsequent episodes occur, conventional reassurance is of limited value. The person begins to fear that more episodes will take place, and at unpredictable times and in any setting. They become anxious and apprehensive, develop a pattern of avoidance and strive to achieve a sense of safety.

In many cases, the occurrence of repeated panics is followed by restrictions of mobility. Sufferers tend to avoid situations in which they feel that a panic may occur and/or situations from which a rapid escape might be difficult. They plan in advance a particular route, time of journey, and escape exits. Places and activities that are commonly avoided include supermarkets, theatres, cinemas, public transport, driving unaccompanied, bridges or tunnels. Being caught in a traffic jam or standing in a long queue are common causes of anxiety. In many instances, the affected person becomes fearful of being alone at home. They need the reassuring presence of a trusted person who can provide safety or take actions to provide safety (e.g. calling a doctor or ambulance) if a catastrophe threatens. If these fears and the consequent avoidance of 'unsafe' places become excessive, the diagnosis of panic disorder is expanded to panic disorder with agoraphobia.

It seems endless

The average duration of an episode of panic is between 5 and 20 minutes, but at the time, it seems to be endless. It is a distressing episode of intense fear during which the person feels that a catastrophe is about to happen. During the episodes, ordinary processes of reasoning are somewhat impaired (i.e. 'My mind goes blank', 'I can't think straight'). It is like a mental dust-storm. At the time of the panic, the person is convinced of a realistic and imminent danger. The most commonly reported intense bodily sensations include rapid heartbeat, sweating, dizziness, shortness of breath and shaking. The most commonly reported thoughts experienced during panic include the following: I am having a heart attack, I am losing control, I am going to faint, I am going to scream, I am going to choke, I am going to suffocate.

One young woman patient had such intense sensations of a pounding heart during panic that she sometimes felt her heart would actually burst right through her ribs. During one panic episode, her heart rate was observed to increase by 25 beats per minute. It is not unusual to see an increase of 20 or more heartbeats per minute during a panic; but in some episodes, little or no increase in heart rate occurs. In a typical episode, people experience at least some of these bodily sensations, and during the most intense panics they report an increasing number of the sensations. In a particularly bad episode, they are flooded by a rush of these disturbing sensations which intensify the imminent danger and threat of losing control. The sensations are intense and intrusive and probably are one of the causes of irrational thinking described earlier. After being buffeted by these disturbing sensations and frightening thoughts, the person is likely to be left feeling anxious, shaken and tired – even exhausted – for between 30 minutes and several hours. As mentioned earlier, episodes of panic leave a residue of anxiety.

During panics, most people experience a feeling of being trapped and their overwhelming need is to escape. This powerful urge to flee can lead to irrational and risky behaviour, such as driving too fast or recklessly or running blindly out of a building. One patient who had experienced many panics became so apprehensive about losing control when driving her car that she restricted herself to driving very slowly, only in the slow lane, and only in the early or late hours of the day. When she sensed the possible onset of a panic, she brought her vehicle to an abrupt halt, almost regardless of the following traffic. In severe cases, patients keep adding to their list of places to avoid, with each new panic adding another dangerous setting to the list, and in the most extreme cases, the affected person ends up being restricted to their own home.

Roughly a third of the initial panics occur in public places, about a quarter while in a car, and approximately a third begin at home. In many cases, it is possible to trace the occurrence of major stress before the first panic (personal conflicts, stress at work, loss or grief, etc.). The person's interpretation of, and reaction to, that first panic depend on the accompanying bodily sensations and the circumstances of the panic. As was evident in the first two case illustrations, it is common for an unexpected panic to occur when a person notices rapid heartbeats, shortness of breath and a sense of danger. If this is interpreted as the start of a heart attack or other medical catastrophe, the person searches for emergency medical help, expecting treatment for a heart condition or some related medical problem. When the doctors conclude from these tests that the person's cardiac system is functioning normally, this produces a great sense of relief – but also leaves unexplained the nature and the cause of the discomfort and the distress. This absence of a satisfactory explanation can become a breeding ground for anxiety.

When a second episode occurs and the absence of cardiac or other medical problems is confirmed, the possibility of an anxiety disorder is considered. Once the person is persuaded by repeated medical reassurance and testing that there is no danger of a medical catastrophe, the fear may change from a worry about illness to an intense fear of having another panic. They begin to fear the panic itself – the fear of fear.

The incidence of panic

Contemporary estimates of the incidence and prevalence of panic disorder, and other psychological and psychiatric problems, are strongly influenced by the results of a large epidemiological study carried out on nearly 20,000 people in five districts of the United States – the Epidemiologic Catchment Area (ECA) study (Klerman 1985). The information was collected by trained lay interviewers who carried out a standardized interview of the respondents. Their findings, which have been criticized on a number of grounds, apparently showed disturbing evidence of widespread mental illness, with an upper estimate that 20 per cent of American adults suffer from mental illness at some point in their life, and that anxiety disorders are the largest mental health problem in the country. It was estimated that women have a 2.1 per cent lifetime prevalence rate for panic disorder and the rate for men was 1.0 per cent. The disorder was most common among people in middle adulthood and uncommon among people over the age of 65, and in these cases, it appeared to arise after a significant illness or injury. These estimates were contested by other researchers who thought that the ECA study exaggerated the prevalence of these disorders.

The ECA study produced some surprising results. For example, they identified a large number of people with agoraphobia, but found that a mere 7 per cent of them had also had a panic disorder. In contrast, a study of 300 anxiety patients assessed in the course of a large-scale collaborative study on the treatment of panic (Ballenger *et al.* 1988) did not find a single person whose agoraphobia had *not* been preceded by panic episodes. In an attempt to reconcile these conflicting findings, Horwath *et al.* (1993) re-interviewed 22 of the subjects who were classified in the ECA study as having agoraphobia without panic, and found that this conclusion was justified in only two of the 22 cases.

The discovery that anxiety disorders are common in the general population is consistent with other information on the subject. In addition, the ECA findings regarding the age of onset (median age of 24) and the peak incidence in middle adulthood are consistent with other findings, as is their determination that the ratio of panic disorder among women is two to three times as great as it is among men.

The debate about panic

Panic disorder has replaced agoraphobia as the anxiety disorder of greatest interest. Agoraphobia is now regarded as a secondary manifestation of panics – 'almost all agoraphobia ... is initiated by spontaneous panics', according to Klein and Klein (1989). Klein argued that panic disorder is a distinctive type of anxiety disorder and is essentially biological in nature. His views gave rise to fruitful discussions about the nature of panic, and arguments for and against the biological and the psychological explanations are the substance of one of the most interesting debates in the whole field of abnormal psychology. The opposing points of view were summarized in this way:

> One model, biomedical, claims essentially that panic is a disorder of the body, is biochemical, with a genetic vulnerability, and appropriately treated by drug therapy. The other, cognitive-behavioral, claims that it is a disorder of the mind based on misinterpretation, with a cognitive diathesis, and suitable for psychotherapy.
>
> (Seligman 1988: 321)

Klein based his claim for the distinctiveness and importance of panic disorder on two main arguments. Patients with a history of panic attacks do not respond to the drugs that produce improvements in patients with other types of anxiety disorder, but they respond well to imipramine, an anti-depressant drug (Klein and Klein 1989: 20). He accidentally discovered the anti-panic effects of imipramine in 1959 while carrying out research on the newly introduced anti-depressant medication imipramine, and decided to test its effects on those patients who were not deriving benefit from anti-anxiety medications such as benzodiazepines.

> The logic behind this was not exactly coercive: it was more a case of our not knowing what else to do for them, and thinking that perhaps this strange, new, safe agent with peculiar tranquilizing powers might work. Several patients volunteered for a pilot trial, primarily because anything was better than being sent home unimproved.
>
> (Klein 1987: 4)

Their unexpected response to anti-depressant medication set them apart from patients with other types of anxiety disorder.

The second piece of evidence on which Klein based his claim for the distinctiveness of panic arose from the fact that panic attacks can be induced in the laboratory by the infusion of lactate to patients who have a history of panic episodes. These two pieces of evidence were combined to reach the conclusion that panic disorders are distinctive – panic patients respond differentially to drug treatment, and panics can be provoked in these patients by a specific drug that leaves other patients unaffected. The concept of panic disorder was established on these two main pillars.

The connection between the two pillars is strengthened by the fact that the induction of a panic by an infusion of lactate can be blocked by the prior administration of imipramine. Additional arguments were introduced later, but they are secondary in importance and timing to the two main arguments. It then became apparent that there is a close connection between episodes of panic and agoraphobia, with a large number of agoraphobic patients recalling experiences of panic episodes.

Klein introduced the idea that episodes of spontaneous panic are 'due to the pathological central discharge of an evolved alarm mechanism, possibly linked to separation anxiety or asphyxia' (Klein and Klein 1989: 37). Still later, Klein homed in on the nature of the dysfunction and argued that spontaneous panics are the result of false firings of a suffocation alarm system (see below).

He assembled a good deal of evidence to support his arguments, and his original observation that imipramine does have anti-panic effects was confirmed. It is also correct that a proportion of people with a history of panic attacks respond positively to the lactate-infusion laboratory test. It was originally claimed that the overwhelming majority of panic patients respond positively, but subsequent research showed a far lower rate. It was also shown that people who are not sufferers from panic disorder can respond positively to the test, and most interestingly, the response to the infusion of lactate was found to be partly dependent on psychological factors.

Klein's claim that episodes of panic can initiate agoraphobia received considerable support. In six surveys and studies, it was found that the percentage of people with agoraphobia who said that their panics had occurred prior to the development of their phobia was never less than 80 per cent, and in one study it went as high as 97 per cent.

The biological theory was subjected to four types of criticism.

1 The numerous attempts to find a biological substrate for the disorder have been unsuccessful.
2 Klein's revised theory provides significantly more detail than the original proposal, but remains unclear on critical points.
3 There is positive evidence that contradicts the theory or its implications.
4 Some critics consider the whole enterprise to have been misguided.

The basis for the original argument, the two main pillars, has been challenged. The initial claim that the induction of panics by lactate infusions is a distinctive, diagnostic symptom of panic disorder was not supported. It turns out that these responses are not specific to panic disorder patients as was originally suggested. For example, the panic rates for patients with depression, those with generalized anxiety, and those with panic disorder do not differ (Ehlers *et al*. 1988). As conceded by Klein, a large number of patients with panic disorder do not respond positively to the lactate-infusion test. The response to the infusion test lacks specificity and sensitivity. Patients with panic disorder are not as distinctly different as Klein had originally postulated.

Noting that so many different chemical agents have been shown to produce a panic effect, Gorman (1987) questioned whether there were any active agents that did not cause a panic. Moreover, as D. M. Clark (1988) commented, the active agents do not have a common chemical property. If panic disorder is indeed a biological dysfunction, it is one that is easily provoked and by diverse chemical agents. The evidence on lactate infusion was criticized on the grounds of methodological shortcomings, including a failure to control for baseline responding (i.e. ensuring comparable levels of baseline responding in the patients with panic disorder and comparison patients before the lactate is infused).

The original observation that led Klein to separate out panic disorder from other types of anxiety disorder was criticized. Contrary to what was originally asserted, the claim that imipramine, and related anti-depressant drugs, have a specific action on spontaneous panics was not confirmed. According to Tyrer (1986), imipramine produces broad effects, and in addition, several classes of medication are capable of blocking spontaneous panic attacks. These include anti-depressant medications of two main types, and certain types of benzodiazepines. A similar view was expressed by Zitrin (1986) and other collaborators of Klein, who pointed out that there are at least three classes of medication that effectively block panics (Zitrin 1986). The claim of an exclusive connection between imipramine and panics was not confirmed.

The biological theory has difficulty in accommodating various findings. Panics can be induced by purely psychological procedures (Rachman 1990). Psychological treatments are followed by significant reductions in the frequency of panics (Marks 1987) and there is good evidence that CBT is particularly effective in reducing panics (Barlow 2002; D. A. Clark and Beck 2010; D. M. Clark 1997, 1999; D. M. Clark et al. 1994; McNally 1995). There is no reason why psychological treatments should be ineffective in modifying panic disorders even if they are biological in character, but these psychological results were not deducible from Klein's theory.

The major demographic features of panic disorders remain unexplained. There is nothing in the biological theory to explain why women are so much more vulnerable to this putative biological disorder, and there is no reason to explain why it should occur most frequently in early adulthood.

Klein's revised theory

After establishing panic disorder as a separable disorder, Klein analysed the implications of this distinction. He set out its connection with agoraphobia, and made assessment and treatment recommendations. At a later stage, he set forward a novel theory, proposing that 'many spontaneous panics occur when the brain's suffocation monitor erroneously signals a lack of useful air, thereby maladaptively triggering an evolved suffocation alarm system' (Klein 1993: 306). He postulated that the suffocation alarm is triggered by physiological mechanisms that detect increasing carbon dioxide and brain lactate values.

According to Klein, the suffocation alarm is activated by increasing levels of carbon dioxide which then produce sudden respiratory distress (sensations of smothering), which promote brief hyperventilation and panic. Obviously such a monitor would be of survival value. When our breathing becomes difficult, nothing else matters.

Klein also proposed that the alarm can be activated by psychological cues to suffocation.

> A no-exit situation or one where stuffy, stale air implies no exit, where there are crowded, immobilized people or someone appears to be smothering, might all elicit panic if the suffocation alarm threshold is pathologically lowered or if the cues are particularly salient.
>
> (Klein 1993: 306)

False alarms, the triggering of the suffocation monitoring system by inappropriate or insufficient stimuli, can then occur. Unexpected panic attacks are the result of a false firing of the suffocation alarm system and are particularly likely to occur in people who have an abnormally low threshold for activation (hypersensitive alarms), as this causes the alarm to misfire in a seemingly irregular and unpredictable manner. It can be seen that Klein's theory, with its allowance for biological and psychological triggers of the alarm system and consequent panic, is essentially psycho-biological in nature. In the earlier version of his theory, Klein attached seemingly equal importance to breathing problems and to separation anxiety, but that association was not convincing (see Thyer *et al.* 1986) and did not feature in his revised theory.

People who have the hyper-sensitive suffocation alarm system can be identified by testing their reaction to inhalation of carbon dioxide or by their response to sodium lactate. Consistent with Klein's theory, Rachman and Taylor (1993) demonstrated that suffocation reactions can be elicited by psychological means. Fears of suffocation are common (Rachman 1990), and the interruption of breathing can give rise to intense distress (e.g. the experiment by Sanderson *et al.* 1963). However, Klein's plausible emphasis on the fear of suffocation rested on a biological basis (the postulated alarm system), to the relative neglect of psychological triggers.

In his elaboration of the postulated alarm system, Klein attached significance to a little known medical condition known as 'Ondine's Curse', congenital central hypoventilation syndrome, which he viewed as exactly converse to the problems that arise from excessively sensitive suffocation detectors. Among a very small number of infants, the hypoventilation syndrome can have fatal consequences. If the child ceases breathing during sleep, hence becoming hypoxic, they can die. Pointing out that when these children are grown up, they are completely insensitive to carbon monoxide and have no sense of suffocation under asphyxiating circumstances, Klein (1996) argued that the absence of a suffocation detector in children with this rare disorder is proof of the *general* existence of a suffocation detector – most people have the detector.

It should follow that children who survive Ondine's Curse – that is, the overwhelming majority of such children – should be relatively immune to the development of panic disorder in adulthood, unless they have the misfortune to have a traumatic experience that induces the disorder. To be precise, these unfortunate children are not suffering from the absence of a postulated suffocation alarm monitor, but from a seriously deficient one. For the most part, their breathing during sleep is maintained at a safe level, with very rare failures of the system.

Incidental evidence in support of part of Klein's theory was provided by Rachman and Taylor (1993) who were prompted by the revised theory to carry out a re-analysis of data collected in an experiment on the nature of claustrophobia that was unrelated to Klein's theory (Taylor and Rachman 1994). The 179 non-clinical participants were divided into those with a high fear of suffocation ($N = 49$) and those with little or no such fear, as assessed on a dependable questionnaire. The participants also completed a number of behavioural tests that included a suffocation challenge of breathing through a narrow straw for two minutes. On re-analysis, it appeared that subjects with a high fear of suffocation reported more panics during the test than those with a low fear of suffocation, namely 18.4 per cent of the whole group versus 1.5 per cent. After the suffocation challenge test, the subjects completed a brief structured interview pertaining to experiences of anxiety and panic. It was found that relative to participants with a low fear of suffocation, the high scorers reported a greater incidence of panic in enclosed spaces (59.2 per cent of the whole group versus 16.2 per cent), and also in other situations (57.1 per cent versus 20.6 per cent). Those with a high fear of suffocation also reported a far greater frequency of unexpected panics (32.7 per cent versus 4.4 per cent). In other words, the participants with a high fear of suffocation were seven times more likely to report having unexpected panics than were those who had little or no fear of suffocation.

In a study that was conducted specifically to test one aspect of Klein's theory, McNally *et al.* (1995) compared the experiences of patients who had experienced panic disorder and those of community participants who had experienced episodes of panic, but did not have panic disorder. They found three cognitive symptoms that discriminated the clinical from the non-clinical panics: fear of dying, having a heart attack, and loss of control. As suggested by Klein's theory, suffocation symptoms had the largest effect size of any physiological symptom, and they pointed out that 'suffocation sensations may be especially likely to generate the catastrophic thoughts that best discriminate clinical from non-clinical panic' (McNally *et al.* 1995: n. p.).

Despite its boldness and several successes, Klein's theory attracted some criticism (e.g. Ley 1994; McNally 1994; Schmidt *et al.* 1996). Complaints were made that the theory is insufficiently detailed to allow for precise evaluation. It also fails to explain why some people die from carbon monoxide asphyxiation – why did their suffocation alarm monitor failed to trigger? Klein answered that carbon monoxide and similar agents may 'disable the suffocation monitor or alarm system' (Klein 1996: 84).

In light of these problems and objections, a word is necessary about the status of Klein's work and the biological theory. It is difficult to defend some of Klein's original arguments, but his work is nevertheless of lasting value. Even though the 'two pillars' on which his original theory was based are best regarded as scaffolding that served a temporary purpose, he successfully drew attention to the significance of the occurrence of episodes of panic, their functional relation to agoraphobia, and the possible involvement of an easily triggered suffocation alarm system. Finally, Klein's introduction of the concept of panic disorder and his advocacy of a biological explanation acted as grist that led to the formulation of competing, psychological explanations.

The cognitive theory of panic

With their long-established interest in and knowledge about fear and anxiety, psychologists were drawn to the new concept of panic disorder, but found the biological explanation unsatisfactory. Two psychological explanations were developed independently by Barlow (1988) and by D. M. Clark (1986), but they overlap and for present purposes the differences between them are not significant. Clark's theory, which has been the subject of a considerable amount of research, is described and analysed, but much of the reasoning in this chapter applies equally well to Barlow's theory.

Clark's theory is stated in an admirably succinct manner: 'Panic attacks result from the catastrophic misinterpretation of certain bodily sensations' (Clark 1986: 462–463). Bodily sensations such as a rapid heartbeat or dizziness are catastrophically misinterpreted as being dangerous; for example, a person might interpret palpitations as evidence of an impending heart attack. Other examples include the misperception of breathlessness as evidence of incipient respiratory arrest, or perceiving dizziness as evidence of an imminent loss of control. A wide range of stimuli are capable of producing episodes of panic, and include some external stimuli, but according to Clark (1988), the triggers for panic are almost invariably internal. Barlow (1988) also attaches considerable significance to the misinterpretation of internal stimuli. If the person makes a misinterpretation in which the threat is exaggerated, but not imminent, it is more likely to arouse anxiety than an episode of panic. Disturbing misinterpretations of bodily sensations that give rise to anxiety about one's health, but pose no immediate threat, are the raw material for hypochondriasis, a problem which is increasingly being re-described as *health anxiety* (Salkovskis and Warwick 1986; see Chapter 10).

The cognitive theory of panic has received research support (Barlow 2002; D. M. Clark 1988, 1997, 1999; D. A. Clark and Beck 2010; Craske 1999; Brewin 1996; McNally 1994) and provided the rationale for a psychological treatment of panic disorder, cognitive behaviour therapy, which is effective (Acierno *et al.* 1993; Barlow 2002; D. M. Clark 1997, 1999; Clark *et al.* 1994; Clark and Fairburn 1997; Craske 1999; Margraf *et al.* 1993), and is recommended by NICE and the NIMH as the treatment method of choice. In support of the cognitive theory, patients with panic disorder have a higher frequency of the cognitions that lend themselves to catastrophic misinterpretation (Clark 1986, 1988, 1997a; Barlow 1988, 2002; Hibbert 1984). They are more likely to experience thoughts of impending loss of control, loss of consciousness, heart attack, and so on, than are people who have anxiety that is not associated with a panic experience. Reports of specific connections between the catastrophic cognitions and the occurrence of panic are encountered in case after case of patients receiving cognitive behaviour therapy. In the clearest examples, the panics are eliminated after the patient's cognitions have been corrected. Between 74 per cent and 95 per cent of patients are panic-free after three months of CBT (Clark *et al.* 1994).

Changes in bodily sensations usually precede an episode of panic (Clark 1988). Experimental studies have shown that patients with panic disorder are significantly more likely to interpret their bodily sensations in a mistaken and catastrophic manner than are patients who do not experience panics (Clark et al. 1994). Furthermore, if a catastrophic misinterpretation is activated, the probability of an experience in panic is increased (Clark 1987). In a review of the data, Ehlers (1992: 3) concluded that 'Panic patients demonstrated an enhanced ability to perceive their heart rate, they tended to shift their attention towards physically threatening cues and they rated bodily symptoms associated with anxiety or panic as more dangerous.' The specificity of the connections between the particular bodily sensations and the associated cognitions is consistent with the theory. So, for example, a combination of breathlessness and dizziness accompanied by a fear of passing out or losing control was associated with panic on 11 out of 13 occasions, but this combination of sensations was never followed by a panic in the absence of a fearful cognition (Rachman 1990).

Unusually within clinical psychology, Clark's theory is causal, and it is difficult to demonstrate definitively that the associations between sensations, cognitions and subsequent panic are more than co-effects. It is possible that the cognitions described by the panic patients are epiphenomena (a view shared by some biological theorists, such as Klein and Klein [1989], and by conditioning theorists such as Wolpe and Rowan [1988]). Perhaps they are merely accompaniments of a fundamentally biological disorder or accompaniments of a conditioned panic reaction.

Even though it is difficult to prove the causal connection, there are several arguments to support the view that cognitions do indeed play an important part in the causation of panics. Instructions given to vulnerable subjects or patients can be important determinants of the occurrence or non-occurrence of a panic. For example, when participants are told that a deliberate provocation, such as the infusion of lactate, might produce a panic, the occurrence of panic increases (Clark 1988). To test the hypothesis that the instructions given to the testee influence the likelihood of a person responding positively to a panic provocation challenge, Clark provided one group of panic patients with instructions designed to reassure them about the sensations they could expect to experience after receiving an infusion of lactate, while participants in the control group were merely told that lactate is safe. All of the participants knew that they could stop the infusion at any time, and consistent with the hypothesis, the rate of panic in the reassured experimental group was significantly lower than it was in the control group. The rate for the experimental group was 30 per cent and that for the control group was 90 per cent.

In addition, links between bodily sensations, fearful cognitions and panic have been demonstrated in the experiments on claustrophobic and panic disorder patients. Episodes of panic were strongly associated with a significant elevation of fearful cognitions, and in the absence of such cognitions, episodes of panic were uncommon or in some samples, absent. Sanderson *et al.* (1989) demonstrated that introducing a degree of personal control reduces the probability of the person panicking under the provocation of inhalations of 5.5 per cent carbon- dioxide-enriched air, which would ordinarily produce panic in a substantial number of participants. In this experiment, the participants were given access to a lever which they were told could control the experimental conditions, and this information succeeded in reducing the rate of panics even though the control was in fact illusory. Carter *et al.* (1995) also showed the power of psychological factors to moderate the reaction to deliberate provocations of panic.

People can be primed for anxiety or panic by receiving alarming information about their own or other people's health (for example, George had a sudden heart attack) and by adverse life events. Episodes of panic increase after such events and the onset of panic disorder often is linked to adverse life events. In addition, some people are primed to misinterpret their own bodily sensations. Brewin (1996) observed that attention has been directed almost solely to the accessible cognitions, but notice should also be taken of the important non-conscious cognitive processes involved in anxiety (pre-attentive processes, memory and attentional biases, etc.).

The theories of D. M. Clark and of Barlow understandably and correctly emphasize the importance of the misinterpretation of bodily sensations, but misinterpretations of other threatening events can also produce a panic.

Any factors that bring about significant changes in bodily sensations, or in *external* threats, increase the opportunity for catastrophic misinterpretations. The common factors include over-breathing, strenuous exertion, taking stimulants such as caffeine or drugs. The priming conditions that increase the likelihood of a person misinterpreting these changes in sensation include adverse life events, alarming information, and a consistently negative style of attributions. The eliciting conditions are threatening information, a menacing context and the absence or loss of safety signals.

The vulnerability to episodes of panic can be reduced by avoiding those actions that provoke excessive bodily sensations (such as high levels of caffeine intake); by adopting or developing safety signals and procedures; and best of all, by making correct interpretations of the changes that do take place. The main thrust of cognitive behaviour therapy is directed at these very misinterpretations and their replacement by more appropriate and reassuring explanations (see Barlow 2002; D. A. Clark and Beck 2010; D. M. Clark *et al*. 1994; Craske 1999; Hawton *et al*. 1989; Margraf *et al*. 1993; McNally 1995; Salkovskis 1996a).

Cognitive theory is a coherent model with successful connections to cognitive psychology, abnormal behaviour and experiences, and therapeutic applications. The therapeutic effects of cognitive behaviour therapy cannot be explained by any other theory. A less obvious advantage of the cognitive theory of panic is that it enables one to accommodate much of the current information on panic which includes the evidence collected and assembled by proponents of the biological theory. The fact that a variety of biochemical and physiological manipulations can induce episodes of panic shows that it is not the specificity of the agent that is important; rather, the common element should be sought in the person's understanding of the procedure and his or her expectation of the effects of the manipulation, especially on their bodily sensations.

The cognitive theory also accommodates the fact that in a minority of instances, episodes of panic can be induced by relaxation, an outcome that is not obviously predictable from the biological theory (unless relaxation disarms the suffocation monitor?). Following the cognitive theory, if the induction of relaxation gives rise to a catastrophic misinterpretation of the changes in bodily sensations that occur during relaxation, a panic can occur. If, for example, the person is frightened of losing consciousness or dying, then bodily sensations of a slowing in breathing, faintness and tingling can be interpreted as threatening and cause a panic. Some patients reject relaxation treatment for this very reason.

Exactly this chain of events occurred in a patient whose panic disorder had been triggered by an unfortunate experience in which she had had an extremely adverse reaction to taking a street drug. It produced intense feelings of unreality and depersonalization, and at its worst, she felt that she was going insane. Thereafter, whenever she began to feel any unusual sensations or feelings that resembled the trigger event, she became extremely anxious and on occasion panicked. It was not possible to teach her relaxation techniques because it provoked adverse reactions.

Vulnerability

Clark (1988, 1997) postulates that certain people are vulnerable to panic because they have an enduring tendency to misinterpret bodily symptoms. There are at least three types of vulnerability. The person might be predisposed to experience intense or frequent bodily sensations, or predisposed to make catastrophic misinterpretations, or both. The second possibility, the inclination to 'catastrophize', has received most attention, and rightly so. Most people experience changes in bodily sensations, even of an intrusive kind, with regularity. Hence, the opportunities for panic are almost limitless, but the occurrence of these episodes is extremely rare. We need to ask, therefore, why and under what circumstances these changes in sensations are catastrophically misinterpreted.

Thus far the research has succeeded in showing that people with a history of panic episodes show an enduring tendency to be highly sensitive to changes in bodily sensations, and also to have a tendency to misinterpret them (Clark 1999). In addition, successfully treated panic disorder patients show a marked reduction in their tendency to make these catastrophic misinterpretations (Clark *et al*. 1994). In some seemingly tame laboratory exercises, even reading a series of statements pertaining to the sensations of discomfort and anxiety has been sufficient to bring people close to a panic (Clark 1988). For example, in one study, panic patients who were asked to respond to words written on index cards were brought close to a panic by exposure to negative words such as 'choking' and 'dying'. Partly as a result of the research on panic disorder, and for some related reasons, attempts have been made to measure enduring tendencies of this type (see, for example, the construction of a special scale, called the Anxiety Sensitivity Index mentioned in Chapter 3 ['Vulnerability'] – Reiss *et al*. [1986]).

All theories need to address the question of the timing and context of episodes of panic, and in early formulations of the cognitive theory, emphasis was placed on the role of over-breathing. Hyperventilation causes an increase in bodily sensations and was believed to be productive of many instances of panic. Hyperventilation can be provoked by strenuous exercise, or by distress, and if the resultant bodily sensations are mistakenly interpreted as signs of an impending medical problem, panic can ensue. Later research led to a de-emphasis on the role of hyperventilation and Margraf (1993) concluded that hyperventilation is related to panic in two ways.

First, it is one of many processes that can lead to the perception of bodily sensations which may trigger positive feedback loops between sensations and anxiety responses. Second, because of the circular nature of such feedback processes, hyperventilation can also be a response to anxiety.

(Margraf 1993: 49)

It will be recalled that in the revision of his biological theory, Klein (1993) postulated that hyperventilation is a response to a false triggering of the suffocation alarm system. In Klein's view, hyperventilation is an attempt to compensate for the feeling of insufficient useable air; but in the cognitive theory, hyperventilation more often is regarded as a precipitant of panic in that it produces bodily sensations which are open to misinterpretation.

Critique

A bold original theory, extensive in its implications and successful in generating an effective therapy, is bound to elicit keen interest, criticism and research. As mentioned earlier, the cognitive theory of panic is one side of the mighty debate between predominantly biological and predominantly psychological explanations for various forms of abnormal behaviour.

Criticisms of the theory were raised by psychologists working within the cognitive framework (e.g. Seligman 1988; Teasdale 1988), by advocates of the original conditioning theory of fear and anxiety (e.g. Wolpe and Rowan 1988) and by advocates of the biological approach (notably Klein and Klein 1989). Among the objections, it was argued that Clark's theory is loosely specified and inconsistent with some evidence; that the effects of various types of drugs on episodes of panic are inconsistent with the theory; that episodes should never occur when patients are relaxed; that nocturnal panics should not occur; and that there are many circumstances and stimuli that increase anxiety, but do not lead to panic. Some of the criticisms, such as the occurrence of relaxation-associated episodes of panic, did not raise serious problems for the cognitive theory (a state of relaxation does not preclude the intrusion of catastrophic cognitions), but did instigate research into nocturnal panics (see Craske 1999). An account of the biological criticisms and the counter-arguments is provided by McNally (1994: 110–115).

The main demographic features of panic disorders (onset in early to middle adulthood, female preponderance) remain to be explained. Why should people begin to 'catastrophize' in early adulthood? Why are women 2–4 times more likely to 'catastrophize'? Why do so few elderly people develop panic – they certainly have greater reason than young adults to be concerned about their bodily sensations and deteriorating health. Seligman (1988) commented that the concept of 'catastrophic misinterpretations' is too loose, and also argued that Clark's theory is not sufficiently different from non-cognitive explanations. It seems to overlap with the conditioning explanation of panic (see Wolpe and Rowan 1988). Seligman also raised the persistently troublesome problem of why it is that certain kinds of fear appear to defy disconfirmation.

Why, he asked, does a person who has experienced hundreds of episodes of panic fail to learn that his heart is *not* defective? Why does he continue to believe that he is about to have a heart attack? Having received ample disconfirming evidence to prove that what he believed was false, the belief should weaken and disappear. It is, however, likely that the original fear of an impending heart attack *is* largely disconfirmed, but is then replaced by a strong fear of experiencing a nasty panic. This fearful cognition is intermittently reinforced, and therefore is difficult to disconfirm. Teasdale (1988) asked why cognitive therapy requires 'back up' from evidence provided by one's own experiences. Even when cognitive interventions do produce changes in thinking, they often need to be bolstered by direct experience.

The occurrence of nocturnal panics is common among sufferers of panic disorder, and progress has been made in research on these panics, but a wholly satisfactory explanation is not yet available. Craske and her colleagues have proposed a cognitive explanation in which the key proposition is that nocturnal panics, like other panics, are caused by catastrophic misinterpretations of certain bodily sensations when the person awakens (Craske 1999, 2003). There is evidence of elevated physiological activity shortly before awakening with a nocturnal panic. However, this may beg the question – why does the elevated activity arise in the first place? It is possible that a proportion of these panics are induced by disturbing dreams, and that in other instances, the person is awakened and then becomes aware of disturbing bodily sensations. These sensations then trigger a panic in vulnerable people. Gathering the information necessary to test these and related explanations is no easy task, but progress has been made (Craske 1999), and encouragingly, there is evidence that CBT based on

Craske's rationale produces significant and lasting improvements in nocturnal panics (Craske 2003).

Another potential problem for the theory of panic disorder is the occurrence of so-called 'non-cognitive panics', in which the person reports having experienced a panic without the accompaniment of a fearful cognition (Rachman *et al.* 1987). These may simply be failures to identify the appropriate thought, but it should be said that each of the patients who reported a non-cognitive panic had on at least one other occasion reported a so-called cognitive panic. It is not merely a matter of dealing with people who are incapable of recognizing and reporting fearful cognitions.

The questions of causality raise difficult problems and there is no simple way to determine whether the cognitions are the cause, the consequence, or merely a correlate of the episodes of panic. The decline in cognitions and in bodily sensations observed after successful treatment is consistent with predictions that flow from the theory, but Seligman (1988) argued that they are open to more than a single interpretation. The decline in cognitions and/or in bodily sensations may well produce the reduction of the panics, but it is also possible that the decline in cognitions and sensations are consequences of the reduced episodes of panic, and not the cause. It is also possible that the decline of cognitions is a correlate of the reduction in the episodes of panic. Other critics suggested that the cognitions and their decline might be mere epiphenomena (Wolpe and Rowan 1988). One reason for giving serious consideration to alternative possibilities arose from an early study of the treatment of panic disorder. Patients who received pure exposure treatment without cognitive interventions showed improvements that were as large and enduring as those patients who received pure cognitive therapy in which exposures were excluded (Margraf *et al.* 1993). Moreover, the cognitions declined to the same extent in both groups. In this instance, it appeared that negative cognitions can decline after direct cognitive treatment, or after non-cognitive treatment. Following refinements of the method, however, the superiority of cognitive treatment has been affirmed (Beck 2005; D. A. Clark and Beck 2010; D. M. Clark 1996, 1999).

Nevertheless, a comprehensive cognitive explanation needs to account for the decline in cognitions that occur after non-cognitive treatments, such as repeated exposures to the fearful situation, or stress-management training. The most obvious possibility is that with each exposure, the patient acquires fresh, disconfirmatory evidence (e.g. no heart attack, did not lose control, and so forth). The accumulation of repeated, personal, direct disconfirmations of a catastrophic event weakens the catastrophic cognitions. However, one is left to wonder why the direct modification of the catastrophic cognitions was not always significantly more effective than the indirect, incidental effects of exposure in the study by Margraf *et al.* (1993), and a similar one by Ost and Westling (1995).

As mentioned, refinements of the cognitive method enhanced their strength, and there are indications that the longer-term effects of cognitive behaviour therapy are superior to other methods. There is also evidence of a relationship between the amount of cognitive behaviour therapy provided and the extent of change. In an important outcome study, panic patients who received added cognitive therapy had a superior therapeutic outcome to those who received indirect treatments (Clark *et al.* 1994). As far as the therapeutic mechanisms of cognitive therapy are concerned, there is a need to determine whether or not the reduction or elimination of key cognitions is the *critical element* in CBT. It is proven that the direct modification of cognitions is a sufficient condition for treatment success, but we also know that direct modification is not a necessary condition for success (e.g. exposure alone can be effective, medications can produce improvements, and so forth). An obstacle to finding answers to these questions arises from a need for control over the timing of the events. Reductions in fear are easy to observe and record, but they can occur slowly, over weeks rather than minutes. In cases of panic, the measures of change in therapeutic trials typically range over days or, commonly, over weeks (e.g. the number of panics experienced per week or even per month). So if the patient records a decrease in panics – say, from four per week to one per week – when exactly did the decline take place? The cognitive changes can be even more difficult to track. Significant changes in cognition can occur suddenly (e.g. Ost 1989; Rachman and Whittal 1989), and are therefore easy to record. However, in many and perhaps most circumstances, clinical or experimental, the cognitive shifts are slow to develop, changing over weeks rather than minutes (e.g. the cognitive therapy group in the Booth and Rachman [1992] claustrophobia study).

To complicate matters, changes in fear and in fearful cognitions can occur even when the person is separated from and out of context from the fear-provoking stimulus (Rachman 1990). It is not possible to determine precisely when the changes occurred. So researchers are left with the difficult task of timing the sequence of changes in the cognitions, and in the episodes of panic, knowing that these changes may take place over an extended period, and that determining the precise point of change is difficult. There are also some indications that cognitive shifts can initiate a process of behaviour/emotional change that only becomes evident sometime later.

The fact that medications can significantly reduce panic, even in the absence of CBT, requires explanation. The problem is a broad one because medications can be effective in the treatment of social phobia (Heimberg *et al.* 1998; see Chapter 11) and of OCD (Rachman *et al.* 1979).

Are the therapeutic effects achieved by CBT or by medications mediated by a common mechanism? It seems unlikely, and in any event the combination of CBT and drugs is not additive. For reasons that are unclear, CBT and medications appear to be independent means of treatment – to the mutual discomfort of proponents of psychological and of biological treatments.

To summarize, the cognitive theory has exceptional explanatory value and has garnered a good deal of support (Austin and Richards 2001 ; Barlow 2002; Beck 2005; D. A. Clark and Beck 2010; D. M. Clark 1999; Craske 1999; Ehlers 1992). It also provided the platform for a demonstrably effective method of therapy. At present, there is no satisfactory explanation for the success of this therapy other than the cognitive theory itself.

The coherence between the theory and its clinical applications is a strength. We now have a reasonably good idea of why and when episodes of panic are likely to occur. Any settings, sensations or cues that increase the opportunity for catastrophic misinterpretations – or that increase the probability of a misinterpretation occurring of an internal or external threatening stimulus– raise the likelihood that the person will experience an episode of panic. Significant changes in the number and intensity of relevant bodily sensations, and/or a strong tendency to interpret these sensations as indicators of imminent danger, can promote panic. We also know that although everybody experiences bodily sensations of the type that can provide an opportunity for catastrophic misinterpretations, very few people make the misinterpretations that induce a panic.

Treatment

Panic disorder is treated by psychological techniques, by medication or a combination of both. Until the introduction of cognitive behaviour therapy (CBT), the main psychological method for treating panics and the associated agoraphobic avoidance consisted of many repetitions of controlled, graded exposures to the feared stimulus (Barlow 1988; Marks 1987; Mathews *et al*. 1981; Rachman and Wilson 1980). This method, *behaviour therapy*, was moderately effective and was supplemented in many cases by training in relaxation, stress-management skills, etc. The inclusion of a large component of cognitive therapy enhanced the behavioural treatment (Beck 2005; D. A. Clark.and Beck 2010; D. M. Clark 1999; Clark *et al*. 1994). Around 80 per cent to 90 per cent of patients who receive CBT are panic-free at the end of therapy (Clark 1997). The treatment consists of two components: the identification of the maladaptive cognitions and their replacement with plausible benign cognitions, plus the provision of exposure exercises designed to facilitate the cognitive changes (Hawton *et al*. 1989). The fact that in some studies, a relatively pure cognitive treatment proved to be as effective as the traditional exposure treatment (e.g. Margraf *et al*. 1993) meant that the explanation for the effects of behaviour therapy had to be reconsidered. Equally, the fact that a pure exposure treatment can be as effective as a cognitive treatment raised comparable questions about the cognitive theory.

Leaving aside these theoretical questions, the potency of CBT is notable and clinicians are able to provide effective help for many people and to do so with well-grounded confidence – an unprecedentedly powerful method (Clark 1997).

In many clinics and general practices, the majority of patients receive the alternative treatment – medication. Imipramine can be effective (Clark *et al*. 1994) and other types of tricyclic anti-depressants are capable of reducing or eliminating panics in many cases. They do, however, produce side-effects and can be difficult to tolerate (Lader 1994). There is also a risk of relapse when the medication is withdrawn. In a large study conducted in four sites, 312 patients were given either cognitive therapy (panic control treatment [PCT]); imipramine; PCT plus a placebo; or PCT plus imipramine (Barlow *et al*. 2000). The groups of patients who received PCT or imipramine were significantly improved. Interestingly, the patients who received PCT plus imipramine did well, but no better than those who received PCT plus a placebo. The drug treatment and the psychological treatment were both independently effective, but when they were combined, no advantage accrued. The effects of the psychological treatment were lasting, but there were many relapses after drug treatment (40–50 per cent within six months).

The risk of relapse is also high (50 per cent or more) with another class of medication, the well-established and widely used anti-anxiety benzodiazepine drugs (e.g. alprazolam). Up to 15 per cent of patients attending general practitioners seek treatment for anxiety, in one or other of its forms, and the standard treatment is anxiolytic medication, especially benzodiazepine (Lader 1994). 'Anti-anxiety drugs suppress the symptoms of anxiety to some extent, sometimes quite effectively, but they do not deal with the root causes of the disorder' (Lader 1994: 323).

Even when psychological therapy is the preferred treatment, facilities are limited. Fortunately, the scant dissemination of CBT procedures and the lack of trained therapists are now being corrected in the UK by the national scheme for providing Improved Access to Psychological Therapies (IAPT) described in the Introduction to the third edition of this book.

As psychological treatment and medication are both effective in reducing anxiety, it is reasonable to expect a combination of the two to be superior to either method used separately. Surprisingly, this is not the case. The majority of studies in which the combination of the two was matched against 'medication only' and 'psychotherapy only' failed to demonstrate a superiority for the combination of methods (e.g. Otto, Gould *et al.* 1996). For example, in an early comparative investigation of the therapeutic effects of behaviour therapy only versus medication only (clomipramine) in 40 patients with severe and chronic OCD, both treatments were shown to be moderately effective (Rachman *et al.* 1979). A comparison group of patients who received a combination of the two treatments did only as well as did the patients who received either the medication or the behaviour therapy. There was no additive effect (see also Foa *et al.* [1992: 279] – 'imipramine did not potentiate the effects of behavior therapy'; Otto, Pollock *et al.* 1996; Marks 1987). When the OCD study was completed, it was suggested that clomipramine might achieve its effects secondarily (Rachman *et al.* 1979), as a consequence of a reduction in depression (clomipramine is an anti-depressant medication). The clomipramine reduces the depression and that relieves the OCD. Some studies failed to confirm this suggestion and the matter is unresolved. Regardless of the explanation for the surprising absence of additive effects, the later comparisons of psychological treatment alone or in combination with medication give the same answer – additive effects are rarely found (Otto, Pollock *et al.* 1996). We appear to have a peculiar therapeutic arithmetic in which $1 + 1 = 1$.

Despite the absence of convincing evidence of its value, the combination of psychological treatment with medication continues to be the method of first choice in many facilities. At present (2013), in day-to-day clinical practice, it often is in the patient's interest to receive both treatments, especially if the panic disorder is accompanied by depression. However, in some combinations at least, the addition of medications can interfere with psychological treatment (Marks *et al.* 1993) and/or increase the risk of relapse. Otto, Pollack *et al.* (1996) reported that 69 per cent of panic disorder patients who took no medication after cognitive therapy remained well for up to two years; whereas only 24 per cent of those who continued to take medication after cognitive therapy remained well in the follow-up period (see also Otto *et al.* 1992).

Summary

Panic is an episode of intense fear of sudden onset and generally lasts between 5 and 20 minutes, leaving a residue of anxiety. Panics are commonly experienced by people with an anxiety disorder, but if the repeated occurrence of panics is the major or only problem, it is diagnosed as a panic disorder.

The original theory of panic disorder states that it is essentially a biological disorder and is appropriately dealt with by medication. The revised biological theory is more specific and traces the problem to an over-sensitivity of the body's alarm system. Panics are false alarms that occur when the alarm system is triggered in the absence of a true threat to the supply of useable air. The theory is supported by some evidence, but does not account for significant aspects of the phenomena. The cognitive theory states that panics result from a catastrophic misinterpretation of certain bodily sensations, and it follows that a correction or elimination of these misinterpretations should prevent recurrent episodes of panic. The theory has garnered considerable support and the deduced therapy is effective, but several problems remain to be solved.

Agoraphobia 8

The original concept of agoraphobia, a fear and avoidance of public places, has been revised and is now linked to the theory of panic disorders. This chapter describes the current view of agoraphobia, its nature and causes, and the prevailing approach to treatment.

The prototypical neurosis

For over 30 years, *agoraphobia* was regarded as the prototypical neurosis and theories that failed to provide a plausible explanation of agoraphobia were of little interest. The main features of agoraphobia are a fear and avoidance of public places and of travelling, especially on public transport. These features sometimes are associated with a fear of being alone, even at home. Affected people report that they are frightened of passing out, having a heart attack, being trapped, losing control, or undergoing some other distressing event. As mentioned in the previous chapter, these cognitions are critical in the onset of panic. People who struggle with agoraphobia experience unpleasant bodily sensations in anticipation of and during excursions from safety, which is in most cases their home. In serious cases, the person is immobilized unless accompanied by some trusted companion, and even then their mobility is constricted. A severely affected patient described his state in these words: 'Everything outside my front door is Vietnam.'

The disorder usually emerges in early adulthood and is at least twice as common in women as in men. It is often associated with other psychological problems, notably panic disorder, claustrophobia, depression. Cases of agoraphobia not associated with episodes of panic are uncommon . As mentioned in Chapter 7, between 80 per cent and 97 per cent of patients reported that they had experienced panics before the development of their agoraphobia (Klein 1987, 1989). The current view is that in the overwhelming majority of cases, agoraphobia is secondary to the development of a panic disorder. Agoraphobia is often associated with other psychological problems, notably depression and, of course, panic. People who suffer from agoraphobia have high levels of general anxiety. Their fears tend to persist for many years, but do show some daily and weekly fluctuations.

The subject of agoraphobia rose to prominence in the early 1950s because of its common appearance in clinics. Learning theorists such as H. J. Eysenck (1957, 1967) and Wolpe (1958) insisted on the need to study observable behaviour and they were quick to recognize that agoraphobia could provide a testing ground for their fresh ideas on the subject of neurosis. The fear was well-suited for treatments by the emerging methods of behaviour therapy because unadaptive avoidance *behaviour* is the central – and accessible – feature of agoraphobia, and hence is a suitable test-bed for explanations of neurosis that concentrate on observable behaviour.

The theorists were guided in their approach by a considerable store of information that had been collected on the behaviour of small animals studied under laboratory conditions. A great deal was already known about the generation and maintenance of *avoidance behaviour* in animals. The advocates of the application of learning theory to abnormal behaviour were familiar with the concepts and methods of studying avoidance, and readily construed agoraphobia in these terms.

Conditioned fear was thought to be the central component of most neuroses, including agoraphobia. In this disorder, it was argued, the conditioned stimuli that evoke the fear consist of public places, public transport, and so on. It was argued furthermore that the conditioned fear gives rise to avoidance behaviour because people learn to avoid those places in which they have experienced fear or pain (Mowrer 1960). For a period, this approach was productive, supported as it was by the laboratory evidence and reinforced by the successful development of treatment techniques that were derived from the theory, but flaws gradually emerged (see Chapter 5).

Among the reports that provided support for the theory was a study of 88 agoraphobic patients by Ost and Hugdahl (1983), who found that 81 per cent of the patients attributed the onset of their agoraphobia to a conditioning experience. On the other hand, Thorpe and Burns (1983) found that although 70 per cent of their agoraphobic respondents did report having experienced a precipitating event, only 38 per cent of the total described it in a way that was consistent with a conditioning explanation. Nonetheless, the accumulating data ultimately showed that most instances of agoraphobia are preceded by episodes of panic (Klein 1987, 1989), and these are plausibly regarded as aversive conditioning events.

As a result of the increasing reliance on cognitive explanations of abnormal behaviour, psychologists began to question whether people with agoraphobia are truly frightened of public places. It was argued instead that people are frightened of *what might happen to them in these places* rather than the places themselves – just as people who feel claustrophobic while going up in a lift are not frightened of the lift, but rather of what will happen to them in the lift (e.g. suffocation, panic).

Klein (1987) introduced the radically alternative idea that agoraphobia is merely a by-product of a more fundamental problem – panic disorder. He argued that people develop agoraphobic avoidance because they are fearful of experiencing episodes of panic, and it is for this reason that they are apprehensive about using public transport, going to public places, sitting in restricted sections of theatres, etc. It is now widely accepted that the most common sequence is episodes of panic followed by the development of agoraphobic avoidance. As a result, there has been a shift away from regarding public places and public transport as contributing to the core of the problem. Instead they are seen as the *context* in which the panic-related fears are made manifest. Given this change of view, attention shifted from the causes and consequences of agoraphobia to the causes and consequences of panic.

The emergence of agoraphobic behaviour after someone has undergone a frightening or painful experience in a public place or while travelling presented few problems for the formerly dominant conditioning theory; but the onset of agoraphobic avoidance after a loss or bereavement, in which there is no convincing evidence of a frightening experience in the place subsequently feared, could not be accounted for in conditioning terms. The fact that agoraphobic reactions can occur after a bereavement or other loss is also a problem for Klein's theory. In a national survey of 900 agoraphobic respondents, Thorpe and Burns (1983) found that 23 per cent of them stated that their agoraphobic avoidance emerged after the death of a relative or friend. Another 13 per cent reported the onset after they had experienced an illness. Survey respondents said that their most common fear was that of having a panic attack. Closely related are fears of fainting or collapsing (Hallam 1978; Thorpe and Burns 1983). In light of this information – namely that people with agoraphobia fear fainting/panics, collapsing, illness, death, etc. – it is understandable that they are most apprehensive about those situations in which they would need assistance if the feared events occurred. They are most apprehensive about situations in which they feel trapped, increasing distance from home or other safety, waiting in a queue, in the centre of a row in the theatre or cinema, travelling unaccompanied, etc.

In considering the onset of agoraphobia after a loss or bereavement, it is useful to view agoraphobic avoidance behaviour as a balance between danger and access to safety. The loss of a relative or friend may seriously undermine one's sense of safety. This is particularly likely among people who are generally anxious and who have developed dependent styles of behaving. Broadly speaking, any important event that threatens one's sense of safety or general sense of security is capable of tilting the balance between danger and safety.

Any changes that increase the person's sense of *safety*, whether occurring naturally or in therapy, will be followed by a decline in fear and avoidance (e.g. Carter *et al*. 1995). A sense of safety can be promoted by developing self-help safety procedures that include relaxation techniques, safe travel procedures, cognitive restructuring, and a range of other plans and activities that increase one's sense of efficacious independence – self-efficacy (Bandura 1977). The greatest benefits can be expected from a sense of safety that is based on the development of satisfactory coping skills, because this enables the person to ensure their own safety, expand their mobility, and reduce the dependency on other people which sometimes brings in its train unwanted problems.

On the contrary side, damage to one's sense of safety can be caused by the experience of failure, personal loss or distressingly aversive events. A single aversive experience appears to have the power to undermine for lasting periods the sense of safety that has developed over long periods. The second contributor to the decreased sense of safety is the loss of protection, especially in the form of a trusted companion. A diminished sense of safety can also occur when the protection loses some of its dependability. In the case of a companion, it only requires one or two instances of unreliability to undermine the sense of security. As far as other safety devices are concerned, people with agoraphobia understandably attach importance to the dependability not only of people, but also motor vehicles, telephones and other forms of safety or access to them. A sense of safety is nurtured by dependability and predictability (Rachman 1984).

Treatment

The traditional treatment of agoraphobia, dating back to the introduction of behaviour therapy, consisted of repeated, planned, controlled excursions into the patient's feared places – repeated therapeutic walks, initially accompanied, and then going solo.

> An impressive collection of outcome studies provide compelling evidence that having agoraphobics confront the situations they fear is sometimes sufficient, frequently necessary, and usually beneficial. Approximately 60–70% of patients treated with in vivo exposure experience moderate or greater reductions in symptoms.
>
> (Shapiro et al. 1993: 187)

See also Mattick *et al.* (1990) and van Balkom and Vorst (1997).

However, as the large majority of cases of agoraphobia develop as a result of repeated episodes of panic, the treatment of agoraphobic avoidance is now secondary to the treatment of panic. Tackling the panic disorder first and then 'mopping up' the agoraphobic avoidance is the preferred treatment (Hawton *et al.* 1989; D. A. Clark and Beck 2010; D. M. Clark and Fairburn 1997).

Summary

The main features of agoraphobia are a fear and avoidance of public places and public transport. It was originally regarded as a prime instance of a conditioned fear pattern and analyses of case material supported this view. The affected person experienced an unpleasant conditioning event in public which gave rise to a persisting conditioned fear. The motivating properties of fear then came into operation and led to the reinforcement of escape and avoidance behaviour – agoraphobia.

It is now agreed that in most cases, agoraphobia is caused by repeated episodes of panic, and that agoraphobia is a secondary problem. In some instances, however, agoraphobia develops after a loss, bereavement or illness.

Cognitive analyses led to the view that sufferers from agoraphobia are not actually frightened of public places as such, but rather are frightened of what might happen to them in these places. This re-analysis led to the introduction of the role of a search for safety or signals of safety. Agoraphobic avoidance is seen as a balance between a sense of danger and access to safety.

The original psychological treatment of this problem by planned, controlled excursions into the places the person fears to enter is moderately effective, but tackling the cause of the fear and/or the associated episodes of panic is the preferred treatment.

Obsessions and compulsions 9

Obsessive-compulsive disorders (OCD) are classed as anxiety disorders. The main features of OCD, obsessions and compulsions, are described in this chapter. Obsessive-compulsive disorder is one of the most complex forms of anxiety disorder and is distressing and even disabling. Psychological and biological theories have been advanced to account for OCD, but they are parallel explanations and neither is conclusive. The psychological explanations are more specific than the biological ones. Current methods of treatment are psychological, pharmacological, or both.

Obsessive-compulsive disorders (OCD) are distressing for the affected person and also for friends and relatives who rarely escape the adverse consequences of this problem. Most patients have a mixture of obsessions and compulsions, with one or other manifestation predominating. Obsessions and compulsions are strongly associated with anxiety, and even driven by anxiety. They are also closely associated with depression. If they are left untreated, these disorders can become chronic.

The compulsive behaviour that is characteristic of many people who suffer from obsessive-compulsive disorders is a pure example of abnormal behaviour. For these people, repeatedly carrying out essentially irrational actions, such as washing their hands over and over again for hours on end, can be a source of considerable distress and even disablement. Compulsions are repetitive stereotyped acts. People whose other behaviour is in most respects within rational borders recognize that their compulsive behaviour is senseless, but it is driven by strong irrational urges and exceedingly difficult to control. The compulsions generate frustration and distress. The classical examples of compulsive behaviour are repetitive, excessive, stereotyped *cleaning* and comparably stereotyped and repetitive *checking*, especially to ensure safety in the home and at work (e.g. repeatedly checking the safety of the stove, electrical appliances, doors or windows).

Obsessions are recurrent, intrusive, repetitive thoughts, images or impulses that are objectionable and give rise to subjective resistance. Common examples are thoughts of harming elderly people, carrying out a violent act, molesting children, blasphemous images. They conflict with the person's principles and morals and are repugnant, but characteristically difficult to block or remove. Affected people recognize that the intrusive thoughts are the production of their own minds and not inserted by external forces or people.

A devout young man was tormented by blasphemous thoughts and images whenever he attended church services. He experienced urges to shout obscenities during prayers, had aggressive sexual images of the Virgin Mary, and was prevented from praying by the intrusion of blasphemous Satanic phrases. The obsessions were interpreted as signs that he was a vile hypocrite and he became increasingly miserable and isolated.

TABLE 9.1

Distinctive features of obsessions and compulsions

Obsessions are intrusive thoughts that:
- are repugnant
- are unwanted
- have aggressive/sexual/blasphemous themes
- provoke internal resistance
- cause distress
- are recognized to be of internal origin
- are recognized to be senseless (insight)
- are ego-alien
- are associated with depression.

Compulsions are repetitive, stereotyped activities that:
- are preceded or accompanied by a sense of compulsion that is recognized to be of internal origin
- provoke internal resistance
- are recognized to be senseless or excessive
- may cause embarrassment or distress
- are difficult to control over the long term
- are purposeful and directed.

People with organic impairments may engage in repetitive acts that:
- lack intellectual content
- lack intentionality
- have a mechanical and/or primitive quality
- are associated with organic dysfunctions.

A 28-year-old accountant was so tormented by thoughts that he might attack his parents with a sharp knife that he avoided visiting them more than occasionally, and always kept out of their kitchen. He was fond of them and a loyal son, and was completely bewildered by his obsessions, but made excellent progress during a course of cognitive therapy.

An accomplished nurse repeatedly refused to work on a paediatric ward because she had recurrent images of touching young children in a sexually inappropriate manner. The images were so repugnant that she completely concealed the nature of her problem until she was referred for psychological treatment after medications had given her no relief during a period of depression. It is understandable that sufferers from repugnant, objectionable and embarrassing obsessions conceal the nature of their private struggle.

The necessary and sufficient conditions for describing repetitive behaviour as *compulsive* are a powerful urge to act, and attributing this pressure to internal sources, not to outside forces or people. Compulsive behaviour is purposeful and intentional, and is unlike mechanical repetitions such as tics or twitches. The person recognizes that the repetitions are excessive and irrational, and feels frustrated. The occurrence of resistance to the compulsive behaviour is a confirmatory feature, but is not necessary or sufficient. Although the compulsions are partly within the person's voluntary control (that is, they can be delayed, extended, postponed or reduced – or even carried out by other people), the urge to carry out the acts is powerful.

The necessary and sufficient features for defining a repetitive thought, impulse or image as *obsessional* are intrusiveness, internal attribution, unwantedness, objectionable and repugnant content, and uncontrollability. The confirmatory indicators are resistance and an alien quality.

Prevalence and course

Obsessive-compulsive disorder (OCD) is a distressing and disabling disorder, but not common. The early estimates were that less than 1 per cent of the population suffered from OCD, but modern findings show that the figure is higher. From surveys carried out in selected cities in the United States, it has been estimated that between 2 per cent and 3 per cent of the population have significant OCD at some point in their lives. These figures possibly err on the side of overestimation, but the data do show that OCD is more common than was originally believed (D. A. Clark and Beck 2010; Rachman and de Silva 2009).

Many people who experience minor OCD-like thoughts and behaviour, such as infrequent obsessions and/or inconvenient compulsive activities, tolerate the problem and are frustrated, but neither distressed nor disabled. Moreover, even among those whose problems are of clinical severity, a significant proportion never seeks professional help. In order to avoid embarrassment or criticism, they conceal their problems. There is no clear preponderance of either males or females who are affected with OCD, but there are some gender differences in the manifestations of OCD (there is a preponderance of females in the subgroup of compulsive cleaners).

The disorder usually emerges in adolescence or early adulthood; and in most cases, is evident before the age of 25. By the age of 30, nearly three-quarters of all cases will have come to be diagnosed. In some instances, a considerable period of time elapses before the affected person comes to a clinic, but this unnecessary delay is becoming less common as public education on the subject of OCD improves and the problem is more readily recognized than it was 30 or more years ago. In roughly half of all cases, the problems develop gradually. Among those with a sudden onset, there is an excess of compulsive cleaners over compulsive checkers.

There is a close and probably causal relationship between compulsive urges and compulsive acts, with the former producing the latter. Obsessions and compulsions are closely related. In a study of 150 obsessional patients, Wilner *et al.* (1976) found that 69 per cent of the patients complained of both obsessions and compulsions, 25 per cent had obsessions only, and 6 per cent had compulsions only. A similar estimate was reached by Akhtar *et al.* (1975) who reported that 25 per cent of their patients had obsessions that were not associated with overt acts.

Types of compulsive behaviour

A broad division can be drawn between the two main types of compulsive behaviour – compulsive washing/cleaning and compulsive checking. Numerous patients have elements of both these forms of compulsion, with one predominating.

Checking compulsions

These repetitive compulsions are intended to avoid harm coming to the affected person or people who are important to them, and almost invariably are oriented towards the future. They can be regarded as a form of preventive behaviour – actively avoiding the possibility of some adverse event. Cleaning compulsions share some of these properties, but have in addition a significant element of passive avoidance; that is, taking steps to avoid coming into contact with contaminating stimuli or situations that might provoke the urge to clean. When passive avoidance fails, the person feels compelled to escape.

Checking compulsions (more often than cleaning compulsions) are associated with doubting and indecisiveness, take a long time to complete, and are accompanied by feelings of frustration. Affected people tend to complain of a loss of memory, but it is generally a loss of confidence in their memory, and they can satisfactorily remember events and actions that are totally unrelated to their compulsive checking (Radomsky *et al.* 2001).

'A precise and liberating memory'

Compulsive checking of the security of the electrical appliances, stoves, doors and windows of her house became such a problem for a young clerk that she was spending up to two hours checking that all was secure before she was able to leave her home each morning. On numerous occasions, she became so uneasy about remembering whether or not she had checked everything before leaving that she was compelled to return home from work in order to carry out a re-check. She recognized that the chances of a mishap occurring were extremely low, but the anxiety was so intense that it could be dampened only by repeatedly checking each potential source of danger over and over again.

The difficulty which compulsive checkers experience in trying to convince themselves of safety is remarkable, and the sheer repetitiveness of their actions is puzzling, even to the affected person: 'I have to do it again and again to make sure.' They have such difficulty remembering if they have checked adequately that they fear losing their memory. However, this is a misinterpretation because they are suffering from a lack of confidence in memory, rather than a memory deficit. They repeatedly strive to achieve what Proust described as a 'precise and liberating memory' (Proust 1981: 55).

A patient was intensely anxious about the possibility that inadvertently she might have injured someone while driving her car. After a journey, even a shortish one, she would have a strong feeling that she had injured a pedestrian or cyclist, but could not remember the details. Any unusual events, such as thumps or bumps encountered during a drive spiked up her anxiety and forced her to retrace the entire journey, carefully searching for any signs of an accident or an injured person. On a few occasions, she dreaded that she might find a corpse.

Another patient felt compelled to ensure that everything was 'right' and therefore engaged in extensive checking. He repeated almost every action that he carried out. His most serious doubts were about the doors, windows and gas taps in his house, which he checked many times before leaving his home and before retiring to bed. He could relate some of his checking behaviour to particular threats, such as the possibility of his house being burgled; but for the rest, he had only a vague notion why it was necessary to carry out these repetitive checks – in order to avoid some unspecified and unspecifiable disaster. All of us are familiar with the feeling that some of our completed tasks seem 'just right', but others leave us with the feeling that they are not quite right. Numbers of people with OCD are tormented by an overwhelming need to ensure that whatever they do, however trivial, must be completely right, and they labour long and hard to achieve that release, repeating their actions over and over again. It can lead to immobilizing procrastination and avoidance, typified by perfectionist students who are seldom satisfied with their work and turn in assignments late or not at all.

Compulsive washing/cleaning

The most common cause of compulsive washing is a fear of contamination (Rachman 2004, 2006). Feelings of contamination drive strong urges to remove the source of the pollution, and the easiest and most common method is washing and/or cleaning. Washing is a universal method for removing dirt and because hands are the main point of contact with the external world, most people engage in handwashing every day. When people feel contaminated they naturally resort to washing, especially handwashing.

A 36-year-old salesman developed an intense fear of disease contamination, especially AIDS, and began washing his hands, his body and his clothing over and over again each day. At its worst, he was having eight showers a day, none of them entirely reassuring because of his pervasive fear of contracting the disease through any contact with 'unclean' people, objects or places. He vigorously avoided any people or places that he felt were potential sources of contamination. Whenever he went out in public, he was frightened of possible contacts with sources of contamination and was especially frightened by the prospect of encountering used condoms. As a result, he carefully scanned the environment for any evidence of signs of danger. So, for example, when walking in a public park, he constantly scanned the area for signs of condoms, often mistaking even the slightest trace of white, such as a discarded tissue, for a used condom. His general level of anxiety was high and his fear of contamination was at a peak. Even though he recognized that the chances of contracting AIDS or other serious diseases by casual contacts in his everyday life were exceedingly remote, and that in any event, repeatedly washing himself would provide no protection, he had an overwhelming urge repeatedly to clean himself. Despite the exaggerated and admittedly senseless quality of his actions, the driving force of the anxiety dominated his behaviour.

Washing/cleaning compulsions are the second most common form of OCD compulsion, exceeded only by compulsive checking. In a sample of 560 people with OCD, Rasmussen and Eisen (1992) found that 50 per cent had fears of contamination. Contaminants fall into four broad classes: possibly diseased items (such as blood, hospital swabs), dirt/pollution, harmful substances, and mental contaminants. Contamination can threaten harm to one's physical health, mental health and social life, and the compulsive washing is intended to reduce or remove a significant threat. Compulsive cleaning is so abnormal – excessive, irrational and even bizarre – that it overrides other behaviour and has become almost definitional of OCD.

Prior to 1994, it was assumed that all washing/cleaning compulsions are provoked by physical contact with a contaminant, such as germs, blood, putrefying food (the word *contamination* comes from the Latin verb *tangere*, to touch, and implies physical contact). Remarkably, however, a fear of contamination can be provoked without any physical contact with a discernible contaminant such as dirt, disease, putrefying food or bodily products (Rachman 2004, 2006).

A feeling of internal dirtiness and/or pollution can develop after enduring an emotional or physical violation. Examples include humiliation, degradation, abuse, betrayals, sexual violations. The feelings of internal dirtiness, *mental contamination/pollution*, are imperfectly connected to observable, identifiable sources of pollution. Even touching items that look clean can evoke feelings of dirtiness. The feelings are easily re-evoked by a memory, image or thought (Rachman 2004, 2006). The source of the mental contamination is always human.

Mental contamination can also develop from one's own actions, thoughts, images or memories. *Self-contamination* can arise from blasphemous thoughts, intrusive repugnant images such as incestuous images, preoccupation with pornography, or other unacceptable ideas and actions. Feelings of mental contamination often have a moral element, and recall the notion of 'mental pollution' introduced by John Bunyan to describe his horrifying blasphemous obsessions. He was tormented by 'tumultuous thoughts' . . . 'masterless hellhounds [that] roar and bellow and make a hideous noise within me' and cause a 'pollution *of the mind*' (Bunyan [1678] 1947: 136).

Feelings of mental contamination do not respond to ordinary cleaning. The site of the contamination is diffuse and inaccessible. The source of the contamination is always human, and not infrequently the contaminated person is unable or unwilling even to mention the name of the contaminator (see Table 9.2 and Figure 9.1, pp. 136–7).

A 43-year-old man suffering from mental contamination for over 20 years was severely dysfunctional and housebound. He felt so contaminated that he washed his hands about 80 times a day. They were so excoriated that every fortnight his dermatologist covered the patient's hands in a thick medicinal cream. Before retiring at night, the patient had to apply a similar cream and he slept with a pair of thick gloves on in order to contain the cream and to avoid further contamination during the night. He was frightened of being contaminated by any contact with government agencies, and official letters – and then all letters – became such a threat that he had to don protective clothing and gloves before touching them. He was housebound because he was frightened of contact with any building, item or person associated with the government.

The fear of contamination started when he was 23 and his marriage broke up, against his will. His wife told him that she had decided to divorce him and he received a court order the following day. Within 24 hours, he lost his wife, his house and his very young son (excepting brief weekly visits). Despite his distress, on his own initiative he arranged with a lawyer for monthly child-support payments to be sent to his wife, but soon started receiving demanding letters from the government support agency, alleging that he was delinquent. He made five visits to the agency and was seen by a different clerk each time, but could not persuade any of them to listen to his account or read the legal documents. He was repeatedly degraded: 'I was treated with contempt.'

He felt so polluted by letters, places and people associated with government that he began washing intensively. As his need to avoid people and places associated with government grew, it became difficult to leave his house, and of course he lost his job. He also learned that his wife had been betraying him during the marriage.

Over the 20 years of his disorder he received a great deal of treatment, including two stays in the specialized OCD ward of a psychiatric hospital. He received a variety of medications and several courses of psychotherapy. The patient derived some benefits, but they seldom lasted.

Ultimately it emerged that he was suffering from mental contamination, caused by the betrayal (see Rachman 2010) and subsequent losses, humiliation and degradation. During cognitive therapy, he learned that forming images of selected scenes in which he had been humiliated and degraded in government offices immediately produced strong feelings of contamination – all over his body. It became evident that his widespread feelings of contamination were easily, frequently and lastingly evoked by intrusive images, memories and thoughts of his violation. Like many patients with this form of contamination, he attributed the exceedingly unpleasant feelings of pollution and internal dirtiness to external cues – official letters and contact with people and places associated with government.

After nine sessions of cognitive therapy that focused on his betrayals and degradation, he was substantially improved – minimal fear of contamination, nil compulsive washing, and freely able to go out and use his home and surroundings. In the following month, he received three booster sessions, and at the one-year follow-up, his substantial treatment gains were stable.

Mental contamination shares some of the features of physical contact contamination, but is distinctive in several ways (Table 9.2). The concept of mental contamination expands the span and significance of fears of contamination and can facilitate the treatment of formerly untreatable cases. It should also reduce the number of incompletely treated patients.

Persistence

One of the most puzzling aspects of obsessive-compulsive behaviour is its persistence. There is no obvious reason for people to engage in this repetitive, tiring, embarrassing and unwanted self-defeating behaviour. Even more puzzling is the persistent recurrence of intrusive, unacceptable and distressing thoughts.

TABLE 9.2

Features of contact contamination and mental contamination

Contact contamination	Mental contamination
Feelings of discomfort/dread	Feelings of discomfort, uneasiness, dread
Provoked by contact with dirt/disease	Physical contact not necessary
Not applicable	Can be generated internally
Feelings evoked instantly with contact	Occasionally, see above
Focused mainly on skin, especially the hands	No typical focus
Generated by contact with external stimuli	Can be generated internally (e.g. urges, images)
Not generated by ill-treatment	Can be generated by perceived ill-treatment
Contaminants are dirty/harmful substances	Primary source is a person, not a substance
Feeling dirty/infected	Internal dirtiness/pollution predominantly
Spreads widely	Some generalization, but
Easily transmissible to others	Rarely transmissible to others
Others considered vulnerable	Uniquely vulnerable
Source known to affected person	Source of contamination obscure to affected person
Site identifiable	Site inaccessible
Tangible contaminant	Intangible contaminant
Contamination re-evocable by contact with dirty/diseased source	Contamination re-evocable by contact with human source
Contamination evocable by secondary 'carriers'	Contamination evocable by secondary sources, 'carriers'
Common in childhood OCD	Rarely occurs in childhood
Pollution rarely re-evoked by mental events	Pollution re-evocable by relevant mental events
Anxiety evocable by relevant mental events	Anxiety evocable by relevant mental events
Lacks a moral element	Moral element common
Revulsion, disgust, nausea, fear	Anxiety, revulsion, anger, shame, guilt, disgust common

TABLE 9.2 *continued*

Contact contamination	Mental contamination
Not applicable	Level/range of contamination fluctuates in response to changes in attitude to contaminator
Generates urges to wash	Generates urges to wash
Generates urges to avoid	Generates urges to avoid
Transiently responsive to cleaning	Cleaning is ineffective
Treatment moderately effective	Treatment under development

Mental Contamination   Contact Contamination

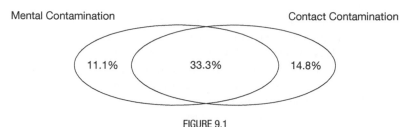

FIGURE 9.1

Co-occurrence of mental contamination and contact contamination

Adapted from Coughtrey *et al.* (2012)

The most favoured answer is that compulsive behaviour persists because it reduces anxiety. As described in Chapter 2, Mowrer's (1939, 1960) two-stage theory of fear and avoidance, stating that successful avoidance behaviour paradoxically preserves fear, was incorporated into explanations of obsessive-compulsive behaviour. The reports given by people who have OCD can be accommodated in Mowrer's view and the theory served well for a period. The inadequacies of the theory gradually became apparent, and although it cannot provide a comprehensive account of obsessive-compulsive behaviour, some of the predictions that followed from the theory were supported.

The prediction that compulsive activities are followed by a reduction in anxiety was tested in a series of connected experiments using a simple procedure (see Rachman and Hodgson 1980). Consistent with Mowrer's theory, when patients with OCD are asked to touch one of their provocative contaminants (e.g. touching dirt), they report a steep increase in anxiety and an accompanying urge to carry out the relevant compulsive act, usually washing. The patients were asked to carry out an action that would give rise to an increase in anxiety, such as touching a dirty carpet, and told that they were free to reduce the ensuing anxiety by washing or any other behaviour of their choice. In the large majority of cases, the completion of the (compulsive) activity, invariably washing, was followed by a reduction in anxiety and in the strength of the accompanying urge. When the compulsive act was carried out, the anxiety promptly declined, as would be predicted by Mowrer's theory.

In other experimental tests, when patients were asked to delay carrying out the compulsive activity, their anxiety level persisted for a while and gradually declined to near zero within three hours. Anxiety can decline spontaneously, albeit slowly, even when no compulsive acts are carried out. This phenomenon is not entirely consistent with the theory.

The slow spontaneous decay of anxiety and urges is a contrast to the rapid reductions achieved by carrying out the relevant compulsive behaviour. It is therefore understandable why compulsive behaviour develops – it produces relief far more quickly. There is, however, a penalty because the efficiency of the compulsive actions generates persisting irrational and burdensome behaviour.

There were very few exceptions to these findings among patients with cleaning compulsions, but a number of exceptions were observed in cases of compulsive *checking*. The completion of the compulsive checking either left the anxiety unchanged or, in exceptional circumstances, was followed by a slight increment in anxiety (Beech 1971, 1974). Notably, the amount of anxiety that could be provoked under these experimental conditions was larger (and easier) among patients with cleaning compulsions than among those who engaged predominantly in checking compulsions. A probable explanation for the exceptions observed in experiments on checking compulsions is that the participants did not feel fully responsible for carrying out the provocative task, and as discussed below, there is a strong relationship between feelings of responsibility and checking behaviour.

It has been postulated that compulsive checking occurs when people who believe that they have a special responsibility for preventing harm to others and to themselves are unsure that the perceived threat has been removed or adequately reduced (Salkovskis 1985; Rachman 2003). In their attempts to achieve certainty that all is safe, they check repeatedly. Unfortunately, checking increases the urge to check again (Radomsky *et al.* 2006). Intensively checking to ensure safety can produce paradoxical effects that fuel a self-perpetuating mechanism.

The first element of this mechanism arises from the person's inability to achieve complete assured safety because the checking rarely reaches a natural terminus. Often it is difficult to achieve certainty that future threats have been totally eliminated. The second element of the self-perpetuating mechanism is a deficit of memory, actually a deficit in confidence about one's memory. With repeated checking, confidence in one's memory declines (Radomsky and Rachman 1999; Radomsky et al. 2001; Radomsky et al. 2006; Radomsky et al. 2010; van den Hout and Kindt 2003). Loss of confidence in memory in turn promotes repeated checking (Radomsky et al. 2001). The third element is a cognitive bias in which affected people feel that the probability of a misfortune occurring is increased when they are responsible for some task, such as securing the house. The fourth element is another bias in which the person's sense of responsibility *increases* after they have checked for safety.

The mechanism can trap people. The presence of four connected elements impedes treatment because even if one element is 'repaired', say if the person's confidence in his/her memory is boosted, the remaining elements are likely to persist.

There is, however, an underlying cause of compulsive checking and if that is dealt with, sound progress can be made (Rachman 2002; Radomsky et al. 2010). Salkovskis (1985, 1988) identified the presence of a highly inflated sense of responsibility in many patients with OCD, an inflation that is particularly important in compulsive checking. It has even been suggested that inflated responsibility is a crucial factor and that compulsive checking does not develop in the absence of inflated responsibility (Rachman 2002).

Intrusive thoughts

Intrusive, unwanted, objectionable, obsessional thoughts or images that give rise to subjective resistance are puzzling and fascinating. Why do people experience them? What is the origin of these unacceptable thoughts, why do they recur so frequently (up to 50 times per day)? What function, if any, do they play, and why are they so difficult to control?

Recurrent blasphemous intrusions, obscene images or impulses in church, aggressive thoughts about harming children or elderly or infirm people, images or impulses about unacceptable sexual acts, such as molesting children, are *repugnant and useless*. To make matters worse, there is a tendency for people who are afflicted by these unwanted intrusions to believe that by having the thoughts or images, they actually increase the likelihood of the objectionable event occurring. An example of this phenomenon, called *thought-action-fusion*, was given by a student who was tormented by repetitive thoughts that his family might be harmed in a serious motor accident (Shafran and Rachman 2004). He felt that every time he had this thought and the accompanying horrific image, he increased the probability that his family would be harmed in an accident. Naturally this raised his sense of responsibility and ensuing guilt, as well as inflating his anxiety.

People who experience obsessions often engage in behaviour that is comparable to escape and avoidance behaviour; this includes the obvious forms of avoidance, but also some less obvious mental neutralizing types of behaviour ('undoing' the thought) and repeated requests for reassurance. These people are not actually seeking information (they know the answers), but are attempting to cope with their anxiety. The reassuring effects of reassurance in OCD, and other disorders such as health anxiety, are transient. The reassurance fades, but the problem does not.

Many of the tactics that people use in their attempts to cope with recurrent obsessions are equivalent to overt compulsions. The majority of naturally occurring obsessions are generated internally, but they can be provoked by external stimulation, such as the sight of a sharp object which is then incorporated into an unacceptable aggressive obsession. For example, a fond mother was tortured by thoughts that she might stab her young children, and was terrified of being left alone with them in the kitchen, near knives or other sharp objects.

Horowitz (1975) demonstrated that after being exposed to stressful events, people tend to experience intrusive and repetitive thoughts. Consistent evidence was collected by Parkinson and Rachman (1980) who studied the experiences of a group of mothers whose children were being admitted to hospital for elective surgery. The mothers experienced a steep increase in unwanted thoughts and images, accompanied by distressingly high levels of anxiety. Reassuringly, the distressing thoughts and anxiety decreased rapidly when the parents were informed that their children were safe again.

Progress in addressing these questions was made when it was demonstrated that most people experience unwanted intrusive thoughts or images which bear a qualitative similarity to obsessions, even though there are considerable differences in frequency and intensity. Intrusive thoughts, images and impulses are common experiences (Rachman and de Silva 2009; Salkovskis 1985). The large majority of non-clinical respondents report experiencing unwanted intrusive thoughts of the type which bear a strong similarity to obsessions. The form and the content of obsessions reported by non-clinical respondents and by obsessional patients are similar, but those experienced by patients with OCD are more frequent, more intense, more vivid and longer lasting. They provoke significantly higher levels of anxiety, and are difficult to resist and difficult to dismiss. It is precisely the anxiety-provoking and distressing obsessions that are most difficult to control. The 'normal obsessional thoughts' reported by the non-clinical respondents are dismissed, blocked or diverted with little difficulty.

It is probable that the distressing effects of obsessional thoughts and their consequent *adhesiveness* are connected, and there is a limited amount of evidence of a correlation between disturbed mood and the difficulty in dismissing an intrusive and unwanted thought (Sutherland *et al.* 1982). The frequency of obsessions is significantly increased by increments in anxiety, even if the anxiety is not directly related to the content of the obsession. In a productive cognitive re-analysis of this and related questions, Salkovskis (1985) and Salkovskis *et al.* (1998) postulated that the distress and adhesiveness of obsessions arise from the person's over-interpretation or total misinterpretation of the significance of the relevant thoughts. Insofar as they interpret their objectionable unwanted thoughts as being of great significance (for example, if they interpret the thoughts as revealing some utterly repugnant but important aspect of their true personality), they experience adverse emotions.

The emotional disturbances in turn interfere with the person's ability to deal with the thoughts satisfactorily. Instead, they are inclined to engage in ultimately futile behaviour, such as repeatedly saying neutralizing phrases, counting numbers, etc. In most instances, these attempts are functionally equivalent to compulsive behaviour. At best, the neutralizing activities provide a temporary relief; but in the long run, they serve to confirm the significance of the intrusive thoughts. Hence they contribute to the persistence of the problem.

These are some example of obsessions described by patients with OCD (de Silva and Rachman 1992; Rachman and de Silva 2009):

- the thought of causing harm to children or elderly people;
- blasphemous thoughts during prayers;
- the thought of 'unnatural' sexual acts;
- the impulse to violently attack and kill a dog;
- the impulse to disrupt the peace at a gathering (for example, shout or throw things);
- thoughts of molesting a child.

The cognitive theory of obsessions

The cognitive theory proposes that obsessions are caused by a catastrophic misinterpretation of the personal significance of one's intrusive thoughts (Rachman 1997, 2003). Everyone has streams of thoughts each day and a proportion of these are unwanted, uninvited and intrusive. Among these uninvited thoughts are some which are objectionable, repugnant, even horrifying. If the person interprets these unacceptable thoughts as being of important personal significance, of being revealing, it can cause distress. The thoughts reveal that 'I am mad, bad, dangerous.'

Attempts to suppress the thoughts often produce a paradoxical increase in their frequency. Virtually everyone experiences unwanted intrusive thoughts and deals with them by dismissing them as insignificant, mere noise. It should be noted that it is exceedingly rare for patients suffering from obsessions to act on their repugnant intrusive images or thoughts. Informal surveys of clinicians with experience of treating patients with OCD have failed to come up with any such cases.

Obsessions are best dealt with by altering the significance attached to the uninvited thoughts and the results of clinical trials of cognitive therapy are positive, but limited in number (Freeston *et al.* 1997; Whittal *et al.* 2010).

Compulsive hoarding

Excessive hoarding resembles a compulsion, but has some distinctive features (Frost and Hartl 2003; Rachman *et al.* 2009; Wheaton *et al.* 2011). In many instances it is associated with OCD, but also occurs among people with mental illnesses and in dementia.

Excessive hoarding has five prominent features:

1 excessive acquisition of large numbers of unnecessary and often worthless objects or items;
2 apparently irrational, emotional attachments to the objects;
3 vigilant protection of the collection;
4 cluttered living conditions; and
5 emotional and behavioural resistance to discarding the objects/ items.

The hoarding is excessive if it seriously interferes with normal daily activities, creates hazards, and provokes complaints from other people or agencies. The social pressure to put an end to the hoarding can be distressing.

People engaging in this behaviour concede that it is perhaps excessive, but regard it as worthwhile and justifiable. In principle, they are not averse to receiving help in managing the excesses, but are unwilling to forgo their collections. Consequently they do not see the need for psychiatric medication. They are open to advice and support, but rarely seek psychological treatment.

A major cause of the confusion about the nature of hoarding arises from the fact that most of our current knowledge about excessive hoarding is based on a skewed sample, indeed on less than one fifteenth of the total population of hoarders. A large number of people who engage in excessive hoarding have no associated psychological problems. Over 5 per cent of the population engage in excessive hoarding (Tolin *et al.* 2008), but most of the research and hence current knowledge about hoarding has been carried out on samples of people with OCD. Hoarding is five times as common as OCD but only about one third of OCD patients, or fewer, have hoarding symptoms (Kessler *et al.* 2005; Samuels *et al.* 2008; Tolin *et al.* 2008). As most of the published research on hoarding is based on OCD samples, it means that current knowledge is based on roughly one fifteenth of the total sample of hoarders.

A significant number of patients with OCD exhibit symptoms of hoarding. The estimates range from 11 per cent (see Steketee and Frost 2003: 908) to 33 per cent, but hoarding is not specific to OCD and occurs in association with other disorders (Abramowitz *et al.* 2008; Wheaton *et al.* 2011). As mentioned, large numbers of hoarders have no associated disorders.

Is excessive hoarding a compulsion?

As described above, the term *compulsion* refers to repetitive, purposeful behaviour that the person feels compelled to carry out. If it is distressing and/or disabling, it is clinically significant. Clinical compulsions are emotionally negative, and typically, frustrating and upsetting. They are preceded by strong urges to carry out the behaviour, and commonly take on ritualistic qualities – precisely repeated, unchanging actions that resemble religious rituals in form but not content. The person has insight into the problem; that is, he or she recognizes that the compulsive behaviour (usually repetitive checking or washing) is basically irrational, and tries to resist it, at least in the early stages. The similarities between excessive hoarding and compulsive behavior are feeling compelled to carry out the actions, strong urges that are hard to resist, and repetitiveness.

However, people who engage in hoarding do not have 'insight', do not regard their hoarding as irrational, and they justify their actions. The acquisition and storing of new items is emotionally positive or neutral. The acquisition and protection of their collections are not distressing, but the unmanageable clutter can be frustrating. The distress that hoarders experience is secondary, mainly in the form of negative social pressure.

Their great difficulty in discarding unnecessary or worthless items is a major obstacle to adaptive changes. Attempts to encourage the person to dispose of the items are tenaciously resisted. This component has no resemblance to compulsions. As set out below, there are some similarities between the acquisition component of hoarding and compulsive actions (Table 9.3). Both are driven by strong urges that are difficult to resist, and both involve repetitive actions. However, the repetitive actions that typify OCD – compulsive checking and/or

TABLE 9.3

Separating excessive hoarding from OCD

Demographic distribution	Hoarding is approximately 15 times as common as OCD. Most current information on hoarding is based on research with OCD patients.
Hoarding unchanging; extremely stable	OCD often varies over time, usually arises in late childhood or early adulthood.
Insight/complaints	Excessive hoarders rarely complain about their 'problem'; rarely seek treatment and have limited 'insight'.
Age at which people seek treatment	Many people with OCD seek treatment, usually in early adulthood.
Purpose	The purpose of OCD compulsions is to reduce threat and/or anxiety; multiple reasons for excessive hoarding including taking advantage of opportunities to add to one's collection.
Emotions	OCD compulsions are emotionally negative. Excessive hoarding is emotionally positive or neutral.
Cognitive analyses	Cognitive analyses of OCD centre on appraisals of intrusive thoughts. No similar conceptualization for excessive hoarding.
Attachment/ sentimentality	People with excessive hoarding often have over-general and over-developed ideas regarding attachment to their possessions.
Treatment response	Excessive hoarding is unresponsive to traditional CBT or medication for obsessive-compulsive disorder.

washing – are repetitions of essentially identical actions day after day, and they become stereotyped. Hoarding involves repeatedly acquiring new objects and is generic, not a repetition of specific actions. It is not a pattern of stereotyped daily behaviour.

Hoarding 'obsessions'?

The use of the term 'obsessional' to describe hoarding is misleading. As described above, obsessions are recurrent, intrusive, unwanted and often repugnant thoughts or images or impulses. They cause considerable distress and are resisted. The term 'preoccupied' is a more accurate description of the hoarder's intense and pervasive interest in adding to their collections and protecting them. The preoccupying thoughts are not intrusive, nor unwanted and certainly not repugnant.

The differences between excessive hoarding and OCD are summarized in Table 9.3 above (Rachman *et al.* 2009).

Some theoretical considerations

The nature of the link between OCD hoarding and anxiety is not clear, but it has been suggested that the hoarded items and the site of the hoarding might provide a sense of safety. 'Possessions come to be associated with feelings of safety and disposing of them feels like a violation of that safety. The safety signal value of their posssessions adds to the emotional turmoil associated with the disposal.' (Frost and Hartl 2003: 174). Presumably the removal of the safety signals arouses anxiety.

The similarities between 'compulsive' hoarding and OCD are outweighed by the differences between them, and the matter can be clarified by separating hoarding from OCD (Rachman *et al.* 2009). Separating the two will promote fresh construals of excessive hoarding and encourage studies of the full range of excessive hoarders and hoarding. The unanswered questions include the hoarders' tenacious resistance to discarding hoarded items, and why attempts to dispose of apparently unimportant trivial items can provoke intense emotional reactions.

The relationship between anxiety and OCD

There is a connection between most forms of obsessive-compulsive problems and fear/anxiety. The relationship between cleaning compulsions and anxiety is particularly close, but the connection between obsessional slowness (Rachman 1974) and anxiety is slender. The psycho-physiological responses to presentations of phobic stimuli and to obsessional stimuli are similar. In both instances, the stimuli produce an increase in autonomic responsiveness and this responsiveness tends to diminish after successful treatment. The subjective responses to obsessional and anxiety-provoking material involve a similar increment in subjective distress. These subjective responses, like the physiological reactions, tend to diminish after successful treatment. Obsessive-compulsive reactions and anxiety reactions frequently are associated with extensive avoidance behaviour, and this too is diminished after successful treatment. Obsessional patients give retrospective reports of having experienced excessive anxiety during childhood and there is an elevated incidence of anxiety neuroses among the relatives of obsessional patients (Rachman 1985).

Treatment

Given the association between obsessive-compulsive phenomena and anxiety, psychological techniques that successfully reduce anxiety should be effective in dealing with obsessive-compulsive problems, and this is the case (e.g. Barlow 2002; D. A. Clark 2003; D. A. Clark and Beck 2010; Freeston et al. 1997; I. Marks 1987; M. Marks 2003; Rachman and de Silva 2009; Radomsky et al. 2010; Stanley and Turner 1995; van Balkom et al. 1994; Whittal et al. 2010). For certain types of problems, notably those caused by a fear of contamination based on physical contact and characterized by observable compulsive behaviour, the prevailing technique of exposure and response prevention (ERP) is dependably effective. The treatment consists of planned, controlled exposures to the situation/stimuli that evoke the fear or discomfort (e.g. repeated, controlled contacts with perceived sources of contamination) followed by response prevention; that is, the inhibition of any consequent or associated compulsive behaviour, such as handwashing. The exercises are planned by the patient and therapist and carried out repeatedly and systematically (Barlow 2002; D. A. Clark and Beck 2010; Marks 1987), but in some cases the problem returns. Fears of mental contamination are more complex and appear to respond best to cognitive therapy, but full control trials need to be completed.

The application of cognitive analyses has generated a fresh form of treatment for obsessions. Following the success of cognitive models to account for panic disorders (D. M. Clark 1986) and OCD (Salkovskis

1985), it was proposed that obsessions are caused by catastrophic misinterpretations of the personal significance of unwanted, intrusive, repugnant images, thoughts or impulses (Rachman 1997, 2003). The objectionable intrusions are believed to be revealing: 'I am a bad, dangerous, mad person.' The therapy is designed to help patients make realistic, benign interpretations of the significance of their intrusions; and to this end, the provision of corrective information about OCD is followed by cognitive analyses of their disorder, the collection of 'survey data' and the completion of behavioural experiments (Rachman 2003). The results are positive, but trials are still limited in number (Freeston *et al.* 1997; Whittal *et al.* 2010).

Detailed accounts of the nature and psychological treatment of obsessive-compulsive disorders are provided by Barlow (2002), D. A. Clark and Beck (2010), Rachman (2003) and Swinson *et al.* (1998).

Fortunately, the gap between research and the dissemination of findings into clinical practice (and hence the extremely limited provision of treatment facilities) is now being corrected by the national scheme to improve access to psychological therapies in England (IAPT).

Psychologists and healthcare providers in other countries are actively interested in the scheme. At present (2013), a majority of patients with OCD receive medication, which can be beneficial (Insel 1991; Insel and Winslow 1992; Stanley and Turner 1995; Swinson *et al.* 1998; Zohar *et al.* 1991), but side-effects are common and there is a risk of relapse in coming off the medication (Otto, Pollack *et al.* 1996). In clinical practice, a combination of medication and psychological therapy is frequently recommended, and in particular cases is the preferred course, but as mentioned in Chapter 7 ('Critique'), the uncomfortable fact is that the research data rarely show that a combination of the two treatments is additive (e.g. Insel 1991; Rachman *et al.* 1979).

Depression is evident in most cases of OCD and patients may require pharmacological treatment prior to or during psychological treatment, or instead of such treatment.

Summary

The major manifestations of OCD are the presence of compulsive behaviour, or obsessions, or a combination of both, but with one of the two symptoms predominating. Compulsions are repetitive, stereotyped acts that the person feels driven to carry out, even though they are recognized to be irrational, or at least excessive. The two most common forms are compulsive cleaning and compulsive checking. These are intentional, purposeful, directed acts that are carried out in order to reduce anxiety or discomfort, or to reduce the likelihood of some anticipated distress/event. Obsessions are repetitive, intrusive, unwanted thoughts and images that the person finds repugnant and attempts to resist. The main themes of these unacceptable thoughts are sexual, aggressive or blasphemous.

In addition to the association with feelings of anxiety, a large majority of people have current or past episodes of depression. Increasingly specific theories are being advanced to account for compulsive checking, compulsive washing, and for obsessions. The two competing explanations for OCD are psychological and biological, and each theory has an associated form of treatment – medication or cognitive behaviour therapy. Each type of treatment is at least moderately effective.

Health anxiety disorders 10

The features of severe health anxiety – intense and persistent anxiety about one's present and future health – are described. In common with other anxiety disorders such as post-traumatic stress disorders, generalized anxiety disorder, obsessive-compulsive disorders, the core of health anxiety disorders (HAD) is distressing, uncontrollable anxiety. The cognitive construal of HAD proposes that health anxiety is caused by catastrophic misinterpretations of the significance of sensations and/or changes in bodily functions and appearance (such as swellings, pain, loss of energy, dizzy spells, memory loss). The nature, causes, triggers, persistence, assessment and treatment of HAD are reviewed, and the present status of the cognitive model is appraised.

The analysis of *health anxiety* introduced by Salkovskis and Warwick (1986) provided a foundation for the concept of health anxiety disorders. The common element that links the various anxiety disorders is the presence of excessive anxiety. In health anxiety, the excessive anxiety is focused on one's present and future health.

Salkovskis and Warwick 1986, 2001) proposed that health anxiety is caused by catastrophic misinterpretations of sensations and symptoms. The application of a cognitive approach to construing health anxiety was a crucial step. In common with all of the anxiety disorders, health anxiety is construed as occurring along a continuum from minimal to clinically significant excessive anxiety: 'Anxiety focused upon health is an almost universal phenomenon . . . and persistent anxiety about health is common both in the community and in the clinic' (Salkovskis and Warwick 2001: 46).

The cognitive theory

> The cognitive theory states that in severe health anxiety . . .
> bodily signs, symptoms, variations, and medical infor-
> mation tend to be perceived as more dangerous than they
> really are, and that a particular illness is believed to be more
> probable than it really is.
>
> (Salkovskis 1996a: 65)

The tendency to overestimate the probability of becoming ill and
the seriousness of the dreaded illness is persistent. The anxiety is
provoked by perceived changes in bodily appearance or functioning,
exposure to negative information about health that is personally
significant and/or by experiences that are catastrophically misinterpreted (e.g. disturbing intrusive images).

Health anxiety is not suspended when a person is actually ill, and
the overestimations of the probability and seriousness of threats to
one's health continue to operate (Salkovskis and Warwick 2001). The
sensitivity to changes in bodily functions and appearance is heightened
during an illness.

The concept of health anxiety emerged from the success of the
cognitive model of panic formulated by D. M. Clark (1986) and
Salkovskis's (1985) cognitive model of obsessive-compulsive disorders. The essence of Clark's model is that episodes of panic are
caused by a catastrophic misinterpretation of certain bodily sensations,
such as a pounding heart: 'My pounding heart means that I am about
to have a heart attack.' The danger is *imminent*.

The panic model did not incorporate the catastrophic misinterpretations of sensations or signs that threaten a *future* danger to one's
health, such as developing cancer. This important difference was a spur
to the formulation of the health anxiety concept. Salkovskis's (1985)
cognitive analysis of OCD led him to connect important features of
that anxiety disorder with inflated fears of threats to one's health. The
cognitive model of health anxiety absorbed some aspects of hypochondriasis, and then expanded the definition, scope, classification,
nature and treatment of severe health anxiety. Health anxiety disorder
is a positive 'diagnosis', or rather a positive classification, of a psychological problem within the existing group of anxiety disorders.

Hypochondriasis and anxiety

Severe health anxiety, the extreme end of a continuum of health anxiety, is often termed hypochondriasis. At times, the two terms – hypochondriasis and severe health anxiety – are used interchangeably, but a distinction is helpful.

'Hypochondria' is an anatomical term. It describes 'those parts of the human abdomen ... which lie immediately under the ribs ... [where] the viscera [are] situated ... the liver, gall-bladder, spleen etc.' (OED 1971: 507). They were believed to be the source of melancholy fumes – 'low spirits for which there is no real cause' (OED 1971: 507). Over time, the meaning of hypochondria expanded into 'a disorder of the nervous system ... chiefly characterized by the patient's unfounded belief that he is suffering from some serious bodily disease' (OED 1971: 597). Hypochondria is classified as a mental disorder (DSM-IV 2005; see Asmundson *et al.* [2001] for the various iterations of 'hypochondria' in the DSM).

The diagnosis of hypochondriasis is categorical: a distorted, strongly held belief that one is suffering from a serious disease, despite all the medical and other evidence against the belief; it is a disease conviction. Hypochondriacal beliefs are resistant to disconfirmation. Unlike health anxiety, in which future dangers are anticipated, in hypochondriasis the danger is present and active, and the belief is fixed. The diagnosis of hypochondriasis has been critically analysed (e.g. Abramowitz and Moore 2007; Asmundson *et al.* 2001; Brown 1996; Creed and Barsky 2004; Deacon and Abramowitz 2008; Fergus and Valentiner 2009, 2010; Olatunji *et al.* 2009; Schmidt 2004; Warwick and Salkovskis 1990; Wells and Hackmann 1993; Wise and Birket-Smith 2002).

Health anxiety: a cognitive construal

The cognitive construal of health anxiety has promoted a substantial increase in knowledge about fears pertaining to one's current state of health and future health (Asmundson *et al.* 2001; Marcus *et al.* 2007; Salkovskis and Warwick 2001; Warwick and Salkovskis 1990). Attention has been paid to the cognitions involved in anxiety about one's health. The inflation of vigilance and the triggers for heightened anxiety have been incorporated in the model. The concept of health anxiety opened a path to the inclusion of fears of *mental* illness as well as physical illness.

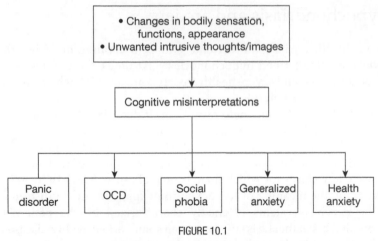

FIGURE 10.1

The anxiety disorders, including health anxiety

Arising out of the cognitive model of OCD, the powerful effects of intrusive images in health anxiety are now under investigation (see below). Health anxiety is dimensional and a range of promising psychometric and other methods of assessment are available or in the process of development. Given the reconsideration of the nature of safety behaviour (Rachman *et al.* 2008; Rachman 2010; Rachman *et al.* 2011; van den Hout *et al.* 2011), the compulsive search for reassurance in patients with health anxiety (Salkovskis and Warwick 2001) has been expanded to include positive safety behaviour. Specific forms of cognitive behaviour therapy (Warwick *et al.* 1996; Clark *et al.* 1998; Sorensen *et al.* 2011) have been deduced from the model and are being subjected to controlled evaluations.

Cognitions about health

The affected people are morbidly preoccupied with their health and greatly overestimate the probability that they have a serious illness and/or that they are at risk of developing a serious illness. They also overestimate the seriousness of the dreaded illness and fear that it will be disabling. Not infrequently, people fear that it will be fatal. Changes in bodily sensations, functions or appearance, and unwanted, disturbing, intrusive thoughts or images or impulses are misinterpreted as indications of an actual or potentially serious illness.

They believe that they are exceptionally vulnerable to illnesses in general and/or exceptionally vulnerable to a particular illness (e.g. cancer, but are relatively unconcerned about cardiac illness). The particular, circumscribed fears are idiosyncratic and originate from the experience of a distressing illness or treatment, or a distressing illness or treatment of a relative or friend. The common fears are a dread of heart attacks, cancer, AIDS, strokes and mental illness. Recognition that anxiety about developing a mental illness is a form of health anxiety will ultimately provide help for sufferers, who are likely to benefit from improved diagnoses and from the CBT that is used to treat health anxiety.

The recent development of scales to assess *cognitions* about one's health (Hadjistavropolous *et al.* 2012) will enhance our knowledge about the content and significance of the cognitions and, most importantly, facilitate experimental evaluations of the cognitive model. In addition to these personally relevant health cognitions, there are indications that people with HAD also have anxiety-evoking *general beliefs* about health and illness, such as beliefs that there is far more illness in the world than people realize, that there must be an explanation for all aches, pains, unusual sensations, and so forth (Fulton *et al.* 2011).

In the cognitive construal, it is the person's (health) cognitions that are critical; that is, the interpretation which the person places on experiences, events, information. These interpretations are *personally significant*. Catastrophic misinterpretations are particularly damaging. General beliefs, held by many other people, are not personally significant, and may play little or no part in HAD.

Pathways to fear

There are three pathways to the acquisition of fears and anxiety. They are acquired by experiencing disturbing or damaging events, by vicarious acquisition (such as a serious illness experienced by a relative or close friend), or by absorbing threatening information (Rachman 1990).

An example of the vicarious acquisition of an intense, specific fear was seen in the case of a middle-aged woman with an unremarkable medical history who was tormented through most of her adult life by a fear that she was going to suffer a catastrophic stroke that would leave her severely incapacitated. When she was ten years old, her mother had a sudden stroke that left her with a mild speech impediment and a disfiguring weakness on the left side of her face. The patient was disturbed by recurrent images of herself with a similar disfigurement. In order to protect herself, she tried to avoid any emotion-provoking situations, restricted her diet by excluding salty or spicy foods and alcohol, measured her blood pressure several times a day, and compulsively checked the appearance of her face. She was little concerned about other threats to her health.

Another patient was extraordinarily preoccupied with potential threats to her health and spent several hours every day reading and re-reading medical guides and scanning the internet for information about health risks. She was so anxious about her health that she maintained a restricted, hypervigilant lifestyle, feeling that at any time she could become seriously ill. She avoided travel, kept to a strict narrow diet, and avoided going near sick people or hospitals.

Following a bout of ill-health and a lengthy period of asthma during childhood, she regarded herself as a weak and vulnerable person, and indeed for approximately three years had been advised to refrain from taking part in sports or other strenuous activities at or after school. At the time of her psychological assessment in adulthood, it was affirmed that her health was not compromised and numerous medical tests and consultations were all negative. The fears were acquired by a lengthy period of adverse health and her feelings of vulnerability were reinforced by her extremely overprotective parents.

Fears of becoming mentally ill can be acquired vicariously by proximity to people who appear to be mentally disturbed. They are avoided in public places, and psychiatric hospitals and wards are strictly off-limits. In one case, the affected man's fear of becoming mentally ill was so intense that each working day he took a four-mile roundabout route to work in order to avoid seeing the local psychiatric hospital. The fear had been generated when he was a boy, and his father insisted on taking him on monthly visits to his severely ill uncle who was a long-term resident in a psychiatric care-home, and rarely spoke or responded to his visitors. Some patients with health anxiety resort to explaining their fear of proximity to disturbed people in terms of contracting 'mind germs' which can affect them. Incidentally, notions of this kind are also expressed by people who are not ignorant or deluded. The idea is that mind germs share some properties of disease germs, including contagiousness.

Fears of losing control of one's mind, of carrying out violent actions, of ending up in a back ward of a long-stay psychiatric hospital, are examples of frightening threats to a person's mental health. Perceived threats to one's sanity are a manifestation of health anxiety and can be as distressing and disabling as perceived threats to one's physical health.

Intense fears of a threat to one's health can be produced by the absorption of disturbing information about epidemics (e.g. SARS, sudden respiratory illness) or by illnesses that can be contracted by contact with sufferers (e.g. AIDS), or by information about potentially harmful foods (e.g. carcinogens). There are several sources of potentially frightening information: friends or relations, the media, internet surfing, advertising. People who are particularly sensitive to threatening information are vulnerable to generalized fears of illness. From a treatment perspective, the specific, idiosyncratic cases of health anxiety are probably more manageable than the generalized forms.

Anxiety about one's health can be generated or exacerbated by pain, bodily sensations, changes in appearance (swellings, blemishes, etc.), injuries, changes in functioning (such as loss of energy, insomnia, loss of memory, fatigue), alarming information about health risks, intrusive images or thoughts, proximity of perceived environmental threats (e.g. blood, putrefying foods), proximity to evidently sick people, thoughts of losing control and behaving in a bizarre manner, episodes of depression, proximity to mentally disturbed people, news of distressing illnesses of relatives or friends, episodic and/or chronic pain, recurrent intrusive images about pain and its consequences.

In a neat experimental investigation, Abramowitz and Moore (2007) demonstrated that when 27 patients diagnosed with hypochondriasis were exposed to personally significant health-anxiety triggers, they promptly experienced large increases in anxiety. The use of personally significant triggers and personally significant safety behaviour is a strength of this incisive experiment.

Pain and health anxiety

Pain is intrusive, frequently distressing, dominating, and often is an alarming symptom. It is a very common reason for seeking medical assistance. Mäntyselkä *et al.* (2001) found that 40 per cent of 5,646 patients attending a primary care facility had pain complaints; and in a Swedish study, the figure was 28 per cent of 6,890 patients (Hasselstrom *et al.* 2002). High levels of health anxiety are common in patients with chronic pain; 59 per cent of 161 patients (Rode *et al.* 2006). Similarly, Hadjistavropoulos *et al.* (2001) found that patients attending a clinic for pain problems had significantly elevated levels of health anxiety. Patients suffering from chronic pain and high health anxiety engage in more safety behaviours than do patients with comparable pain but low health anxiety, and the resort to safety behaviours is correlated with catastrophic thoughts about the pain (Tang *et al.* 2007).

Many sufferers from chronic pain report frequent and distressing intrusive images that are comparable to those described by patients with health anxiety. In a study carried out on 59 attendees at a rehabilitation clinic, Philips (2011) found that pain-related images evoked strong emotional reactions which included elevated anxiety. The images were assessed by structured interviews and experimental probes, and 78 per cent of the participants reported one or more recurrent images when in pain. When asked to form their most distressing (index) image, their pain levels rose and negative emotions increased. In addition, their negative cognitive appraisals worsened during and after the image formation. Most of the images were 'forward' and involved dreaded long-term consequences of the chronic pain (e.g. incapacitation, severe disablement). Before taking part in the study, most of the participants were unaware of the recurrent nature of their pain-related images. When they described the images, many had a strong emotional reaction within minutes or even seconds.

The 'prevalence of physical symptoms within the American population at any given time is remarkably high' according to Pennebaker (1982: 5), and he was able to compile a list of 54 common symptoms, including headaches, coughing, nasal congestion, constipation, toothache, dizziness, back pain and muscle soreness. The formidable list of potential triggers of health anxiety is consistent with this high base rate of symptoms and signs. Notwithstanding the remarkably high prevalence of symptoms and potential triggers of alarm, we seem to manage tolerably well. As Taylor and Brown (1988) explained, most people are unrealistically optimistic about their health.

This raises an intriguing question about the continuum of health anxiety. If physical and mental symptoms are so common, and exposures to ubiquitous external and internal information are so prevalent, we need to understand how people find the time to cope with the many threats to their health. Taylor and Brown (1988) suggest that the unrealistic optimism about one's health is an illusion. If so, it is one of the effective illusions.

The persistence of health anxiety

Why does unadaptive behaviour persist? This question arises in all analyses of anxiety disorders and was termed the 'neurotic paradox' by Mowrer (1960). Anxious and distressing images and thoughts about one's health, and associated behaviour, are unadaptive, but they persist. The thoughts and fears persist despite the negative results of medical tests and the provision of repeated reassurances.

The belief that one's health is under serious threat produces hypervigilance; attention is attuned to signs of threat (Eysenck 1992). The active search for these signs 'succeeds' in detecting dangers, and the successes inflate the person's anxiety. This in turn reinforces the need for vigilance and continuous searching. The content of the fear directs the person's search for safety. Affected people are attuned to the triggers that pertain to their particular fear and scan their social, physical and internal environments for signs of danger. They are seldom 'off-duty'. Health anxiety is persistent and pervasive.

Memories of threatening information are available, emerge spontaneously, are recalled deliberately, and even 'rehearsed' as in the post-event processing of upsetting social events (Clark and Wells 1995; Rachman, Gruter-Andrew *et al.* 2000). The deliberate recall and replaying of events or information that appear to threaten one's health (post-event processing) contribute to the maintenance of health anxiety.

Threatening images

Memories of these threats can also recur in the form of disturbing unwanted intrusive images that evoke considerable fear. A good deal of attention has been paid to unwanted, intrusive thoughts, and after a long period of neglect, the power of *unwanted images* has now become a subject of considerable interest (Arntz 2012; Brewin *et al.* 2010; Hackmann *et al.* 2011; Philips 2011). Intrusive images that involve *future* dread rather than recollections are particularly common in cases of health anxiety (Muse *et al.* 2010). In their interview study of 55 patients diagnosed with hypochondriasis, the large majority of participants reported experiencing recurrent intrusive and distressing images: 'the majority of the patients (86.05%) classified their image as relating to the future. Imagining a future event has been shown to increase an individual's perception that that the imagined event will occur' (Muse *et al.* 2010: 7). For example, 'I have a recurrent image of myself severely disabled by the illness and unable to feed, clean or care for myself.' The characteristic response to these disturbing images is to suppress them, but unfortunately these attempts often go wrong and increase rather than decrease the frequency of the images (Rassin 2005), thereby adding to the anxiety.

The clinical significance of intrusive images was recognized by Beck (1976): 'In employing systematic desensitization, for instance, I customarily ask for a detailed description of each image. The patient's report is often very informative and, on many occasions, reveals new problems that had not been previously identified' (Beck 1976: 221). 'Many times, maladaptive ideation occurs in a pictorial form instead of, or in addition to, the verbal form' (Beck 1976: 242). He then went on to help the patient modify the images by 'decentering' or 'distancing' them. This was an early, prescient example of rescripting (see p. 178).

Given some of the similarities between OCD and health anxiety, it is to be expected that significant intrusive images are experienced by sufferers from health anxiety. Intrusive images in OCD can be powerful and provoke intense emotional reactions. They are primarily visual, usually vivid, effortless, fully formed, of short duration (because the person 'stops' the image), and the content is remarkably stable (Rachman 2007). Some of them remain unchanged for a lifetime. Wells and Hackmann (1993) described a pilot study of ten patients with health anxiety who were selected because they had intrusive images, observed that the main themes were illness and death, and many were forward-oriented rather than past images. As mentioned, Muse *et al.* (2010: 1) found that a large majority of hypochondriacal patients experienced 'recurrent, distressing intrusive images'. The most significant (index) image was experienced 3.77 times per week. The majority of the images were either a memory of an event or associated with a memory, but were future-oriented, and almost all were on the theme of serious illness or death. Some of their findings resonate with prominent aspects of obsessive-compulsive disorders: 'participants reported responding to experiencing intrusive images by engaging in avoidance, checking, reassurance-seeking, distraction and rumination' (Muse *et al.* 2010: 1). The recurrence of the disturbing images and thoughts stirs up anxiety, and leaves the person vulnerable to persisting anxiety.

Muse *et al.* (2010: 7) raise the plausible possibility that these recurrent future-oriented images of illness and death 'serve to maintain anxiety about health by increasing the participants' estimation of the likelihood of these events occurring'. This resembles the effects of the cognitive bias thought-action-fusion encountered in cases of OCD (Shafran and Rachman 2004). Recurrent intrusive thoughts of feared misfortunes (e.g. losses, accidents or illnesses) are believed by the affected person to increase the probability of the misfortune actually occurring. The modification of thought-action-fusions can be relatively straightforward with non-clinical participants (Zucker *et al.* 2002; Marino-Carper *et al.* 2010), but the bias is less easily modified in patients.

With a view to the possible introduction of rescripting into CBT for health anxiety, preliminary research has shown that rescripting can significantly reduce the distressing reactions to the images (Philips and Samson 2012). The mere repetition of the formation of the index images does not reduce the emotional reactions. The long-term effects of rescripting exercises remain to be determined.

Cognitive biases

The operation of various cognitive biases can sustain and reinforce health anxiety. For example, *ex consequentia* reasoning (Arntz *et al.* 1995) can provoke and sustain health anxiety. This bias arises from the usually latent belief that, 'If I am anxious it must mean that there is danger; so, if I am made anxious by the pain in my head that means there is a significant danger lurking.' Similarly, confirmatory biases can reinforce the anxiety: 'As a result' of confirmatory biases 'patients selectively notice and remember information consistent with negative beliefs about their problems' (Salkovskis 1996a: 69).

One of the two thought-action-fusion (TAF) biases, inflated likelihood of occurrence, can play a part in health anxiety. In this bias, the affected person believes that thoughts of a particular misfortune, such as a thought about developing cancer, actually increase the probability that the misfortune will occur: the likelihood form of TAF (Shafran *et al.* 1996). Recently it has been suggested that intrusive *images* are also subject to the likelihood bias. Philips (2011) encountered 'image-action fusion' in a sample of sufferers from chronic pain who were attending a rehabilitation clinic. Many participants endorsed a belief that their recurrent unwanted intrusive images about the pain and its disabling consequences increased the probability that the dreaded consequence would actually occur. This finding is consistent with early research by Sherman *et al.* (1985) who demonstrated that health-related images that are easy to form are followed by increased estimates of the probability that one will develop the illness. Images that the participants had difficulty in forming were not followed by significant increases in the estimated probabilities. Over-predictions of the intensity of an anticipated fear, a robust phenomenon, is another bias that can increase health anxiety (Rachman and Bichard 1988).

Safety behaviour

Safety behaviour is a prominent feature of HAD, as it is in other anxiety disorders, and is almost universally regarded as undesirable. Sufferers from HAD attempt to cope with threats to their health by carrying out safety behaviours that are emblematic of the disorder. There are four main forms of safety behaviour: avoidance, checking, information-seeking and requests for reassurance. None of them appear to be helpful. The fear of serious illness raises the person's level of vigilance which is manifested in scanning for internal symptoms and signs discernible on one's body. The external environment is scanned for items, situations or people that are potential threats to one's health, and when detected they increase the person's anxiety and hence initiate avoidance behaviour. The avoidance of other people precludes acquiring reassuring information about the perceived threat, and does nothing to disconfirm the maladaptive cognitions. The fundamental overestimations of the probability of becoming ill and of the probability of the illness being very serious persist.

Many affected people engage in repeated and increasingly intense checking of their bodies and bodily functions. Regrettably, the checking generally increases their anxiety, partly because of the enhanced attention paid to the seemingly suspicious signs and symptoms; and partly because repeated checking tends to produce a loss of confidence in one's memory (Radomsky and Rachman 1999; Radomsky et al. 2006; Radomsky et al. 2001; van den Hout and Kindt 2003 – see Chapter 9). Compulsive checking causes more checking, not less checking (Radomsky et al. 2010).

There is ample evidence that safety behaviour can reinforce unadaptive behaviour and interfere with the progress of therapy (Rachman et al. 2008). In a well-conceived experiment, Olatunji et al. (2011) demonstrated that engaging in hygienic safety behaviours, such as repeatedly using sanitized wipes, exacerbated 'symptoms' of health anxiety, and increased scores on measures of HAD. Safety behaviour can interfere with a prevailing treatment technique – exposure – because it disrupts or undermines the effects of the exposure exercises.

Recently, the role and effects of safety behaviour were reconsidered because of accumulating evidence that in specifiable circumstances, 'judicious safety behaviour' can *facilitate* therapeutic progress (Rachman *et al.* 2008). It has been shown to be facilitative in the ERP treatment of agoraphobia (de Silva and Rachman 1984; Rachman *et al.* 1986); in the treatment of snake phobia (Bandura *et al.* 1974; Rachman, Hammond *et al.* 2000; Milosevic and Radomsky 2008); in treating acrophobia (Ritter 1969); fear of spiders (Hood *et al.* 2010); reducing claustrophobia (Powers *et al.* 2004; Sy *et al.* 2011); and in reducing feelings of contamination, disgust and anxiety in non-clinical participants who react strongly to contact with a contaminant (Rachman *et al.* 2011; van den Hout *et al.* 2011). In none of these experiments was there evidence that the use of the safety behaviour prevented the desired changes in maladaptive cognitions. Increasing attention is being paid to reconsidering the effects of safety behaviour (Parrish and Radomsky 2010; Parrish *et al.* 2008; Sy *et al.* 2011). Just as there is bad cholesterol and good cholesterol, there is bad safety behaviour and good safety behaviour (Rachman 2012).

Repeated requests for reassurance are a characteristic feature of health anxiety, and can be frustrating and exasperating. They are generally unsuccessful and can be an impediment to treatment. Reassurance can be helpful, but for 'people suffering from severe or persisting health anxiety it is likely at best to be useless and at worst to be counter-productive' (Salkovskis and Warwick 2001: 56).

The medical advice is generally *exclusionary* ('no, you do not have a sexually transmitted disease'; 'this blemish, lump, is not cancerous'; 'your disturbing thoughts are not a sign of schizophrenia') and can leave the patient without a satisfying explanation for their recurrent pain, disturbing thoughts, changes in bodily function or appearance. It is an ineffective form of safety behaviour (Parrish and Radomsky 2010). The development of an acceptable and effective form of reassurance, perhaps following along the lines of 'judicious safety behaviour' (Rachman 2010) will be a useful forward step. For people who are not affected by health anxiety, authoritative reassurance and plausible explanations enhance the person's feelings of safety.

In sum, several factors contribute to the persistence of health anxiety: hypervigilance, enhanced selective attention to threatening information about health risks, an accumulation of threatening memories, disturbing intrusive images, post-event processing, cognitive biases such as *ex consequentia* reasoning, changes in bodily functioning, pains, changes in appearance, intrusive thoughts and images, and the resort to safety behaviour which reinforces the maladaptive interpretations of certain bodily sensations.

Health anxiety and panic disorder

There are important connections between health anxiety and panic disorder. The first is a similarity of certain features of both disorders, and the second is that the prevailing explanations of health anxiety and panic disorder share an essential cognitive element. In both theories it is postulated that the anxiety and fear are caused by a catastrophic misinterpretation of certain bodily sensations (Clark 1986; Salkovskis and Warwick 2001).

The experience of intensified autonomic sensations, such as a pounding heart, can evoke anxiety. If these sensations are misinterpreted as signs of a catastrophic threat, a panic can occur. However, in health anxiety, the potentially threatening sensations are wider, and the triggers for anxiety include recurrent intrusive images, thoughts, loss of energy, perceived loss of memory, and other changes in functioning or appearance.

In panic disorder, the misinterpretation of the bodily sensations provokes an intense fear of imminent danger, often of a heart attack (Rachman and de Silva 2010). The fear involves autonomic arousal, arises sharply, lasts in the region of 5–20 minutes, and gradually subsides only to leave a residue of anxiety. The episodes of panic tend to occur in particular situations such as public places, and the disorder is associated with agoraphobia. In contrast, the misinterpretations of bodily sensations or functions, disturbing thoughts, intrusive images, and so on that provoke health anxiety create a persisting well of anxiety that generates pervasive hypervigilance. The cognitive content of health anxiety can be circumscribed (e.g. AIDS) or general – a dread of a range of possible illnesses. Some patients are tormented by both types of cognition.

Health anxiety and OCD

The repeated, even compulsive, requests for reassurance bear a resemblance to compulsive OCD behaviour, but there is a defining difference between the two. Sufferers from OCD obsessions and compulsions resist them because they recognize that they are unwanted and not rational. Many of them are embarrassed by their thoughts and behaviour and conceal them (Newth and Rachman 2001). Sufferers from health anxiety regard their fears as rational and openly seek reassurance.

In both disorders, the affected person grossly overestimates the probability of a catastrophic threat to their health or well-being, and this inflated probability multiplies with a major overestimation of the danger of the anticipated threat. The multiplicative effects of the overestimations cause distress and extremely elevated levels of vigilance, safety behaviour and checking (Rachman 2002). Both disorders are associated with depression (Noyes 1999, 2001).

In both disorders, the sufferers experience recurrent intrusive and disturbing images. The content of some of the images is similar, but those which are experienced by people with health anxiety are focused on threats to their health and the feared consequences of a serious illness (Muse *et al*. 2010). In addition to disturbing thoughts about their health, many/most patients with OCD are tormented by unwanted intrusive thoughts, impulses and images that are repugnant and generate waves of self-doubt (Rachman and de Silva 2010; Rachman and Hodgson 1980).

There are no precise figures on the issue at present, but a minority of patients with health anxiety and a minority of patients with OCD fear that they are vulnerable to mental illness, and both groups avoid proximity to people who behave in a bizarre manner in public or are known to be suffering from a mental illness. The underlying fear is that mental illness is an *illness* and might be physically or socially contagious.

Given the similarities in the compulsive checking manifested by the two disorders, the approach to treatment has some identical elements. The prevailing treatment is exposure and response prevention (ERP), but this is expanding to include cognitive analyses and techniques.

Assessment

Some tests of health anxiety are available, but the need for improvements and additional tests is evident. The Health Anxiety Inventory (HAI) was developed specifically to assess health anxiety (Salkovskis *et al*. 2002), and has satisfactory psychometric properties (Abramowitz and Moore 2007; Alberts *et al*. 2011; Fergus and Valentiner 2009).

Consistent with the cognitive model, it has two main factors: probability of illness and severity of illness (Abramowitz *et al.* 2007; Alberts *et al.* 2011), and can be used to assess therapeutic improvement (Clark *et al.* 1998; Sorensen *et al.* 2011). Given the broadening perspective of health anxiety, the HAI will benefit from an expansion of items pertaining to fears of developing a serious mental illness, and also items that assess a generalized fear of a variety of health risks and items that address circumscribed, idiosyncratic fears of a particular illness.

There is a need for measures of HAD cognitions. At present there is the Health Cognitions Questionnaire (Hadjistavropolous *et al.* 2012) and the Irrational Health Beliefs Scale (Fulton *et al.* 2011). The former covers cognitions that are relevant to the cognitive model and is suitable for experimental analyses of HAD. It has a useful parallel form for people who are currently ill. The inclusion of cognitions pertaining to mental illness would be an advance. The measurement of the person's degree of disease conviction (Warwick *et al.* 1996; Clark *et al.* 1998) is essential and the simple rating scale currently used warrants development and validation. An assessment of disease conviction can be added to a cognitions inventory, such as that constructed by Hadjistavropolous *et al.* (2012), or developed as a separate scale; either way, provision should be made for assessing changes in conviction.

The two key premises of the cognitive model, namely the inflated estimations of the probability of developing the illness and of the seriousness of the dreaded illness, remain to be fully evaluated.

The predisposing factors that underlie health anxiety are not clearly delineated, but high levels of anxiety sensitivity, neuroticism, depression, and a preoccupation with health and well-being are probably involved (Williams 2004; McClure and Lilienfeld 2001). There is evidence of elevated scores on scales of neuroticism in people with health anxiety (Williams 2004), but little to suggest a unique or even specific contribution of neuroticism.

In routine clinical use, the HAI, Health Cognitions Questionnaire, the degree of disease conviction, estimations of the probability and seriousness of the feared illness, an improved vigilance scale, safety behaviour scale, cognitive bias scale, medical utilization scale, and a depression scale – the Beck Depression Inventory (BDI) – are available for assessing progress (Rachman 2010).

An assessment battery suitable for use in conducting a randomized treatment trial (RCT) should comprise clinical interviews, including a standardized interview schedule, measures of health cognitions, tests of disease conviction, tests of intrusive imagery and thoughts, the

BDI, the Yale–Brown Obsessive Compulsive Scale–Hypochondriasis (YBOCS–HC), and independent blind assessments of clinical status pre- and post-treatment and follow-ups.

Treatment

Evaluating the results of treatment can be difficult because of the confusion between severe health anxiety and hypochondriasis. Most of the published treatment trials include 'hypochondriasis' in the title, even when the substance of the report describes the selection, assessment and treatment of health anxiety, usually by cognitive behaviour therapy. However, the number of controlled randomized trials of treatment for health anxiety is growing.

In 1996, Warwick *et al*. reported successful results in the treatment of 32 patients with severe health anxiety (the term 'hypochondria' appears in the title). Health anxiety and disease conviction were significantly reduced at the end of 16 sessions of cognitive behaviour therapy, and the improvements were sustained at the three-month follow-up. The dramatic reduction in disease conviction is particularly important. As is common in studies of hypochondria and of health anxiety, the patients had elevated depression – perhaps a manifestation of the 'fumes of melancholy' referred to in the OED (1971) definition of hypochondria. The significance of the results is somewhat limited because the comparison condition was a passive waiting-list condition, a single therapist carried out the treatment, and the follow-up period was too brief.

In an extended replication trial reported two years later, Clark *et al*. (1998) added an active therapy comparison condition (stress-management training [SMT]), deployed eight therapists, extensive treatment (16 sessions plus three booster sessions), a range of assessment measures, and three follow-up assessments (at 3, 6 and 12 months). Forty-eight patients participated. In most of them, the health anxiety was focused on fears of cancer or cardiac illness. The two active treatments produced significant reductions in health anxiety and distress, and in associated behaviour (e.g. checking, reassurance). These changes exceeded the minimal changes observed in the waiting-list control condition. As Warwick *et al*. (1996) found, the cognitive treatment was followed by a dramatic reduction in disease conviction. In all measures except those pertaining to mood, the cognitive behaviour therapy results surpassed those of the SMT condition at post-treatment. The CBT improvements declined somewhat between the 6-month and 12-month follow-up periods, but remained significantly superior to the pre-treatment scores. Most of the differences between SMT and CBT had faded by the 12-month follow-up. Overall, the results of this admirably designed and executed randomized control trial provide strong evidence of the effectiveness of CBT in the treatment of severe health anxiety.

Sorensen *et al.* (2011) carried out a randomized control treatment trial on 76 patients diagnosed with hypochondriasis. Unusually, they compared the effects of CBT with another form of therapy, short-term psychodynamic therapy (SSTP). This method is commonly used in Denmark, where the trial took place, to treat patients with this diagnosis. Sixteen sessions were provided over a six-month period, and the main outcome measure was the Health Anxiety Inventory (HAI). The results of the CBT group were superior to the waiting-list control on all measures, and superior to the SSTP on the main measure and one measure of depression. The differences between the two therapy groups diminished during the six-month follow-up period.

The results of the trial are interesting because of the comparison between methods. There are some limitations, however. All of the SSTP was conducted by the same therapist, and the assessment measures were insufficient. Nevertheless, the findings are consistent with those from other trials. Cognitive behaviour therapy appears to be an effective method for treating severe health anxiety.

Hedman *et al.* (2011) compared the effects of internet provision of a mainly CBT protocol ($N = 40$) with a minimal attention control condition ($N = 41$) in the treatment of hypochondriasis. The diagnoses were made on the telephone. Using the internet, the participants filled in measures of mood, symptoms and engagement on a regular basis. At the end of the treatment, 67 per cent of the CBT participants were no longer diagnosed as suffering from hypochondria, and a mere 5 per cent of the attention control group showed this improvement. The CBT participants were significantly less depressed post-treatment. The results were sustained at the six-month follow-up. The large changes are seemingly remarkable after a remote, mixed CBT protocol provided on the internet. A few unsatisfactory assessment measures were used (e.g. the Clinical Global Impression [CGI] scale; Ruhe *et al.* 2005), but the significant declines in the Health Anxiety Inventory merit consideration.

There are several weaknesses of the study. Diagnosis by telephone is dubious and no information is provided about the validity of this method; the attention control condition was minimalist and according to the authors proved to be valueless; there was no control for demand factors; and the analysis of the results did not control for the significant decline in depression in the CBT group. It is possible that engaging in an active internet programme produced the reported declines in depression. It would not be unusual for reductions in depression, however achieved, to be reflected in changes in related negative psychological states, such as health anxiety (Watson and Pennebaker 1989). In the attention control condition, there was no decline in reported depression and virtually no decline in health anxiety.

Prior to the completion of conventional trials, the evidence pertaining to the effects of psychological treatment on health anxiety (often titled as hypochondria) was promising despite limitations such as small samples, unsatisfactory protocols, and inadequate control conditions (e.g. Avia *et al.* 1996; Barsky and Ahern 2004; Visser and Bouman 2001). Overall, the results of the randomized control trials are encouraging – CBT substantially reduced severe health anxiety and disease conviction – but definitive conclusions await further trials.

Present status of the cognitive model

Research into health anxiety has produced many interesting findings and the results of indirect tests of the cognitive model are certainly promising, but direct tests of the cognitive model remain to be carried out. Is health anxiety caused by catastrophic misinterpretations of the threatening significance of certain changes in bodily functions and/or appearance? Is it caused by catastrophic misinterpretations of the significance of a pain? Is it caused by catastrophic misinterpretations of unusual intrusive thoughts and/or conduct? Broadly, do sufferers from health anxiety greatly overestimate the probability and/or the seriousness of threats to their health?

The results of several indirect tests are encouraging. The implications of the results obtained with cognitive behaviour therapy, which is directly derived from the cognitive model, are important. Cognitive behaviour therapy has been found to be effective in reducing severe health anxiety (Clark *et al.* 1998; Nakao *et al.* 2011; Sorensen *et al.* 2011; Warwick *et al.* 1996), and the results are consistent with the model. Importantly, the treatment procedure is a product of the theory. It is not a self-generated *ad hoc* treatment. In a comparison with an active treatment, CBT was far more effective than short-term psychotherapy, which is of course differently derived.

It is noteworthy that in all of the trials, CBT was followed by broad improvements in addition to the reduction in health anxiety. There were reductions in unadaptive behaviour such as reassurance-seeking, and from the point of view of the cognitive theory, the large and significant reductions in disease conviction are particularly interesting. This finding comes close to providing a test of the core of the cognitive theory (Salkovskis 1996a; Salkovskis and Warwick 2001). Endorsement of an exaggerated, fixed conviction that one has a significant disease is a very important negative cognition, and the primary aim of CBT is to remove or reduce maladaptive cognitions. Disease conviction was substantially reduced after CBT (Warwick *et al.* 1996; Clark *et al.* 1998). This line of research remains to be pursued, including specific assessments of the person's estimations of the probability and seriousness of the feared illness. Mediation analyses to ascertain the functional relationships between changes in cognitions and reductions in health anxiety will be necessary.

Prior to participating in the randomized trials, the patients had elevated scores on the measures of negative health-related cognitions – the absence of such evidence would have left a gap in the theory. Other results that are consistent with the model include the fact that the negative cognitions were significantly reduced post-treatment, and the therapeutic effects were impressively large.

However, 'reverse engineering' precludes definitive conclusions; the effectiveness of the treatment cannot confirm the model. Other explanations are possible. For example, the patients who received stress-management training in the Clark trial also reported some significant clinical improvements.

Is severe health anxiety the result of catastrophic maladaptive cognitions? Barsky *et al.* (2001) found that hypochondriacal patients did not regard themselves as having an elevated risk for non-medical misfortunes, such as robbery, but did feel at elevated risk for illnesses. This specific bias was significantly related to a tendency to amplify their bodily sensations. Hadjistavropolous *et al.* (2011) tested their Health Cognitions Questionnaire on 208 patients with medical problems and 273 community controls. After controlling for depression and anxiety, they found that the scale scores successfully 'predicted health anxiety'. Interestingly, high scores on the Health Cognitions Questionnaire were associated with a poor response to reassurance. In a slightly different approach, Fulton *et al.* (2011) studied some of the *beliefs* that are associated with health anxiety. They tested their specially constructed Irrational Health Beliefs Scale on two large non-clinical samples and obtained results comparable to those of

Hadjistavropolous et al. (2011). The scores on their beliefs scale were correlated with health anxiety.

In their meta-analytic review, Marcus et al. (2007) found evidence of elevated self-assessment of health risk in a variety of predominantly non-clinical studies, and evidence that people who endorsed such risks were prone to amplifying their bodily sensations. Marcus et al. commented on some inconsistencies in the data, notably some differences between the results from clinical and non-clinical samples, and also drew attention to gaps in our knowledge.

In a direct investigation of health anxiety triggers, Abramowitz and Moore (2007) showed that exposure to personally significant health-related stimuli provokes anxiety. They tested three hypotheses about safety behaviour, namely: exposure to personally significant health-related stimuli will provoke anxiety and urges to perform safety behaviour; carrying out the safety behaviour will reduce the anxiety and urges; and these reductions will occur more slowly when the safety behaviours are not performed (i.e. they will show a slow spontaneous decline). The results confirmed their three hypotheses, all of which are consistent with the cognitive theory. Their investigation is a clear example of how exposure to health-related stimuli can trigger anxiety. It is also one of the few experimental demonstrations of the operation of safety behaviour in HAD, and substantiates one of the similarities between HAD and obsessive-compulsive disorders. As mentioned above, their use of personally significant triggers is a strength, and can be exploited in experimental investigations of the cognitive model. Their results provide support for the model.

They also traced the slow spontaneous decay of the anxiety that has been observed in patients with OCD. This finding is relevant for the rationale given for ERP, which assumes that repeated exposures facilitate habituation to the anxiety-evoking stimuli. However, it remains possible that direct modifications of the key cognitions in HAD might prove to be a superior method.

It has been shown that distressing intrusive images are common in patients with health anxiety and in patients suffering from chronic/episodic pain. Sherman et al. (1985) found that troubling images about health were easy to imagine, and increased the participants' estimations about the probability of their becoming ill. As mentioned earlier, Muse et al. (2010) plausibly suggested that the high frequency of recurrent health-related images reported by hypochondriacal patients might increase their estimations of the probability of an illness. These are early indications that intrusive distressing images can indeed exacerbate and/or trigger increases in health anxiety.

The results of an experiment by Tang *et al.* (2007) have an interesting, albeit indirect, bearing on the subject of triggering. They studied the behaviour of 20 patients with chronic back pain and high health anxiety when carrying out two physical tasks, and compared the results with those of 20 patients with low health anxiety, and those of a pain-free control group. The participants with high health anxiety displayed more safety-seeking behaviour than those with low health anxiety, consistent with the cognitive model. As to the triggering of anxiety, it is particularly interesting that the safety behaviour was correlated with 'catastrophizing thoughts'. This result is consistent with the cognitive theory.

The available evidence of the contribution of negative health-related cognitions to the development and maintenance of HAD is positive, but piecemeal. Most of it is consistent with the cognitive theory, but a systematic programme of research is desirable.

Conclusion

The putative cause of severe health anxiety is a persisting over-estimation of the probability and seriousness of being affected by a dreaded illness. At the other extreme, there are very many people who significantly *underestimate* the probability that they will develop an illness and/or its seriousness – unrealistic optimism (Taylor and Brown 1988). Knowledge about severe health anxiety is too limited at present to warrant a fruitful comparison, but in time a comparative analysis of severe health anxiety and the pervasiveness of unrealistic illusions about one's health will be fascinating.

Summary

The core of health anxiety disorders (HAD) is distressing, uncontrollable anxiety about one's present and future health. The cognitive construal of HAD proposes that health anxiety is caused by catastrophic misinterpretations of the significance of sensations and/or changes in bodily functions and appearance (such as swellings, pain, loss of energy, dizzy spells, memory loss). The nature, causes, triggers, persistence, assessment and treatment of health anxiety are reviewed, and the present status of the cognitive model is appraised.

Social anxiety 11

Social anxiety is defined and described. Affected people experience intense anxiety prior to and during social occasions. It develops in adolescence or early adulthood, is chronic and often associated with other psychological problems, notably depression. Few people are unfamiliar with feelings of apprehensiveness on some occasions, but clinicians and clinical researchers focus on the most extreme forms of social anxiety, often referred to as social phobia. The cognitive theory is described and evaluated, and trends in treatment are adumbrated.

The definition of social anxiety

The essential feature of the disorder is an intense and persistent fear of social occasions and/or performance situations. Entry into one of these situations evokes anxiety, but a formal diagnosis is appropriate only if the anxiety is intense and interferes significantly with the person's life or causes extreme distress. In severe instances, it is so restricting that it clouds a person's entire life. The terms social anxiety and social phobia are used interchangeably.

Social anxiety is an intense and persistent fear of social occasions and/or performance situations. Affected people are fearful of possible scrutiny and anxious that they might behave in a manner that is embarrassing, inept, unacceptable or all of these. The manifestations can include: sweating or trembling in public, excessive blushing, an inability to write or eat in public, a reluctance or inability to speak in public, stage fright. It is a source of distress, concern and shame. Anticipation of social occasions generates considerable anxiety.

Some people fear and avoid a range of different social situations, but for others the fear is circumscribed and evoked only in a specific context such as public speaking (Rapee 1995). The most commonly feared situations include, in descending order, fear of public speaking, attendance at parties, meetings, and speaking to figures in authority. In recognition of the difference between multiple and circumscribed fears, it is common to distinguish between generalized social anxiety (Mannuzza *et al.* 1995) and specific social anxiety. Generalized social anxiety is associated with other psychological problems, such as depression. The circumscribed social phobias are more often preceded by specific traumatic experiences (Sternberger *et al.* 1995) and affected people are prone to experience unwanted and distressing trauma-associated images (Hackmann *et al.* 2000; Hackmann *et al.* 1998).

Socially phobic people engage in extensive avoidance behaviour, but some social interactions are unavoidable and hence a cause of anticipatory anxiety as well as situational anxiety. Social phobia is unchanging, the most chronic of the anxiety disorders, and has a lifetime prevalence of 7.8 per cent (Wittchen and Fehm 2003). Social phobias tend to emerge in adolescence or early adulthood – 15–25 years of age (Barlow 2002; Schneier and Johnson 1992; Wittchen and Fehm 2003). For specific manifestations of social anxiety, such as a fear of public speaking, the prevalence can go as high as 70 per cent (Pollard and Henderson 1988). Survey data collected by Weiller *et al.* (1996) indicate that social phobia is under-recognized (Stein and Stein 2008) and a risk factor for depression and / or alcoholism (Wittchen and Fehm 2003).

The connection with alcohol abuse is illustrated by a lawyer who sought treatment for his intense social anxiety because it was making court appearances a torment. He attempted to control his anxiety by drinking increasing amounts of alcohol before appearances, as a form of 'self-medication'. On some occasions, he needed so much alcohol that his speech was slurred.

It is widely believed that alcohol reduces anxiety and there is persuasive evidence that this can happen. However, as Wilson (1988) pointed out, there are exceptions in which drinking alcohol is followed by an increase in anxiety, and several moderating factors have to be taken into account when assessing the relation between alcohol and anxiety. These include the social setting in which the drinking takes place, the person's previous history of drinking, the interpretation which the drinker places on bodily and psychological changes that occur during drinking, and so forth. It is also possible that the same episode of drinking can have anxiety-reducing effects and later, anxiety-elevating effects. This sequence is not uncommonly reported by patients with anxiety disorders who describe an initial period of reduced anxiety during the drinking episode itself, only to be followed the next morning by uncomfortable jittery feelings that resemble anxiety.

This pattern of early relief and later jitters is illustrated by a patient who had social anxiety and agoraphobia. In the early stages of a course of behavioural treatment, he made slow, steady progress in overcoming his social anxiety and in regaining the ability to walk about freely. However, he continued to have troublesome weekends during which he frequently experienced a return of anxiety and an inability to venture through those parts of the city which he was able to manage on most days. It turned out that he celebrated the end of the working week by drinking on Friday night, only to wake up on Saturday morning feeling agitated and fearful. He subsequently decided to curtail his drinking and this was followed by a decline in his weekend anxiety.

The distinction between social phobics and people with avoidant personality disorder was teased out by Heimberg (1996). People affected by social phobia recognize that their anxiety constitutes a problem and ideally would like to overcome it. A person with an avoidant disorder expresses no wish to have a more active social life and adopts an isolated life by choice. People who suffer from persistent social anxiety frequently complain of the unpleasant intrusiveness of the bodily manifestations accompanying these problems, especially blushing, twitching, palpitations, sweating.

Social phobics tend to rate their social skills as deficient. There is a debate about whether people who suffer from intense social anxiety lack the appropriate social skills, or whether they have the skills, but experience difficulty in deploying them; or whether they deploy the skills appropriately, but nevertheless *feel* that they have not done so. The consensus appears to be that a significant minority of people with intense social anxiety do indeed have deficits in social skills, but the extent of these deficits and the exact role that they play in social anxiety are not clear.

The general finding that people with anxiety disorders tend to have multiple problems (Barlow 2002) is evident in social phobia. According to Rapee's (1995) estimate, approximately 50 per cent of people with intense social anxiety also suffer from other manifestations of anxiety, in addition to depression. Among social phobics one commonly encounters: agoraphobia, generalized anxiety disorder, obsessive-compulsive problems. Or to put it the other way around, people who suffer from anxiety disorders such as obsessional problems or agoraphobia have a high chance of suffering from concurrent social anxiety.

Because of some practical difficulties involved in carrying out experimental analyses of social behaviour, many clinical researchers administer self-report questionnaires. These instruments provide useful information, but assume that the respondents have greater self-knowledge than is justified (see Nisbett and Wilson [1977], for a description of how people tend to tell more than they can know). Assessment of the personal beliefs that are given so important a place in the cognitive theory of social phobia rests on similar assumptions about self-knowledge, and also tends to assume that there is greater generality of these beliefs than is the case.

Cognitive theory of social anxiety

The cognitive theory of *panic* proposed by D. M. Clark (1986) was used as a springboard for a theory of social anxiety. Clark and Wells (1995) analysed clinical and experimental evidence pertaining to social phobia and formulated a cognitive model that promoted fresh thinking and research on the subject. The model provides structure and direction to work on this previously amorphous subject.

> The core of social phobia appears to be a strong desire to convey a particular favourable impression of oneself to others and marked insecurity about one's ability to do so ... In particular they believe that when they [social phobics] enter social situations, (1) they are in danger of behaving in an inept and unacceptable fashion and (2) that such behaviour will have disastrous consequences in terms of loss of status, loss of worth, and rejection.
>
> (Clark and Wells 1995: 69)

The authors assume that the cognitive biases described in other types of anxiety disorder also operate in social phobias; namely, that affected people have a strong tendency to over-predict the probability and the seriousness of aversive (social) events. Social phobics are also prone to a variety of information-processing biases (Clark and McManus 2002; Hirsch and Clark 2004). They interpret social situations in a threatening fashion because of a series of distorted assumptions which they make about themselves and the way in which they should behave in social situations. Clark and Wells (1995) set out the main categories of dysfunctional beliefs: unconditional beliefs about the self, conditional beliefs about social evaluation, and excessively high standards for social performance. Examples of the first include beliefs such as, 'I am stupid', 'I am boring'. Examples of the second type include, 'If they really knew what I was like, they would reject me', 'If I appear to be uncomfortable they will think that I am stupid'. Examples of the third type include, 'I must make intelligent and witty conversation', 'I must conceal that I am feeling anxious'. People with a social phobia also tend to have dysfunctional beliefs about other people, in addition to their erroneous self-evaluations. There are clusters of dysfunctional beliefs about other people: the belief that other people are closely attentive to and concerned about one's appearance and/or conduct; that other people can 'read' one's emotions; and that people are quick to reject anyone who appears to be inept.

When affected people with these cognitive distortions enter a novel or demanding or important social situation, an 'anxiety program' is activated, and the person begins to experience signs of autonomic arousal including palpitations, blushing, trembling, sweating, shortness of breath. These intrusive bodily sensations interfere with the person's ability to process the ordinary exchanges that occur in social gatherings, and then their negative self-evaluative thoughts are triggered. The sensations are taken as confirming their inadequacy, oddness and unacceptability. When they feel anxious, they tend to behave in a non-friendly manner, which in turn elicits corresponding behaviour from the people they are with. These reactions confirm the phobic person's fears that other people disdain or disapprove of them. In potentially troublesome social circumstances, the person experiences a significant increase in self-focused attention (Ingram 1990; Hofmann and Barlow 2002), initiation of safety behaviour, and the emergence of behavioural deficits that are induced by anxiety. The self-focused attention sharpens directly the person enters the feared situation, and the monitoring of one's internal sensations has the unfortunate effect of enhancing the anxious feelings. As a result, the person 'equates feeling humiliated with being humiliated, feeling out of control with being observedly out of control, and feeling anxious with being noticeably anxious' (Clark and Wells 1995: 71).

There is evidence that socially anxious people overestimate the extent to which their anxiety is observable (D. A. Clark and Beck 2010; McEwan and Devins 1983). Because of their preoccupation with their internal sensations and their negative interpretation of these feelings, they are less attentive to what is going on around them and may feel out of touch with other people. To make matters worse, because of their cognitive biases, the words and behaviour of their companions tend to be misinterpreted as being negative and critical.

In an attempt to reduce the risk of receiving a negative evaluation from other people, social phobics are prone to engage in safety behaviour. Unfortunately, these safety actions may prevent the unrealistic beliefs from being disconfirmed. For example, the person might avoid making eye contact in order to prevent the expected criticism, but by doing so, they also ensure that they fail to learn that making direct eye contact is not followed by nasty consequences. There is a further difficulty here, not included in the original theory, but which may well be consistent with it. Given that much of what troubles the socially phobic person arises from their fruitless attempts to guess what other people think of them – almost always negative, of course – these pessimistic beliefs are inherently beyond confirmation. It is not possible, except by indirect, difficult and uncommon means, to learn exactly what other people are thinking about one at a particular time. These types of beliefs are out of the arena and not open to disconfirmation. Clark and Wells (1995) make a sound case for the untoward effects of certain kinds of safety behaviour, but some forms of safety behaviour can be constructive and positive (Rachman *et al.* 2008). Preparing and practising a speech is a safety behaviour that can be most helpful. We all engage in mental and physical safety actions in novel or potentially threatening situations, and generally with useful results.

Another process that is activated on entering a potentially threatening situation is a change in performance that is induced by anxiety. The person's preoccupation with his or her internal sensations and their meaning makes them relatively inattentive to what is going on around them. This is easily perceived as a lack of interest or plain unfriendliness, and may well make the other people behave correspondingly; that is, they will feel less friendly towards the affected person and show signs of it. For example, Curtis and Miller (1986) showed that when people were told that the person they had been talking to in a staged experiment disliked them, their subsequent conversation with this person was regarded as less friendly and less warm. So if the social phobic's inattentiveness and apparent disinterest evoke a corresponding withdrawal of interest from the other people, the phobic's fears of rejection are strengthened.

Clark and Wells attach importance to the effects of 'post-event processing', the strong tendency for social phobics to spend a good deal of time and effort thinking about past social experiences, analysing their failures, recalling and 're-living' other failures, and so forth. It is postulated that this processing contributes to the persistence of social anxiety. Developments in the study of unwanted, intrusive images raise the probability that negative images play a significant part in post-event processing (Hackmann *et al.* 2000; Hirsch *et al.* 2003).

Evidence of the negative effects of post-event processing in social phobias has accumulated (Brozovich and Heimberg 2008; Dannahy and Stopa 2007; Rachman, Gruter-Andrew *et al.* 2000). These 'post-mortems' appear to intensify and consolidate one's negative experiences, increase anxiety in anticipation of social occasions and even undermine therapy (Price and Anderson 2011); these researchers also showed that CBT reduces post-event processing. The growing evidence of such processing in social anxiety will inevitably lead to investigations of post-event processing in all of the anxiety disorders.

The cognitive theory is enlightening and stimulating, but complex. It combines maladaptive cognitions, biased information processing, excessively self-focused attention, distorted self-images, self-defeating safety behaviour, post-event processing. The maladaptive cognitions comprise erroneous beliefs about oneself, and about how other people perceive one. The catalogue of information-processing biases in social phobia was summarized by Hirsch and Clark (2004), and by Clark and McManus:

> [S]ocial phobia is characterized by biases in the following: interpretation of external events, the balance of attention between external and self-processing, the use of internal information to make inferences about how one appears to others, recall of negative information about one's perceived observable self, and by a variety of problematic anticipatory and post-event processing.
>
> (Clark and McManus 2002: 92)

Negative images

There is evidence that people who are socially phobic form powerful negative self-images that impair their conduct (Hirsch *et al.* 2003), and as mentioned, these may intensify post-event processing. Hackmann and her colleagues (2000) also reported important evidence of recurrent negative images in people with social phobia: 'Early unpleasant experiences may lead to the development of excessively negative images of their social selves that are repeatedly activated in subsequent social situations and fail to update' (Hackmann *et al.* 2000: 601). The images are usually from the standpoint of a self-observer and the content is of oneself appearing to be incompetent, pathetic, bumbling, neurotic, pitiful. They are generally accompanied by uncomfortable sensations such as blushing, shaking, sweating. The persistence and apparent ubiquity of these images are remarkable, and may go some way to explaining the success of the original fear-reducing technique of systematic desensitization introduced by Wolpe (1958). This involved the repeated evocation (and therapeutic modification) of fearful images. It was on target in a way that was not apparent at the time.

Fortunately, the effects of unwanted negative intrusive images can be dampened by exercises in rescripting (Philips and Samson 2012), and in a pilot study on social phobics carried out by Wild *et al.* (2008), the rescripting led to significant reductions in negative beliefs, distress and anxiety. Rescripting is a technique for altering the content and nature of disturbing intrusive images. It is seemingly simple, but often is remarkably effective when used in the course of therapy. As noted, it is capable of reducing distress and can produce important changes in the person's appraisal of the significance of the image/s.

The disturbing image is described in detail and evoked as a test. The person is advised that forming the image may be upsetting, but it can readily be erased if they wish. Some people are so sensitive to the possible effects of the image that they decline to evoke it. If it is vivid and easily evoked, the sufferer is asked how he/she would like to change it – 'What would you prefer?', 'How should it end?' The person almost invariably comes up with preferred endings, or other desired changes. Rescripting is a valuable technique, but is best used in the context of a course of therapy.

In a straightforward illustration, a woman receiving cognitive behaviour therapy for a complex set of OCD problems was tormented by recurrent images of harming other people. The most upsetting image was one of striking her elderly mother, whom she was caring for and loved deeply. She chose a preferred image of hugging and kissing her mother. After practising the switch from an image of striking her mother to hugging and kissing her instead, she became adept at doing so, and experienced declining tension. She practised the rescripting five times per day for two weeks, and gained complete control of the tormenting intrusions.

The evidence

Comprehensive accounts and discussions of social anxiety are provided by Barlow (2002), D. A. Clark and Beck (2010), Hofmann and Barlow (2002), Rapee and Heimberg (1997), Rapee and Spence (2004), Spurr and Stopa (2002), among others. The cognitive theory is a multi-component model, and the interconnections and interactions of the components are complex.

There is convincing evidence pertaining to some of the components, notably the adverse effects of self-focused attention, the presence of a variety of maladaptive cognitions that include erroneous beliefs and seriously faulty interpretations, biased judgemental and interpretive processing, the unhelpful effects of diverse forms of safety behaviour, and the negative effects of post-event processing. Evidence of cognitive biases has been reported by Hirsch et al. (2006), Voncken et al. (2003), ; maladaptive information processing by Clark and Ehlers. (2004); excessive self-focusing by Hofmann and Barlow (2002) and Spurr and Stopa (2002); unadaptive safety behaviour by McManus et al. (2008); post-event processing by Brozovich and Heimberg (2008) and Dannahy and Stopa (2007).

There is evidence that socially anxious people do endorse more negative self-evaluative thoughts than do other people, are excessively self-focused in social settings, are inclined to interpret ambiguous social situations as being threatening, underestimate their social performance, and misinterpret information provided to them about their behaviour. Socially anxious people also are inclined to overestimate the visibility of their anxiety, and to feel judged and criticized. Their belief that others find them boring or dislike them can promote unfriendly behaviour towards other people, and hence their fears about being disliked become self-fulfilling.

Relief can be obtained by redirecting the intense internal focusing of socially phobic patients towards external cues, and after successful treatment, the excessive self-focusing is diminished (Barlow 2002; D. A. Clark and Beck 2010; Hofmann 2000; Hofmann et al. 2004). This technique, and the associated one of discouraging the person's futile attempts to guess what other people are perceiving and thinking about them, are consistent with the cognitive model. Similarly, useful effects are being reported from discouraging post-mortem ruminations about social failures, behavioural experiments to check the assumed visibility of one's own anxiety, and so on. From the therapeutic point of view, redirecting the self-focused attention when one is feeling socially anxious can be critical, but it is not easy.

Social anxiety within the general framework of anxiety

The cognitive theory can be accommodated within the framework of anxiety set out in Chapter 2. It is possible to substitute for each stage in the anxiety sequence, cues and cognitions that are specific to social phobia. The beliefs that are said to contribute to the social schemata in social phobics include: perfectionistic standards for social performance, false beliefs about social evaluation, and negative views about the self (Clark and Wells 1995). These beliefs plus a temperamental predisposition to anxiety give rise to hypervigilance when the person enters the social situation and starts a process of global scanning that is followed by an intensification of attentional focus. 'One of the most significant changes that occurs when a social phobic enters a feared situation is a shift in attentional focus' (Clark and Wells 1995: 70).

Much of this attention is focused on their internal sensations (and their perceived significance, including whether their emotional state is visible to others). In addition, it is probable that they experience perceptual distortions, particularly in their view of the emotional reactions which they observe in others. If they believe that their disturbed emotional state is evident to other people, they are inclined to interpret it as confirming their inadequacy, ineptness and unacceptability. They are likely to interpret the behaviour and gestures of other people as indicating that others are paying undue attention and doing so in a critical fashion. Favourable remarks or gestures are discounted and negative ones accepted as confirmatory of the phobic's negative self-appraisals. If, however, the affected person succeeds in making a benign interpretation of their sensations and the behaviour of the people around them, minimal anxiety will follow. If the interpretation is predominantly negative, the phobic person will feel rejected and anticipate being shunned in the future. This sequence culminates in feelings of intense anxiety, followed by attempts to escape from the situation.

Treatment

Research into the processes involved in the causation and persistence of social anxiety is inviting, but can be laborious and time-consuming. Technological advances are, however, proving helpful. Given the large number of people whose lives are severely restricted by their social fears, there is understandable pressure to develop and test effective and efficacious methods of treatment as soon as possible. Notwithstanding the inevitable time-gap between the basic research and the drive to develop effective techniques, it is reassuring that significant progress is being made.

The early psychological techniques were predominantly behavioural; that is, they consisted mainly of behavioural exercises designed to reduce the person's fears and avoidance. The frequently repeated exercises of exposing the person to social situations that evoke high anxiety were moderately effective in reducing the anxiety (Barlow 2002; Heimberg *et al*. 1995; Juster and Heimberg 1995; Hofmann and Barlow 2002; Hofmann and Barlow 2002; Ponniah and Hollon 2008; Powers and Emmelkamp 2008b), and the modern techniques of cognitive behaviour therapy (CBT) are a definite advance.

Cognitive behaviour therapy combines the techniques that are deduced from the cognitive theory with the prevailing behavioural methods, but the emphasis has moved towards analysing the person's fearful *cognitions* and interpretive biases, plus rescripting of intrusive images, and testing the effects of engaging in post-event processing.

Cognitive behaviour therapy has been shown to be effective (D. A. Clark and Beck 2010; Mortberg *et al*. 2007; Ponniah and Hollon 2008; Powers and Emmelkamp 2008b), superior to interpersonal therapy (Stangier *et al*. 2011) and to applied relaxation (Clark *et al*. 2006), and equal to (Powers and Emmelkamp 2008b) or superior to exposure therapy (Clark *et al*. 2006). It is effective in treating unadaptive safety behaviour (McManus *et al*. 2008), self-focused attention (Bögels and Mansell 2004; Hofmann 2000, 2004) and post-event processing (Price and Anderson 2011).

It is directly deduced from the cognitive theory of social phobia and gains credibility from the successful deployment of CBT in treating other anxiety disorders. Even at this comparatively early stage, some inventive refinements are under development. Analyses of the separate and joint effects of the several components of CBT, along the lines investigated by Hirsch *et al*. (2006), remain to be completed.

A variety of medications have been tried in treating social phobia with some success (e.g. phenelzine; Heimberg *et al*. 1998), but none have been notably effective. Given the close association between social anxiety and depression, the use of anti-depressants is common and can be helpful, but unfortunately the medications have some drawbacks (significant relapse rates, food prohibitions, side-effects, etc). Given the risks associated with pharmacotherapy and lack of evidence that it is more effective than psychological treatments, medication may best be viewed as a back-up plan under most circumstances.

Summary

Social anxiety is an intense and persistent fear of social or performance situations. Anxiety is evoked when the person feels under scrutiny or that he/she is being evaluated. The most commonly feared situations are meeting new people, public speaking, attendance at parties, meetings, talking to people in authority. A distinction is made between generalized social anxiety and specific, circumscribed social anxiety (e.g. writing in public). Social anxiety has a high lifetime prevalence rate, is usually chronic, and is associated with depression and/or generalized anxiety. It is a distressing and restricting psychological problem.

According to the cognitive theory, the core of the disorder is persisting anxiety in social situations which results from a serious lack of confidence in one's ability to convey a favourable impression to others, and catastrophic misinterpretations of actual or perceived failures to succeed in these attempts. Affected people over-predict the probability of their social failures and the seriousness of the anticipated consequences. Since the early 2000s, significant progress has been made in developing effective psychological treatments.

Generalized anxiety disorder 12

The nature of generalized anxiety is described and its relation to other problems is set out. The approach to treatment and the efficacy of prevailing methods are evaluated.

The nature of generalized anxiety

The description of generalized anxiety disorder (GAD) set out in the DSM classification is excessive anxiety and worry that persists for longer than six months. It is chronic, pervasive, very difficult to control, and tends to be distressing and impairing. The content of the worry and anxiety is generally about one's work, finances, health, personal relationships, family.

In GAD, the anxiety and worry are out of proportion to the probability of an unfortunate event occurring, and an exaggeration of the seriousness of the event should it occur. These dysfunctional cognitions are common to all of the anxiety disorders: the probability that seriously adverse events, even catastrophes, will occur is over-estimated, as are the expected seriousness and consequences of the feared event.

Generalized anxiety disorder is accompanied by a number of physical signs, notably elevated arousal and muscle tension. Other bodily symptoms, such as nausea, urinary frequency, queasy stomach, difficulty swallowing, are commonly described. Affected people are hypervigilant and restless as if expecting some unfortunate event to occur. The worrying often takes the form of unsuccessful attempts to prevent the dreaded event from occurring. Unlike ordinary attempts to solve one's problems constructively, these futile attempts at problem solving lapse into circularity. The affected people have difficulty in concentrating, become irritable and are easily tired.

A 32-year-old teacher described himself as a chronic worrier. He was persistently anxious about his health and was constantly ruminating about his aches and pains. Any threats to the health of his relatives provoked sharp anxiety; each trip was preceded by anticipatory anxiety, he could not rest until his family returned home safely each night, and he felt tense every day of his life.

Barlow (1988, 2002) noted that many of the features of GAD are evident in anxiety disorders and even in disorders of mood. For example, people who are suffering from obsessive-compulsive disorders commonly report prolonged periods of tense worrying, as do many people who are suffering from depression or from social phobia or health anxiety. Roughly half of the people who develop GAD trace its onset to childhood or adolescence, but onset after the age of 20 is not uncommon. The lifetime prevalence rate for this disorder is estimated to be 5.7 per cent (D. A. Clark and Beck 2010), and approximately 12 per cent of patients attending anxiety disorder clinics are diagnosed as having GAD (Barlow 1988: 577).

Boundary problems

Generalized anxiety disorder is so strongly associated with other psychological disorders, notably depression, health anxiety, social phobias, that 'boundary problems' arise (D. A. Clark and Beck 2010). In addition, there is some confusion between 'worry' and anxiety, and between futile problem solving and successful problem solving, and the connections between GAD and mood disorders.

A problem with the concept of GAD is that many features of the phenomenon are observed across other types of anxiety disorder, and none of the features of GAD are exclusive to or specific to GAD. They occur across the board. There are comparable symptoms of GAD (muscle tension, autonomic arousal, vigilance and scanning, apprehensive expectation) in all forms of anxiety disorder (Barlow 2002). This calls into question the value of regarding GAD as a separable problem. Unlike panic disorders, OCD, specific phobias and PTSD – all of which have some clearly distinctive qualities – the cardinal features of generalized anxiety (worry and anxiety) are so common that diagnostic decisions are necessarily quantitative. Does the person worry more often, more intensely than other people?

Most of the worries dwell on anticipated difficulties and/or misfortunes, but troubling worries about *past* events are overlooked in many accounts of generalized anxiety. As described in the previous chapter, post-event processing, recalling and ruminating about upsetting past events contributes to the persistence of (social) anxiety. Another aspect of GAD that tends to be overlooked is the presence of an inflated sense of responsibility. Affected people worry about their own problems, but also worry about other people. They feel responsible for the well-being, safety and health of themselves, their children, relatives and friends, and the resulting anxiety generates worrying.

Some critics complain that GAD is a 'residual category', serving as a receptacle for those disorders which cannot be fitted into one of the existing categories. This objection is extreme, but relative to the other anxiety disorders, all of which are reasonably well specified and have distinguishing features, GAD is untidy.

Barlow argues that GAD is separable because the apprehensiveness which affected people experience is general and covers 'multiple life circumstances' (Barlow 1988: 572). People with GAD are the so-called chronic worriers. In addition, he points out that GAD often persists well after the successful treatment of co-existing anxiety disorders and is therefore best regarded as being relatively independent of the original disorder.

There are important similarities between GAD and social phobia, with the possible exception that people who suffer from the latter disorder manifest their difficulties only or mainly when they are in contact with other people. It is true that several of the worries expressed by people with GAD are social in content (Eysenck 1992), but the chronic worrier is in play at all times and not bound by his or her social context.

In searching for distinctive features of GAD, Dugas *et al.* (1998) concluded that an intolerance for uncertainty is conspicuous, and may be the key variable in this disorder. They advanced a model of GAD that includes maladaptive cognitions, cognitive avoidance, poor problem orientation and intolerance of uncertainty. They gathered support from psychometric studies of the disorder, and obtained satisfactory results from a treatment trial in which the derived CBT focused on the modification of intolerance of uncertainty (Ladouceur *et al.* 2000; Dugas and Robichaud 2007). The effects of the treatment were compared to a waiting-list control condition in a group of 26 GAD patients. After CBT, the intolerance of uncertainty was reduced and broad clinical gains were recorded. The intolerance of uncertainty is a significant concept and may be linked to the striving for safety that is characteristic of anxious people (see below). Uncertainty is no basis for the attainment of feelings of safety. Rather, uncertainty is linked to insecurity.

Persistently high levels of arousal are characteristic of people who suffer from chronic feelings of anxiety and Michael Eysenck's (1992; Eysenck *et al.* 2007) analysis of hypervigilance is particularly relevant to generalized anxiety. He postulates that people with high levels of anxiety engage in rapid scanning of potential threat stimuli ('everything rustles'), followed by a narrowing of attention while the stimuli are being processed. Participants with generalized anxiety disorder show 'attentional biases favouring stimuli that signal threat or danger' (Brewin 1988: 84). Although Eysenck's cogent analysis of hypervigilance is implicitly based on a model of GAD, it is also applicable to other anxiety disorders.

Barlow (1988, 2002) observed that people with GAD engage in a different kind of avoidance behaviour, including forms that are more subtle than the characteristic flight behaviour that one associates with bursts of intense fear. Their avoidance behaviour takes the form of passive avoidance as well as active avoidance; the active avoidance includes excessive precautionary behaviour and repeated requests for reassurance.

Michael Eysenck used GAD as the exemplar when constructing his theory of cognitive vulnerability, emphasizing that particular cognitive biases appear under conditions of stress or high state anxiety.

> The main support for a latent vulnerability factor comes from the interactions between trait and state anxiety or stress . . . it appears that cognitive biases in information processing can be obtained most readily in individuals who possess a cognitive vulnerability factor and who are also in stressed conditions or high in state anxiety.
>
> (Eysenck 1992: 155)

Cognitive biases are also observed in other anxiety disorders, such as social phobias and OCD, and these can be incorporated into Eysenck's concept of cognitive vulnerability.

The search for safety

Generalized anxiety can be viewed as an interplay between signals of threat and signals of safety (Rachman 1984). When the search for safety fails, the perceived threat persists. Affected people consequently engage in persistent, often ill-organized and sometimes frantic searches for safety in order to cope with anticipated threats to family, friends, health and self. Generalized anxiety disorder can be construed as an unsuccessful search for safety (Woody and Rachman 1994), and the behaviour that is typical of GAD is a manifestation of this failure. Their repeated and persistent searches for safety seldom provide lasting satisfaction and they consult widely, seeking reassurance from family, friends and authorities. As in OCD, the relief from reassurance quickly evaporates – 'Are you sure? Are you quite sure?' Affected people go to great lengths to avoid risks, engage in repeated checking, pursue and recommend cautious behaviour, regulate their diet carefully, practise the most hygienic habits and generally engage in over-protective behaviour. They advise their nearest and dearest to take heed and follow their unfailingly cautious style of managing. Despite all of these attempts, they seldom achieve a sense of safety, of calmness or even of contentment, and remain vigilant and over-active.

They perceive a wide range of threats, most of them involving the possibility of future misfortune. Their anxiety is generalized because of the absence or insufficiency of safety procedures or safety signals, and because they overestimate the probability and seriousness of the anticipated aversive events. 'Simply put, the threats are ubiquitous, but there are very few safe places' (Woody and Rachman 1994: 744). The loss, or anticipated loss, of a source of safety, whether it is human or other, will provoke an increase in generalized anxiety and worry, leading to an intensification of the safety-seeking behaviour. The increase in anxiety and vigilance is related to the magnitude of the anticipated or actual loss.

In order to deal with the extraordinary persistence of the anxiety and avoidance behaviour, the addition of a safety-signal perspective is worthwhile. Given that avoidance behaviour, such as that which is observed in all of the anxiety disorders, can persist even in the absence of fear, Gray (1971) made a strong case for the importance of safety signals, defined as the rewarding properties of stimuli which occur in association with the omission of an anticipated punishment. The safety signals exert a powerful influence on the persisting avoidance behaviour, even in the absence of anxiety. The idea is that anxiety generates escape and avoidance behaviour, and a search for safety. Cues that signal the presence of safety reduce the avoidance behaviour. Safety signals de-limit the range and the duration of the threat, and hence of the anxiety. In the presence of an established safety signal, the person is assured of safety from threat in that place at that time. Having achieved a sense of safety, the person can rest and reduce vigilance for a time.

A therapeutic example of the operation of safety signals is provided by one of the tactics used in the treatment of OCD. The patient is trained to take 'off-duty' periods in specified circumstances (Rachman 2003).

> For instance, each evening try to ensure that you are mentally 'off-duty' for one hour; during this off-duty period you are not responsible for planning or carrying out any of your preventive behaviour. Imagine that you are an air-traffic controller, and during your off-duty periods you are not required to keep scanning the screen of aircraft. There is no need to be super vigilant. You are off duty. When traffic controllers take one of their frequent breaks, they can hear the aircraft overhead, and noises from the runway, but they continue reading, conversing, eating – they are off duty.

If a safety signal weakens or disappears, the threats revive or return and hence fear emerges. This sequence has been repeatedly illustrated in research on laboratory animals that have been subjected to aversive stimulation in a confined space. They engage in vigorous, even frantic, searches for a safe spot or a safe time. If they succeed in locating safety, then their agitated and fearful behaviour subsides. If they fail to achieve safety, the frantic search persists. Safe times and safe places are easier to establish if the aversive stimulus is predictable. Conversely, if the anticipated aversive event is unpredictable or irregular, then the establishment of a dependable safety signal is difficult or impossible. If the search for safety fails, the vigilance and over-activity continue and fatigue ensues, perhaps to be followed by longer-term emotional consequences.

Woody and Rachman (1994) give everyday examples of the operation of safety signals that include the behaviour of young children. In the presence of a parent or other safe figure, the child will mix and play contentedly. However, if the mother disappears from view or shows signs of leaving, agitated and anxious behaviour is readily evoked. The close connections between a safe figure and contented activity, and the connection between the absence of a safe figure and anxiety, are constantly present in childhood. These connections are more enduring and tighter if the child is excessively dependent.

Following the safety signal perspective, the similarities between GAD and social phobia become evident. In both of these problems it is difficult for the affected people to achieve continuing safety. People with social anxiety can never know for certain whether others are scrutinizing them and/or being covertly critical. Social interactions are impossible to avoid entirely. They can arise when you least expect them, creating unpredictable sources of anxiety. Likewise, because the anxiety in GAD occurs so often in the absence of specific cues, particularly as the content of the worry often involves future and unknowable events, it is impossible to avoid and difficult to predict. To some extent, the sense of safety provided by interactions with other people is also difficult to predict and control, given the considerable variations in interpersonal interactions. People who are prone to experience persistent generalized anxiety may well be excessively dependent on the sense of security provided by their closest family and friends. If so, interruptions or threats to those relationships are likely to be manifested quickly and prominently in increases in anxiety. Conversely, the strengthening of the personal relationships which convey a sense of safety almost certainly are followed by reductions in the generalized anxiety.

Treatment

As with most anxiety disorders, the treatment of GAD can be psychological or pharmacological, or both. Psychological methods have been developed for managing GAD, and on the prevailing evidence, cognitive behaviour therapy is the favoured method. It is specifically recommended by the UK's National Institute for Health and Clinical Excellence (NICE) Committee and hence is used in the nationwide IAPT psychotherapy service mentioned in the Introduction to the third edition of this book.

Since the early 2000s, a good deal of research on the effects of psychological therapy has been conducted, and several meta-analytic reviews, covering dozens of published studies, have been carried out. The meta-analytic reviews that cover GAD exclusively or in part include Covin et al. (2008), Mitte (2005), Norton and Price (2007), and reviews and evaluations have been published by Barlow (2002), D. A. Clark and Beck (2010), Dugas and Robichaud (2007), Durham et al. (1994), Butler et al. (1991), Chambless and Gillis (1993), Clark (1989), Harvey and Rapee (1995), Ladouceur et al. (2000) and others.

The treatment of GAD is effective, but the contributions of the several components (such as the modification of maladaptive cognitions, development of judicious safety behaviour, extinguishing unadaptive safety behaviour, dealing with the intolerance of uncertainty, inhibiting post-event processing, reducing the inflated sense of responsibility, rescripting of negative images) need to be sorted out. Medications can be helpful in treating anxiety disorders, but at present no specific medication has proven to be of exceptional value in treating GAD.

Summary

Generalized anxiety disorder is excessive anxiety and worry in which the probability and the seriousness of aversive events are exaggerated. The worries generally involve work, finances, loss of status, perceived threats to the health and well-being of oneself, relatives and friends. The anxiety is pervasive, persistent, uncontrollable and usually accompanied by physical signs such as elevated muscle tension, nausea, urinary frequency, and restlessness.

The psychological and physical features of GAD are also encountered in so many other disorders that the distinctiveness of GAD has been questioned. However, GAD can persist even if related anxiety disorders are reduced.

It is suggested that in addition to the fearful component in GAD, there is an important counterbalancing search for safety. Affected people engage in persistent attempts to achieve safety, but when they do not succeed, the restless search continues – the threats are ubiquitous, but there are few safe places.

The treatment of GAD can be psychological or pharmacological or both.

Post-traumatic stress disorder (PTSD) 13

The main features of PTSD are described, and the central psychological processes are analysed. People suffering from PTSD feel under serious current threat, are disturbed by re-experiencing aspects of the trauma, grapple with disturbances of memory, and are excessively aroused. Approaches to therapy are discussed.

It has long been recognized that traumatic events often produce profound psychological effects that are distressing, damaging and long-lasting. In recent years, the effects of trauma (from the Greek word meaning *wound*) have been fully described, and classified as a form of anxiety disorder, namely post-traumatic stress disorder. A full description and analysis of the disorder is provided in a companion volume in this series – *Stress and Trauma* by Patricia A. Resick (2001).

The modern concept, PTSD, arose out of observations of soldiers' reactions to combat, 'war neuroses', and was incorporated into the American Psychiatric Association Classification, the DSM III in 1980, partly in response to the intense concern aroused by the experiences of veterans of the Vietnam War. The inclusion of PTSD as one of the anxiety disorders is justified because two of the major features of anxiety disorders, fear/anxiety and avoidance, are prominent and intense in PTSD. However, PTSD also includes a number of distinctive features, such as disturbances of memory in which affected people remember too much and too little. They re-experience bursts of emotion associated with the trauma, disturbing intrusive thoughts, but also have troubling gaps in their memory for the traumatic events. They are subject to a wide range of associated emotions such as: anger, blame, guilt, detachment, emotional numbing. The features and phenomenology of PTSD are numerous and complex, and some of them, such as flashbacks that can evolve into a temporary detachment from reality, are unique.

An important fact

All analyses and discussions of PTSD must be considered against the very important fact that most people who experience a traumatic event absorb the disturbance naturally (Ehlers and Clark 2000, 2003). The 'vast majority recover without professional help' (McNally *et al.* 2003). This natural recovery is a telling example of the operation of the psychological immune system (Gilbert 2007). Cases of PTSD can be construed as failures of the immune system; the system is inhibited, impeded or impaired.

Why do some people continue to suffer for prolonged periods? The answer given by Ehlers and Clark (2000) is that they continue to feel under *current serious threat*.

The signs and symptoms of PTSD fall into three broad categories. If a person repeatedly 're-experiences' the traumatic event, has disturbances of memory, heightened vigilance and catastrophic misinterpretations of the trauma and its sequelae, it is probable that a post-traumatic stress disorder has developed. During the episodes of re-experiencing, the person feels that the disturbing event is taking place 'here and now', and unsurprisingly, this generates a feeling of serious *current* threat. Disturbances of memory – re-experiencing distressing events and having great difficulty in recalling some significant but puzzling events – are distinctive of PTSD, and not evident in any other anxiety disorders. The disturbances of memory can be involuntary re-experiencing of sensory images of the traumatic event and/or considerable difficulty in attempting to recall aspects of the traumatic event and/or its immediate after-effects.

A second set of signs consists of fear and avoidance of the places or people associated with the the trauma, plus strenuous efforts to avoid thinking about or talking about the trauma or its associations. Persistently increased arousal (including disturbed sleep, nightmares, irritability and anger, startle reactions and extreme vigilance) is a third indicator of PTSD. Detailed accounts of PTSD are given in a number of texts, including those by Barlow (2002), Brewin (2003), Ehlers and Clark (2000), Friedman *et al.* (2007), Resick (2001) and Yule (1999).

There is debate about the definitional details of the concept of PTSD (e.g. what defines and limits a trauma?), and the forthcoming fifth version of the DSM (2013) is likely to introduce changes (Friedman *et al.* 2011). Recently it has been suggested that the concept should be expanded from life-threatening trauma to include negatively *life-altering* traumatic events such as grievous losses, degradation, humiliations, threats of physical assault or sexual abuse, failures of profoundly significant relationships, betrayal (Rachman 2010). Some traumas are enduringly and deeply disturbing even though there is no 'wound', no skin is broken. The life-altering traumatic events are followed by a sense of current threat, fear and avoidance, hyper-arousal and some disturbances of memory – involuntary re-experiencing and difficulties in voluntarily recalling aspects of the traumatic event. Re-experiencing of the trauma that evolves into a temporary detachment from reality is rarely, if ever, encountered. The proposed extension to include life-altering traumatic events may well be contested.

One of the most famous cases in the literature of psychopathology, an exemplar of neurosis that stimulated the development of psychoanalysis, was Freud's case of Anna O. A life-altering grievous bereavement was followed by the emergence of multiple incapacitating neurotic symptoms (Freud 1948, 1949; Jones 1954). She had been suppressing her emotions while caring for her ailing father and the symptoms began to appear shortly after his death (see p. 195 below).

The man described on p. 134 suffered from a host of psychological disturbances for over 20 years after being traumatized by a double betrayal in which he lost his wife, young child and home, all within 24 hours of experiencing a major betrayal.

The distressing case of a man who experienced a delayed onset of PTSD illustrates some of the features of the disorder. An accomplished 52-year-old lawyer had to undergo a series of intrusive and uncomfortable medical procedures, but became so anxious that he decided to avoid essential treatment. To his surprise, for he was a resilient person, he felt shaky, trembled uncontrollably, sweated and felt his heart pounding whenever the subject of his treatment was raised. He began to suffer from recurrent nightmares about his three-year imprisonment in a Japanese prisoner of war camp nearly 30 years earlier, and woke in a terrified state. During the intrusive diagnostic procedures, he experienced vivid flashbacks of his imprisonment and of episodes of the physical torture inflicted on him. His memory of the three years of imprisonment was patchy and he was unable to recall large chunks of time. Fortunately he benefitted from psychological therapy and was able to complete the necessary medical treatment.

A young woman who had been injured in a serious motor collision two years earlier continued to suffer from frighteningly vivid flashbacks of the vehicle approaching her car in the seconds before the crash. She also had nightmares involving collisions and was so frightened of travelling by car that she moved home in order to be close enough to walk to work. She too benefitted from treatment, rather more slowly than the lawyer described above. Her sleep disturbances came to an end and she was able to resume travelling by car, but not without tension.

Post-traumatic stress disorder is unique among the anxiety disorders in that the precipitating event, the trigger, is almost always evident. The site, time and nature of the trauma are known to the victim and to others. The connection between the trauma and the fear is evident and fits in well with the conditioning theory of fear acquisition. There are exceptions, however, especially if the person has experienced numerous or repeated events, such as sexual abuse and/or emotional abuse over a lengthy period.

The wounding, shocking, distressing and damaging events that can produce these profound psychological reactions are dismayingly wide and diverse, ranging from motor vehicle accidents to combat disasters, bereavements, natural disasters, abuse, financial catastrophes, betrayals, medical crises, and so forth. The events and sequelae that have been studied most intensively are sexual trauma, vehicle accidents and combat trauma.

Notwithstanding this disarming list of catastrophes, misfortunes and disasters, most people cope tolerably well and it is only a small minority who develop PTSD or prolonged adverse psychological effects. As mentioned, a satisfactory understanding of PTSD must explain why the majority of people are able to absorb the effects of a 'wounding', are able to cope and persist, and how they succeed in processing the emotions provoked by the trauma.

Explanations

A number of attempts have been made to explain the nature, occurrence and persistence of PTSD, but this is no easy task, partly because of the complex mixture of features of the disorder; and partly because the trauma range from combat disasters to accidents, natural disasters, bereavements, and so forth. It is a tall order to expect an explanation that is sufficiently comprehensive to encompass such a wide array of causes and effects.

The current construals of PTSD range from conditioning theories to cognitive theories, information-processing theories and beyond

(Brewin and Holmes 2003). Three prominent explanations are emotional processing, Brewin's dual representation theory, and the Ehlers–Clark cognitive theory.

Early attempts to explain the effects of trauma emerged from the experimental work of Pavlov (1941). Having shown that dogs develop disturbed behaviour, even severely disturbed behaviour, after one or more exposures to trauma or to unsolvable conflicts, Pavlov introduced a conception of neurosis that was used in the development of a comprehensive theory. The central idea was that the evolution of neurotic behaviour is best understood as a process of conditioning. As a result of an association with traumatic unconditioned stimuli, the animal or person develops abnormal conditioned reactions to previously neutral stimuli (Eysenck and Rachman 1965; Wolpe 1958). These early versions of the conditioning theory of neurosis were essentially theories of traumatic conditioning, somewhat modified by the later inclusion of the possibility that neuroses can be conditioned not only by a traumatic episode, but also by repeated sub-traumatic events. The conditioning theory was influential for a period, until it became evident that fear and neurotic behaviour can also be generated by processes other than conditioning, namely by vicarious experiences and by the transmission of negative information. Aspects of the conditioning theory were later incorporated into the concept of emotional processing, described below.

Emotional processing of traumatic events

The connection between traumatic events and a form of re-experiencing was recognized over a century ago. In one of his famous early papers, Freud said that hysterical patients suffer from 'reminiscences', and postulated that 'their symptoms are the remnants and the memory of symbols of certain traumatic experiences' (Freud 1910: 8). These ideas were richly illustrated by descriptions of the famous case of Anna O, who was treated by Breuer, a colleague of Freud (Jones 1954).

> Anna O's problems originated at the time when she was caring for her sick father and her symptoms could only be regarded as memory symbols of his sickness and death. They corresponded to mourning and a fixation of thoughts of the dead so

short a time after death is certainly not pathological but rather corresponds to normal emotional behaviour.

(Freud 1910: 8)

While caring for her ailing father, the patient had to suppress her strong emotions instead of expressing them in words and actions. As a result of this failure to express the appropriate emotions, she was later handicapped by a range of neurotic symptoms, and according to the account given by Breuer and Freud in various versions (Jones 1954), Anna O derived considerable if transient benefit (Eysenck 1986) from talking to Breuer about her symptoms and their origins – the famous *talking cure*.

The idea that emotional experiences can reverberate for a considerable length of time and continue to disrupt one's behaviour for many years after the event was revived in a modern form when PTSD became a topic of prominence. Indeed, PTSD can be regarded as a prime example of long-term reverberation and re-experiencing of emotional events. For the most part, people do absorb their disturbing emotional experiences satisfactorily. Even in these successful instances, however, it is not uncommon to find that the emotions return, at least in part, after an absence and sometimes to the considerable surprise of the person experiencing the return. In cases of PTSD, flashbacks are a vivid example of such unexpected, puzzling, fragmentary returns of emotional experiences.

Emotional processing is a process in which emotional disturbances are absorbed and decline to the extent that other experiences and behaviour can proceed without disruption (Rachman 1980). Anna O. was treated by Breuer and overcame most of the disturbing symptoms. She seemingly resumed a fruitful way of life for a period of time, but the long-term outcome may have been less than satisfactory (Eysenck 1986).

If the emotional disturbance is *not* absorbed satisfactorily, some troubling signs become evident. They are likely to recur intermittently, and may be direct and obvious, or indirect and subtle. The central and indispensable index of unsatisfactory emotional processing is the persistence or return of intrusive signs of emotional activity such as obsessions, flashbacks, nightmares, fears, pressure of talk, expressions or experiences of emotions that are out of context or out of proportion, maladaptive avoidance. The indirect signs include restlessness, difficulties in concentrating, irritability and other signs of heightened arousal that are characteristic of PTSD.

It is easier to come to grips with failures of emotional processing than with successes. Successful processing can be gauged from the person's ability to talk about, see, listen to, or be reminded of the significant events without experiencing distress or disruptions. All three of the major features of the current diagnostic basis for PTSD appear in the model of emotional processing; namely, heightened arousal, abnormal avoidance and re-experiencing. The concept of emotional processing addresses the mighty fact that the large majority of people do cope, do 'recover' from trauma. But the model, especially as applied to PTSD, makes insufficient allowance for cognitions, and is relatively silent about the memorial disturbances that are a feature of PTSD (Rachman 2001).

The therapeutic implications of the concept are that the transformation or neutralization of emotion-provoking stimuli or memories is facilitated by promoting adaptive and benign cognitions, by repeated controlled presentations, and by the planned presentation of disturbing stimuli in a progressive sequence for certain minimal durations, preferably during low levels of arousal. The transformation, the satisfactory processing, will be impeded by the persistence of maladaptive cognitions, negative appraisals, cognitive biases, unduly brief presentations, intense and unpredictable stimulation, or by a state of elevated arousal.

An elaborated analysis of the therapeutic implications of emotional processing was proposed by Foa and Kozak (1986) as a rationale for exposure treatments, especially a method known as 'exposure and response prevention'. Their analysis has some stimulating aspects, but erroneously assumes that in order for fear reduction to occur, the person's 'fear structures' must be activated. The notion of 'fear structures', the core of their analysis, is not free of definitional and conceptual problems. Moreover, fears can reduced without activating the putative fear structures (Rachman 1990). Fears can be reduced by the provision of information, by observing non-fearful behaviour, by acquiring self-efficacious behaviour (Bandura 1977), by cognitive therapy (e.g. Whittal *et al.* 2010), by anxiolytic drugs and even after taking placebos. In most forms of cognitive behaviour therapy for anxiety disorders, much or most of the effort goes into cognitive analysis and modification. The activation of fear in or between therapy sessions is not uncommon, but it is not necessary for fear reduction (e.g. in the treatment of obsessions, panic disorders). Examples of fear reduction taking place without the evocation of the fear structures are occasionally dismissed on the grounds that some marginal or fragmentary exposure might have occurred, but this resort makes the hypothesis untestable. The deliberate, planned, repeated 'exposures' used in the treatment of some anxiety disorders are not marginal, brief or fragmentary (Powers and Emmelkamp 2010).

Dual representation theory

In contrast to the model of emotional processing, the centrepiece of Brewin's (2001, 2003, 2011) theory of dual representation is memory and its vicissitudes. He postulates that the pathological features of PTSD arise when memories of the trauma become dissociated from the ordinary memory system and suggests that 'recovery involves transforming them into ordinary or narrative memories' (Brewin and Holmes 2003: 356). There are, it is proposed, at least two systems of memory, and information about trauma is represented primarily in one of the two systems. 'Ordinary memories' are mediated by a 'verbally accessible memory' (VAM) system; but memories of trauma are represented in a different system, entitled the 'situationally accessible memory' (SAM) system. The memories are thought to be simultaneously represented in both systems (Brewin 2003).

The two systems of memory are differentially affected by extreme levels of stress (Brewin 2001, 2011). The situationally accessible memory system is triggered involuntarily by cues associated with the trauma and is best illustrated by the operation of flashbacks. These intrusive memories are more emotional and vivid than ordinary memories, and rarely accessible by verbal means. They are poorly integrated into the person's autobiographical knowledge and are difficult for the person to describe. It is argued that the emotions which accompany SAM memories are confined to the primary emotions that were experienced during the trauma. The ordinary memory system, the VAM, consists of oral or written narratives that can be retrieved at will and are well integrated with the person's autobiographical knowledge. Broadly, the distinction between these two memory systems is that between a conscious memorial system and one that is ordinarily outside of conscious manipulation, one that is not easily accessible. Brewin (2001) raised the original idea that flashbacks, re-experiencing and related phenomena may facilitate the transfer of information from the situational memory system to the more accessible verbal system.

Situationally accessible memories present difficult problems because they are disturbing and intrusive, but not accessible. In order to reduce the negative emotions that are produced by cognitive appraisals of the trauma and its consequences (the major aim of cognitive therapy), conscious analysis and re-analysis may be insufficient. It is implied that a purely cognitive form of therapy would leave relatively untouched the verbally inaccessible but powerful SAM memories.

The emphasis on the important memorial disturbances of PTSD is an original approach, and draws strength from its connections with cognitive science and neuropsychology (verbally accessible memories are said to be 'hippocampally-dependent'). Aspects of Brewin's theory are incorporated in the cognitive theory.

A cognitive theory

The cognitive theory of PTSD proposed by Ehlers and Clark (2000) opens with the central question of why post-traumatic signs and symptoms persist. Why are these disturbances not processed? Given that the large majority of people satisfactorily absorb the effects of traumatic events naturally, Ehlers and Clark address the core question of why the important minority fail to do so.

The signs and symptoms persist because the person feels under *current serious threat*. 'PTSD occurs only if individuals process the traumatic event and/or its sequelae in a way that produces a sense of serious current threat' (Ehlers and Clark 2000: n.p.). The sense of current threat 'arises and persists as a consequence of: (1) excessively negative appraisals of the trauma and/or its sequelae; and (2) a disturbance of autobiographical memory characterized by poor elaboration and contextualization, strong associative memory and strong perceptual priming' (Ehlers and Clark 2000: n.p.).

It is proposed that incomplete or failed processing of the traumatic experience leaves the affected person feeling that they are under an external threat to their safety, or an internal threat to their stability, functioning and future. Two mechanisms contribute to this threat: negative appraisals of the event and its consequences; plus the nature of the memory of the trauma itself. 'Individual differences in the appraisal of the trauma' and individual differences 'in the nature of the memory for the event and its link to other autobiographical memories' combine to produce a sense of serious current threat (Ehlers and Clark 2000: 320). The feeling of a current threat is accompanied by intrusive images, thoughts or memories, distressing re-experiencing of events, heightened arousal and fear. These events (e.g. intrusive image/s, flashbacks, etc) and vivid re-experiencing are interpreted by affected people to mean that they are under current threat. Examples of the negative appraisals that might trigger or maintain a feeling of current threat include the following: 'I have been permanently damaged', 'I am ruined', 'I am a dead person', 'My brain is damaged', 'I feel in danger; nowhere is safe', 'I will never get over this', 'I will lose my children'.

Cognitions of this character are so distressing that the person attempts to block the thoughts or images, and even takes steps to avoid any threatening cues, including people, that might evoke or exacerbate the negative appraisals. Attempts to avoid the threatening cues – whether they are internal or external in nature – are self-defeating and tend to sustain the disorder.

Dealing with the paradox of PTSD memories, remembering too much and remembering too little, Ehlers and Clark (2000) proposed that the victim has difficulty in recalling details of the event because of their fragmented and poorly organized memory of the trauma. They used the metaphor of trying to remember the contents of a cluttered, muddled mess in one's cupboard. Recall is greatly assisted when the items are tidied, sorted and arranged in an understandable system. During therapy, the fragmented, muddled and poorly connected memories of the trauma are sorted, organized and re-assessed.

Involuntarily triggered intrusive memories are poorly elaborated and difficult to integrate with normal autobiographical memories. The fragmented, involuntary memories tend to be vivid, are certainly intrusive, and often intensely emotional. They also have a puzzling quality because they are so poorly elaborated and loosely connected to the person's normal bank of autobiographical memories. These qualities are likely to generate or reinforce the person's negative appraisals about the traumatic event: 'My disturbed memory is out of control; it means that I have incurred serious and permanent psychological damage.'

The theory is skilfully used to account for a number of features of PTSD, such as cases of delayed onset PTSD, a feeling of being locked into the past, a pervasive sense of doom, an avoidance of and dislike of talking or thinking about the trauma.

The treatment derived from the theory consists of three main elements. First, the trauma memory needs to be elaborated and 'integrated into the context of the individual's preceding and subsequent experience in order to reduce intrusive reexperiencing' (Ehlers and Clark 2000: 335). Second, the negative and maladaptive appraisals of the trauma and its consequences need to be analysed and modified. Third, the unadaptive methods that the person has adopted to reduce or avoid the stress need to be identified and extinguished. These include the avoidance of people and places, the many and varied attempts to refrain from thinking about the trauma and its associations, and the unadaptive avoidance of talking about the trauma and its consequences. It is this last tendency that accounts for the fact that patients recommended for treatment are not the most dependable and regular attenders at the arranged sessions, some of which can be extremely disturbing. The controlled and graded re-exposure to the trauma or its associations can play an important part in treatment, and often this is supplemented by the restorative use of modified images to overcome the vivid, emotional PTSD images. The power and significance of emotional images is recognized (Hackmann *et al.* 2011; Holmes and Mathews 2010) and the potential value of rescripting the disturbing images is discussed by Arntz (2012).

The results produced by this treatment are most encouraging, and need to be consolidated (Brewin 2003; Bisson *et al.* 2007; Clark *et al.* 2006; Ehlers and Clark 2000; Ehlers *et al.* 2003; Friedman *et al.* 2007). The therapy derives credibility and strength from the fact that it is derived from a coherent theory. In addition, there is a considerable amount of evidence for the efficacy of related, earlier forms of this type of treatment in dealing with other types of anxiety disorder (Marks *et al.* 1998; Resick 2001; Barlow 2002; Harvey *et al.* 2003; Whittal *et al.*, 2010).

It has been established that successful treatment is associated with the reduction of negative appraisals, better integration of trauma-related memories, and changes in self-defeating safety behaviour (Gillespie *et al.* 2002; Halligan *et al.* 2003). Incisive investigations of the core concept of the theory, that affected people feel under current serious threat, are planned. Does the outcome of therapy depend on a significant reduction of the sense of current threat? Are the reductions in current threat produced by changing the negative appraisals, integrating the disturbing trauma memories, and overcoming self-defeating safety behaviour, or by all of these mechanisms?

Gillespie *et al.* (2002) attempted to apply the treatment techniques in a community setting. Ninety-one people who developed PTSD after experiencing the bomb explosion that took place in Omagh, Northern Ireland, in 1998, were treated with an abbreviated form of the treatment. The therapists were given training in these specialist procedures, and the participants received an average of eight sessions. 'Significant and substantial improvements' were achieved, and the degree of improvement was comparable to that reported in research trials.

The expectation that de-briefing after a traumatic event is beneficial has not been confirmed (Ehlers and Clark 2003; Mayou *et al.* 2000; McNally *et al.* 2003), and it may even have adverse effects. It is possible that de-briefing sessions provided too soon after the traumatic event may leave the sense of serious current threat untouched, particularly if it takes place in or close to the traumatic surrounding and/or in the presence of other survivors who are still in great distress.

Given the widening of the concept of PTSD from traumas that are life-threatening to now include traumas that are life-altering, cognitive behaviour therapy will develop further. The life-altering traumas involve negative, even catastrophic appraisals, self-defeating safety behaviour, and some disturbances of memory. The occurrence of mental defeat, in which the person experiences a loss of psychological autonomy, self-denigration, numbing, helplessness, diminished self-efficacy, also needs to be addressed.

The Ehlers–Clark theory overlaps to some extent with each of the two other approaches – emotional processing and the dual representation theory. The concept of emotional processing is an attempt to construe the responses to trauma as a normal psychological process, a function of the psycho-immune system, which occasionally fails. The signs of PTSD are seen as a disruption of the way in which people naturally process emotional material. It is intended to assist in understanding how the large majority of people succeed in coping with traumatic events, and to set out the conditions under which this normal process is disrupted. It provides a platform for specifiable techniques that can help to promote and sustain ordinary emotional processing.

The focus of the dual representation theory is on the disturbances of memory and emphasizes the differences between PTSD re-experiencing, flashbacks and all, and the recall of ordinary events. The theory is broadened by making connections with cognitive science and neuropsychology, and in this way prepares the ground for expansion. It does not address the full range of PTSD signs and symptoms and would benefit from an infusion of more clinically relevant cognitive concepts and analyses.

The cognitive theory has the widest explanatory value of current psychological accounts of PTSD. The introduction of the idea that sufferers feel under current serious threat is an important addition, and helps to explain why the disorder persists. The links between maladaptive appraisals of the threat and memory disturbances are original and stimulating. The model provides the foundation for a coherent, theory-driven form of treatment. Unravelling the nature of the fascinating, paradoxical memory disturbances, their interplay, and the connections with the maladaptive appraisals, invites a great deal of research.

Eye-movement desensitization and reprocessing (EMDR)

The originator of the EMDR technique, Shapiro (1995), observed that she was able to overcome some of her troubling thoughts by repeatedly moving her eyes from left to right, and so encouraged, attempted to use the method of rapid eye movements with some of her patients. Sufferers were asked to form images associated with the trauma, and then engage in rapid eye movements from side to side. She claimed remarkable success in treating people suffering from trauma, and the early case descriptions by Shapiro and her trainees aroused considerable attention.

However, despite the early claims of therapeutic efficacy (e.g. Acierno and Cahill 1999; Shapiro 1995), EMDR aroused scepticism. Evidence that failed to support the claims of therapeutic efficacy was published (e.g. Herbert *et al.* 2000; Lohr *et al.* 1999; McNally 1999; Barlow 2002; Devilly and Spence 1999), and doubts were expressed about Shapiro's unconvincing rationale. Importantly, the element of the treatment that was said to be crucial, rapid eye movements, was shown to be dispensable (Herbert *et al.* 2000; McNally 1999). Other types of repetitive movements were said to be as effective as rapid eye movements. Eye-movement desensitization and reprocessing was criticized for lacking a theoretical basis (Barlow 2002).

Notwithstanding the criticisms, in numerous studies EMDR has now been shown to be effective and the National Institute for Health and Clinical Excellence (NICE) in the UK added it to their recommended treatments for PTSD.

For a period, EMDR was a therapeutic effect in search of an explanation. However, van den Hout and his colleagues (van den Hout and Engelhard 2010, 2011; Engelhard *et al.* 2011) carried out a programme of neat experiments to test their hypothesis that making rapid eye movements during the recall of traumatic memories is 'beneficial because they tax working memory' (van den Hout and Engelhard. 2011: 92). The vividness and emotionality of the images are reduced. For example, the effects of doing mental arithmetic during the recall of traumatic memories produced effects comparable to EMDR, but listening to non-taxing binaural beeps during such recall produced only weak effects. Carrying out a task that involves working memory while recalling aversive memories is effective; carrying out tasks that involve working memory only minimally or not at all is not effective. This well-conceived line of research is making impressive progress and may well provide the missing rationale.

The main hypothesis might additionally promote a fruitful reconsideration of Wolpe's (1958) original success with his anxiety-reducing technique, systematic desensitization, in which anxious patients were asked to form a graded series of images that evoked anxiety. The feelings of anxiety were then inhibited by inducing progressive relaxation. Conceivably, the act of systematically carrying out the relaxation exercises involved working memory.

The working memory hypothesis advanced by Marcel van den Hout, Engelhard and colleagues (van den Hout and Engelhard 2010, 2011; van den Hout 2012) may also throw light on the remarkable distress-reducing effects of the technique of rescripting negative images, described in this chapter and Chapter 10.

Summary

If a person feels under serious current threat for a prolonged period after an actual or threatened death or injury, and repeatedly re-experiences the event in the 'here and now', and suffers from disturbances of memory and elevated arousal, then the possibility of PTSD is considered. The disorder is generated by a life-threatening or negatively life-altering event. Three psychological models of PTSD are described and assessed: emotional processing, dual representation theory and the cognitive theory. The therapy derived from the cognitive model has produced encouraging results and is under continuing evaluation.

Some concluding remarks

The phenomenon of anxiety is exceedingly interesting and psychologists have devoted a great deal of thought to the subject and conducted many investigations. The focus of the work is on the distressing, disturbing and disabling qualities of anxiety. It is an unpleasant negative emotion and much effort goes into overcoming anxiety and preventing it.

However, anxiety is not always negative. It is stimulating and not always in a negative way. Anxiety also stimulates creative activity, small and large. It stimulates attempts to find means and methods of controlling anxiety, some of them ingenious. Anxiety also stimulates creative artistic activities from superb writings to mighty operas.

Suggested reading

There are several excellent accounts of 'anxiety and its disorders' and of methods for overcoming these difficulties. These advanced texts include the comprehensive and authoritative book by D. A. Clark and A. T. Beck (2010) *Cognitive Therapy of Anxiety Disorders*, Barlow's (2002) classic *Anxiety and its Disorders*, Brewin's (2003) *Post-Traumatic Stress Disorder:Malady or Myth?*, D. A. Clark's (2004) *Cognitive Therapy for OCD*, D. M. Clark and C. Fairburn's (1997) *Science and Practice of Cognitive Behaviour Therapy*, Craske's (1999) *Anxiety Disorders*, Friedman, Keane and Resick's (2007) *Handbook of PTSD: Science and Practice*, Hawton, Salkovskis, Kirk and D. M. Clark's (1989) *Cognitive Behaviour Therapy for Psychiatric Problems*, Heimberg, Liebowitz, Hope and Schneier's (1995) *Social Phobia*, Resick's (2001) *Stress and Trauma*, among others. Also, Franz Kafka's ([1925] 1977) *The Trial*.

The emphasis of the present book is on anxiety as a psychological phenomenon.

References

Abraham, K. (1927). *Selected papers*. London: Hogarth Press.

Abramowitz, J. S. and Moore, E. L. (2007). An experimental analysis of hypochondriasis. *Behaviour Research and Therapy*, 45, 413–424.

Abramowitz, J. S., Olatunji, B. O. and Deacon, B. J. (2007). Health anxiety, hypochondriasis, and the anxiety disorders. *Behavior Therapy*, 38, 86–94.

Abramovitz, J., Wheaton, M. and Storch, E.(2008). The status of hoarding as a symptom of OCD. *Behaviour Research and Therapy*, 48, 1026–1033.

Acierno, R. and Cahill, S. (Eds) (1999). Advances in conceptualization and research into the efficacy and mechanism of EMDR. *Journal of Anxiety Disorders*, 13, 1–236.

Acierno, R. E., Hersen, M. and Van Hasselt, V. B. (1993). Interventions for panic disorder: A critical review of the literature. *Clinical Psychology Review*, 13, 561–578.

Agras, S., Sylvester, D. and Oliveau, D. (1969). The epidemiology of common fears and phobias. *Comprehensive Psychiatry*, 10, 151–156.

Akhtar, S., Wig, N., Verma, N., Pershad, D. and Verma, S. K. (1975). A phenomenological analysis of symptoms in obsessive-compulsive neurosis. *British Journal of Psychiatry*, 127, 342–348.

Alberts, N., Sharpe, D., Kehler, M. and Hadjistavropolous, H. (2011). Health anxiety: A comparison of the latent structure in medical and non-medical samples. *Journal of Anxiety Disorders*, 25, 612–614.

Arntz, A., Rauner, M. and van den Hout, M. (1995). 'If I feel anxious, there must be danger': *Ex-consequentia* reasoning in inferring danger in anxiety disorders. *Behaviour Research and Therapy*, 33, 917–925.

Arntz, A. (2012). Imagery rescripting as a therapeutic technique. *Journal of Experimental Psychopathology*, 3, 189–208.

Arrindell, W., Cox, B., van der Ende, J. and Kwee, M. (1995). Phobic dimensions-II. Cross-national confirmation of the multidimensional structure underlying the Mobility Inventory. *Behaviour Research and Therapy*, 33, 711–724.

Asmundson, G. J. G., Taylor, S. and Cox, B. J. (Eds) (2001). *Health anxiety: Clinical and research perspectives on hypochondriasis and related conditions*. Chichester and New York: Wiley.

Austin, D. and Richards, J. (2001). The catastrophic misinterpretation model of panic disorder. *Behaviour Research and Therapy*, 39, 1277–1292.

Avia, M. D., Ruiz, M. A., Olivares, M. E., Crespo, M., Guisado, A. B., Sanchez, A. et al. (1996). The meaning of psychological symptoms: Effectiveness of a group intervention with hypochondriacal patients. *Behaviour Research and Therapy*, 34, 23–31.

Aylward, E. H., Harris, G. J., Hoehn-Saric, R., Barta, P. E., Machlin, S. R. and Pearlson, P. D. (1996). Normal caudate nucleus in obsessive-compulsive disorder assessed by quantitative neuroimaging. *Archives of General Psychiatry*, 53, 577–584.

Baker, T. B., Cannon, D. S., Tiffany, S. T. and Gino, A. (1984). Cardiac response as an index of the effect of aversion therapy. *Behaviour Research and Therapy*, 22, 403–411.

Ballenger, J. McDonald, S., Noyes, R., Rickels, K., Sussman, N. and Woods, S. (1988). Alprazolam in panic disorder and agoraphobia: Results from a multicenter trial. Efficacy in short-term treatment. *Archives of General Psychiatry*, 45, 413–422.

Bancroft, J. (1989). *Human sexuality and its problems* (2nd ed.). Edinburgh: Churchill-Livingstone.

Bandura, A. (1969). *The principles of behavior modification*. New York: Holt, Rinehart and Winston.

Bandura, A. (1977). *Social learning theory*. New York: Prentice Hall.

Bandura, A., Jeffery, R. and Wright, C. (1974). Efficacy of participant modeling as a function of response aids. *Journal of Abnormal Psychology*, 83, 56–64.

Barlow, D., Gorman, J. M., Shear, M. K. and Woods, S. W. (2000). Cognitive behavior therapy, imipramine, and their combination for panic disorder: A randomized controlled trial. *Journal of the American Medical Association*, 283, 2529–2536.

Barlow, D. H. (1985). The dimensions of anxiety disorders. In A. H. Tuma and J. D. Maser (Eds), *Anxiety and the anxiety disorders*. Hillsdale, NJ: Erlbaum.

Barlow, D. H. (1988). *Anxiety and its disorders: The nature and treatment of anxiety and panic*. New York: Guilford Press.

Barlow, D. H. (2002). *Anxiety and its disorders* (2nd ed.). New York: Guilford Press.

Barlow, D. H. and Craske, M. (1988). The phenomenology of panic. In S. Rachman and J. Maser (Eds), *Panic: Psychological perspectives*. Hillsdale, NJ: Erlbaum, pp. 11–36.

Barsky, A. J. and Ahern, D. K. (2004). Cognitive behavior therapy for hypochondriasis. *Journal of the American Medical Association*, 291, 1464–1470.

Barsky, A. J., Ahern, D. K., Bailey, E. D., Saintfort, R., Liu, E. B. and Peekna, H. M. (2001). Hypochondriacal patients' appraisal of health and physical risks. *American Journal of Psychiatry*, 158, 783–787.

Beck, A. T. (1976). *Cognitive therapy and the emotional disorders*. New York: New American Library.

Beck, A. T. (2005). The current status of cognitive therapy: A 40-year retrospective. *Archives of General Psychiatry*, 62, 953–959.

Beck, A. T. and Rush, A. J. (1985). A cognitive model of anxiety formation and anxiety resolution. Special Issue: Stress and anxiety. *Issues in Mental Health Nursing*, 7, 349–365.

Beck, A. T. and Clark, D. A. (1997). An information processing model of anxiety. *Behaviour Research and Therapy*, 35, 49–58.

Beck, A. T. and Emery, G. (with Greenberg, R.) (1985). *Anxiety disorders and phobias: A cognitive perspective*. New York: Basic Books.

Beech, H. R. (1971). Ritualistic activity in obsessional patients. *Journal of Psychosomatic Research*, 17, 417–422.

Beech, H. R. (Ed.) (1974). *Obsessional states.* London: Methuen.

Bisson, J., Ehlers, A., Mathews, R., Pillay, S. and Richards, D. (2007). Psychological treatments for chronic PTSD: Systematic review and meta-analysis. *British Journal of Psychiatry*, 97, 97–104.

Bögels, S. and Mansell, W. (2004). Attention processes in the maintenance and treatment of social phobia. *Clinical Psychology Review*, 24, 827–856.

Booth, R. and Rachman, S. (1992). The reduction of claustrophobia: I. *Behaviour Research and Therapy*, 30, 207–221.

Boring, E. G. (1991). The history of introspection: II (Trans. A. V. Roshchin and I. V. Tverdovskiy). *Vestnik Moskovskogo Universiteta – Seriya 14: Psikhologiya*, 3, 54–63.

Bower, G. H. (1981). Mood and memory. *American Psychologist*, 36, 129–148.

Bradley, B. P., Mogg, K. and Williams, R. (1995). Implicit and explicit memory for emotion-congruent information in clinical depression and anxiety. *Behaviour Research and Therapy*, 33, 755–770.

Bregman, E. (1934). An attempt to modify the emotional attitudes of infants by the conditioned response technique. *Journal of Genetic Psychology*, 45, 169–196.

Brewin, C. (2001). A cognitive neuroscience account of PTSD and its treatment. *Behaviour Research and Therapy*, 39, 373–393.

Brewin, C. (2003). *Post-traumatic stress disorder: Malady or myth?* London: Yale University Press.

Brewin, C. (2011). The nature and significance of memory disturbances in PTSD. *Annual Review of Clinical Psychology*, 7, 203–227.

Brewin, C. and Holmes, E. (2003). Psychological theories of PTSD. *Clinical Psychology Review*, 23, 339–376.

Brewin, C. R. (1988). *Cognitive foundations of clinical psychology.* London: Erlbaum.

Brewin, C. R. (1996). Theoretical foundations of cognitive-behavior therapy for anxiety and depression. *Annual Review of Psychology*, 47, 33–57.

Brewin, C. R., Gregory, J., Lipton, M. and Burgess, N. (2010). Intrusive images in psychological disorders. *Psychological Review*, 117, 210–232.

Broadbent, D. E. (1958). *Perception and communication.* New York: Pergamon Press.

Broadbent, D. E. (1971). *Decision and stress.* London: Academic Press.

Brown, T. (1996). Validity of the DSM-III-R and DSM-IV classification systems for anxiety disorders. In R. Rapee (Ed.), *Current controversies in anxiety disorders.* New York: Guilford Press, pp. 21–45.

Brozovich, F. and Heimberg, R. (2008). An analysis of post-event processing in social anxiety disorders. *Clinical Psychology Review*, 28, 891–903.

Bunyan, J. ([1678] 1947). *An anthology* (edited by J. Stanley). London: Eyre and Spottiswoode.

Burish, T. G. and Carey, M. P. (1986). Conditioned aversive responses in cancer chemotherapy patients: Theoretical and developmental analysis. *Journal of Consulting and Clinical Psychology*, 54, 593–600.

Burstow, B. (2005). A critique of PTSD and the DSM. *Journal of Humanistic Psychology*, 45, 429–445.

Butler, G., Fennell, M., Robson, P. and Gelder, M. (1991). A comparison of behavior therapy and cognitive behavior therapy in the treatment of generalised anxiety disorder. *Journal of Consulting and Clinical Psychology*, 59, 167–175.

Cairns, E. and Wilson, R. (1984). The impact of political violence on mild psychiatric morbidity in Northern Ireland. *British Journal of Psychiatry*, 145, 631–635.

Carter, M. M., Hollon, S. D., Carson, R. and Shelton, R. C. (1995). Effects of a safe person on induced stress following a biological challenge in panic disorder with agoraphobia. *Journal of Abnormal Psychology*, 104, 156–163.

Cella, D. F., Pratt, A. and Holland, J. C. (1986). Persistent anticipatory nausea, vomiting and anxiety in cured Hodgkin's disease patients after completion of chemotherapy. *American Journal of Psychiatry*, 143, 641–643.

Ceschi, G., van der Linden, M., Dunker, D., Perroud, A. and Bredarts, R. (2003). Further exploration of memory bias in compulsive washers. *Behaviour Research and Therapy*, 41, 737–748.

Chambless, D. and Gillis, M. (1993). Cognitive therapy of anxiety disorders. Special section: Recent developments in cognitive and constructivist psychotherapies. *Journal of Consulting and Clinical Psychology*, 61, 248–260.

Chambless, D. and Hope, D. (1996). Cognitive approaches to the psychopathology and treatment of social phobia. In P. Salkovskis (Ed.), *The frontiers of cognitive therapy*. New York: Guilford Press, pp. 345–382.

Claparède, M. (1911). Recognition et moiité. *Archives de Psychologie Genève*, 11, 79–90.

Clark, D. A. (2003). *Controlling obsessions and compulsions*. New York: Guilford Press.

Clark, D. A. (2004). *Cognitive behavior therapy for OCD*. New York: Guilford Press.

Clark, D. A. and Beck, A. T. (2010). *Cognitive therapy of anxiety disorders*. New York: Guilford Press.

Clark, D. M. (1986). A cognitive approach to panic. *Behaviour Research and Therapy*, 24, 461–470.

Clark, D. M. (1987). A cognitive approach to panic: Theory and data. In *Proceedings of the 140th Annual Meeting of the American Psychiatric Association*: Chicago, IL: APA.

Clark, D. M. (1988). A cognitive model of panic attacks. In S. Rachman and J. Maser (Eds), *Panic: Psychological perspectives*. Hillsdale, NJ: Erlbaum, pp. 71–90.

Clark, D. M. (1989). Anxiety states: Panic and generalised anxiety. In K. Hawton, P. Salkovskis, J. Kirk and D. M. Clark (Eds), *Cognitive behaviour therapy for psychiatric problems: A practical guide*. Oxford: Oxford Medical Publications, pp. 52–96.

Clark, D. M. (1996). Panic disorder: From theory to therapy. In P. Salkovskis (Ed.), *The frontiers of cognitive therapy*. New York: Guilford Press.

Clark, D. M. (1997). Panic disorder and social phobia. In D. M. Clark and C. Fairburn (Eds), *Science and practice of cognitive behaviour therapy*. Oxford: Oxford University Press.

Clark, D. M. (1999). Anxiety disorders: why they persist and how to treat them. *Behaviour Research and Therapy*, 37, Supplement 1, S5–S27.

Clark, D. M. (2012). The English Improving Access to Psychological Therapies (IAPT) program. In R. McHugh and D. Barlow (Eds), *Dissemination and implementation of evidence-based psychological interventions*. Oxford: Oxford University.Press, pp. 61–77.

Clark, D. M. and Wells, A. (1995). A cognitive model of social phobia. In D. M. Clark and A. Wells (Eds), *Social phobia: Diagnosis, assessment and treatment*. New York: Guilford Press.

Clark, D. M. and Fairburn, C. (Eds) (1997). *Science and practice of cognitive behaviour therapy*. Oxford: Oxford University Press.

Clark, D. M. and McManus, F. (2002). Information processing in social phobias. *Biological Psychiatry*, 51, 92–100.

Clark, D. M. and Ehlers, A. (2004). Post-traumatic stress disorder: From cognitive theory to therapy. In R. L. Leahy (Ed.), *Contemporary cognitive therapy: Theory, research and practice*. New York: Guilford Press, pp. 141–160.

Clark, D. M., Salkovskis, P., Hackmann, A., Middleton, H., Anastasiades, P. and Gelder, M. (1994). A comparison of cognitive therapy, applied relaxation, and imipramine in the treatment of panic disorder. *British Journal of Psychiatry*, 165(4), 557–559.

Clark, D. M., Salkovskis, P. M., Hackmann, A., Wells, A., Fennell, M., Ludgate, J. *et al.* (1998). Two psychological treatments for hypochondriasis: A randomised controlled trial. *British Journal of Psychiatry*, 173, 218–225.

Clark, D. M., Ehlers, A., Hackmann, A., McManus, F., Fennell, M., Grey, N., Waddington, L. and Wild, J. (2006). Cognitive therapy versus exposure plus applied relaxation in social phobia: A randomized controlled trial. *Journal of Consulting Clinical Psychology*, 74, 565–578.

Cloitre, M., Heimberg, R. G., Holt, C. S. and Liebowitz, M. R. (1992). Reaction time to threat stimuli in panic disorder and social phobia. *Behaviour Research and Therapy*, 30, 609–617.

Coles, M. and Heimberg, R. (2002). Memory biases in the anxiety disorders. *Clinical Psychology Review*, 22, 587–627.

Constans, J. I., Foa, E. B., Franklin, M. E. and Mathews, A. (1995). Memory for actual and imagined events in OC checkers. *Behaviour Research and Therapy*, 33, 665–671.

Cook, E. W., Melamed, B. G., Cuthbert, B. N., McNeil, D. W. and Lang, P. J. (1988). Emotional imagery and the differential diagnosis of anxiety. *Journal of Consulting and Clinical Psychology*, 56, 734–740.

Costello, C. G. (1982). Fears and phobias in women: A community study. *Journal of Abnormal Psychology*, 91, 280–286.

Coughtrey, A., Shafran, R. and Lee, M. (2013, in press). Mental contamination in OCD.

Covin, R. *et al.* (2008). A meta-analysis of CBT for pathological worry among clients with GAD. *Journal of Anxiety Disorders*, 22, 108–116.

Craske, M. (1999). *Anxiety disorders.* Boulder, CO: Westview Press.

Craske, M. (2003). *Origins of phobias and anxiety disorders.* Amsterdam: Elsevier Press.

Craske, M. and Pontillo, D. (2001). Cognitive biases in anxiety disorders and their effect on cognitive treatment. *Bulletin of the Menninger Clinic*, 65, 58–77.

Craske, M. *et al.* (2005). Cognitive behaviour therapy for nocturnal panic. *Behavior Therapy*, 22, 43–54.

Craske, M. G., Sanderson, W. C. and Barlow, D. H. (1987). The relationships among panic, fear and avoidance. *Journal of Anxiety Disorders*, 1, 153–160.

Creed, F. and Barsky, A. (2004). A systematic review of the epidemiology of somatisation and hypochondriasis. *Journal of Psychosomatic Research*, 56, 391–408.

Crews, F. C. (Ed.) (1998). *Unauthorized Freud.* New York: Viking Press.

Curtis, R. C. and Miller, K. (1986). Believing another likes or dislikes you: Behaviors making the beliefs come true. *Journal of Personality and Social Psychology*, 51, 284–290.

Dalgleish, T. (1994). The relationship between anxiety and memory biases for material that has been selectively processed in a prior task. *Behaviour Research and Therapy*, 32, 227–231.

Dannahy, L. and Stopa, L. (2007). Post-event processing in social anxiety. *Behaviour Research and Therapy*, 45, 1207–1209.

Davey, G. (1988). Dental phobias and anxieties. *Behaviour Research and Therapy*, 27, 51–58.

Deacon, B. J. and Abramowitz, J. S. (2008). Is hypochondriasis related to OCD, panic disorder, or both? An empirical evaluation. *Journal of Cognitive Psychotherapy*, 22, 115–127.

Deffenbacher, J. L. (1978). Worry, emotionality and task-generated interference in test anxiety: An empirical test of attentional theory. *Journal of Educational Psychology*, 70, 248–254.

de Silva, P. and Rachman, S. (1984). Does escape behaviour strengthen agoraphobic avoidance? A preliminary study. *Behaviour Research and Therapy*, 22, 87–91.

de Silva, P. and Rachman, S. (2009). *Obsessive–compulsive disorder: The facts*. Oxford: Oxford University Press.

Devilly, G. and Spence, S. (1999). The relative efficacy and treatment distress of EMDR and a cognitive-behavior treatment protocol in the amelioration of PTSD. *Journal of Anxiety Disorders*, 13, 131–157.

Dickinson, A. (1987). Animal conditioning and learning theory. In H. J. Eysenck and I. Martin (Eds), *Theoretical foundations of behaviour therapy*. New York: Plenum Press, pp. 45–61.

di Nardo, P. A., Guzy, L. T. and Bak, R. M. (1988). Anxiety response patterns and etiological factors in dog-fearful and non-fearful subjects. *Behaviour Research and Therapy*, 21, 245–252 .

Dixon, N. F. (1981). *Preconscious processing*. Chichester: Wiley.

DSM-IV (2005). Diagnostic and statistical manual of mental disorders (4th ed.). Arlington, VA: American Psychiatric Association.

Dugas, M. and Robichaud, M. (2007). *Treatment for generalized anxiety disorder*. London: Routledge .

Dugas, M., Gagnon, F., Ladouceur, R. and Freeston, M. (1998). Generalized anxiety disorder: A conceptual model. *Behaviour Research and Therapy*, 36, 215–226.

Durham, R. C., Murphy, T., Allan, T., Richard, K., Treliving, L. and Fenton, G. (1994). Cognitive therapy, analytic psychotherapy and anxiety management training for generalised anxiety disorder. *British Journal of Psychiatry*, 165, 315–323.

Edelmann, R. J. (1992). *Anxiety: Theory, research and intervention in clinical and health psychology*. Chichester: Wiley.

Ehlers, A. (1992). Interoception and panic disorder. *Advances in Behaviour Research and Therapy*, 115, 3–21.

Ehlers, A. and Clark, D. M. (2000). A cognitive model of PTSD. *Behaviour Research and Therapy*, 38, 319–345.

Ehlers, A. and Clark, D. M. (2003). Early psychological intervention for adult survivors of trauma: A review. *Biological Psychiatry*, 53, 817–826.

Ehlers, A., Margraf, J., Davies, S. and Roth, W. (1988). Selective processing of threat cues in subjects with panic attacks. *Cognition and Emotion*, 2, 201–219.

Ehlers, A., Clark, D. M., Hackmann, A., McManus, F., Fennell, M., Herbert, C. and Mayou, R. (2003). A randomized controlled trial of cognitive therapy, a self-help booklet, and repeated assessments as early interventions for PTSD. *Archives of General Psychiatry*, 60, 1024–1032.

Emmelkamp, P., Krijn, M., Mulsbosch, L., de Vries, S. and Schuemle, M. (2007). Virtual reality therapy in treating acrophobia. *Behaviour Research Therapy*, 40, 509–516.

Engelhard, I., van den Hout, M. and Smeets, M. (2011). Taxing working memory reduces vividness and emotionality of images about the Queen's Day tragedy. *Journal of Behavior Therapy and Experimental Psychiatry*, 42, 32–37.

Eysenck, H. J. (1957). *The dynamics of anxiety and hysteria*. London: Routledge.

Eysenck, H. J. (Ed.) (1960). *Behavior therapy and the neuroses*. Oxford: Pergamon Press.

Eysenck, H. J. (1967). *The biological basis of personality*. Springfield, IL: Thomas.

Eysenck, H. J. (1985). *Decline and fall of the Freudian empire*. London: Penguin Books.

Eysenck, H. J. and Rachman, S. (1965). *The causes and cures of neurosis*. London: Routledge & Kegan Paul.

Eysenck, H. J., Wakefield, J. A. Jr. and Friedman, A. F. (1983). Diagnosis and clinical assessment: The DSM-III. *Annual Review of Psychology*, 34, 167–193.

Eysenck, M. W. (1992). *Anxiety: The cognitive perspective*. Hove: Erlbaum.

Eysenck, M. W., Derakshan, N., Santos, R. and Calvo, M. G. (2007). Anxiety and cognitive performance: Attentional control theory. *Emotion*, 7, 336–353.

Fenz, W. and Epstein, S. (1967). Gradients of physiological arousal in parachutists. *Psychosomatic Medicine*, 29, 33–51.

Fergus, T. and Valentiner, D. (2009). Reexamining the domain of hypochondriasis. *Journal of Anxiety Disorders*, 23, 760–766.

Fergus, T. A. and Valentiner, D. P. (2010). Disease phobia and disease conviction are separate dimensions underlying hypochondriasis. *Journal of Behavior Therapy and Experimental Psychiatry*, 41, 438–444.

Field, A., Argyris, N. and Knowles, K. (2001). Who's afraid of the big bad wolf: A prospective paradigm to test Rachman's indirect pathways in children. *Behaviour Research and Therapy*, 39, 1259–1276.

Flanagan, J. (Ed.) (1948). *The Aviation Psychology Program in the Army Air Forces*. USAAF aviation psychology research report No. l. Washington, DC: US Government Printing Office.

Foa, E. B. and Kozak, M. J. (1986). Emotional processing of fear: Exposure to corrective information. *Psychological Bulletin*, 99, 20–35.

Foa, E. B., Steketee, G. S., Kozak, M. J. and Dugger, D. (1987). Effects of imipramine on depression and obsessive-compulsive symptoms. *Psychiatry Research*, 21, 123–136.

Foa, E. B., Kozak, M. J., Steketee, G. S. and McCarthy, P. R. (1992). Treatment of depressive and obsessive-compulsive symptoms in OCD by imipramine and behaviour therapy. *British Journal of Clinical Psychology*, 31, 279–292.

Follette, W. C. (1996). Introduction to the special section on the development of theoretically coherent alternatives to the DSM system. *Journal of Consulting and Clinical Psychology*, 64, 1117–1119.

Follette, W. C. and Houts, A. C. (1996). Models of scientific progress and the role of theory in taxonomy development: A case study of the DSM. *Journal of Consulting and Clinical Psychology*, 64, 1120–1132.

Frances, A., First, M. B. and Pincus, H. A. (1995). *DSM-IV guidebook*. Washington, DC: American Psychiatric Press.

Freeston, M., Ladouceur, R., Gagnon, F., Thibodeau, N., Rheaume, J., Letarte, H. and Bujold, A. (1997). Cognitive behavioral treatment of obsessive thoughts. *Journal of Consulting and Clinical Psychology*, 65, 405–413.

Freud, S. (1905). *On psychotherapy*. London: Hogarth Press.

Freud, S. (1910). Reprinted in J. Rickman (Ed.), *General selection from works of Freud*. London: Hogarth Press.

Freud, S. (1948). *An autobiographical study*. London: Hogarth Press.

Freud, S. (1949). *Introductory lectures on psycho-analysis*. London: George Allen and Unwin Ltd.

Freud, S. (1950). The analysis of a phobia in a five-year-old boy. In *Collected papers of Freud, Vol. III*. London: Hogarth Press.

Freud, S. (1953). *A general selection from the works of Sigmund Freud* (Edited by J. Rickman). London: Hogarth Press.

Friedman, M., Keane, T. and Resick, P. (Eds) (2007). *Handbook of PTSD: Science and practice*. New York: Guilford Press.

Friedman, M., Resick, P., Bryant, R. and Brewin, C. (2011) Considering PTSD for DSM 5. *Depression and Anxiety*, 28, 750–769.

Frost, R. and Hartl, M. (2003). Compulsive

hoarding. In R. Menzies and P. de Silva (Eds), *Obsessive compulsive disorders*. Chichester: Wiley, pp. 163–180.

Fulton, J. J., Marcus, D. K. and Merkey, T. (2011). Irrational health beliefs and health anxiety. *Journal of Clinical Psychology*, 67, 527–538.

Fyer, A. J. (1987). Simple phobia. *Modern Problems of Pharmacopsychiatry*, 22, 174–192.

Gerull, F. and Rapee, R. (2002). Mother knows best. *Behaviour Research and Therapy*, 40, 279–287.

Gilbert, D. (2007). *Stumbling on happiness*. New York: Random House.

Gillespie, K. *et al.* (2002). Community based cognitive therapy in the treatment of PTSD following the Omagh bomb. *Behaviour Research and Therapy*, 40, 345–358.

Gorman, J. (1987). Panic disorders. In D. Klein (Ed.), *Anxiety*. Basel: Karger.

Gray, J. A. (1971). *The psychology of fear and stress*. London: World University Library.

Gray, J. A. (1982). *The neuropsychology of anxiety: An enquiry into the functions of the septo-hippocampal system*. Oxford: Oxford University Press.

Gray, J. A. (1986). The neuropsychology of anxiety. In C. D. Spielberger and I. G. Sarason (Eds), *Stress and anxiety*. Washington, DC: Hemisphere Publishing.

Gray, J. A. (1987). *Psychology of fear and stress* (2nd ed.). Cambridge: Cambridge University Press.

Grinker, R. and Spiegel, J. (1945). *Men under stress*. Philadelphia and London: Blakiston and Churchills.

Grunbaum, A. (1977). Is psychoanalysis a pseudo-science? In R. Stern, L. Horowitz and J. Lynes (Eds), *Science and psychotherapy*. New York: Raven Press.

Hackmann, A., Surawy, C. and Clark, D. M. (1998). Seeing yourself through others' eyes. *Behavioural Cognitive Psychotherapy*, 26, 3–12.

Hackmann, A., Clark, D. M. and McManus, F. (2000). Recurrent images and early memories in social phobia. *Behaviour Research and Therapy*, 38, 601–610.

Hackmann, A., Bennett-Levy, J. and Holmes, E. (2011). *The Oxford guide to imagery in cognitive therapy*. Oxford: Oxford University Press.

Hadjistavropolous, H., Owens, M., Hadjistavropolous, T. and Asmundson, G. (2011). Hypochondriasis and health anxiety among pain patients. In G. J. G. Asmundson, S. Taylor and B. J. Cox (Eds), *Health anxiety*. New York: Wiley, pp. 298–323.

Hadjistavropoulos, H. D., Janzen, J. A., Kehler, M. D., Leclerc, J. A., Sharpe, D. and Bourgault-Fagnou, M. D. (2012). Core cognitions related to health anxiety in self-reported medical and non-medical samples. *Journal of Behavioral Medicine*, 32, 169–178.

Hall, G. S. (1897). A study of fears. *The American Journal of Psychology*, 8, 147–249.

Hallam, R. S. (1978). Agoraphobia: A criticial review of the concept. *British Journal of Psychiatry*, 133, 314–319.

Halligan, S. *et al.* (2003). PTSD following assault. *Journal of Consulting and Clinical Psychology*, 71, 419–431.

Hammersley, D. (1957). Conditioned reflex therapy. In R. Wallerstein (Ed.), *Hospital treatment of alcoholism*. Menninger Clinic Monographs No. 11.

Harlow, H. (1954). Motivational forces underlying learning. In D. K. Adams, O. H. Mowrer, R. B. Ammons, D. Snygg, J. M. Butler, K. W. Spence, R. B. Cattell, D. D. Wickens, H. F. Harlow, J. R. Wittenborn and N. R. F. Maier, *Learning theory, personality theory and clinical research: The Kentucky Symposium*. New York: Wiley.

Harvey, A. and Bryant, R. (2002). Acute stress disorder: A synthesis and critique. *Psychological Bulletin*, 128, 886–902.

Harvey, A., Bryant, R. and Tarrier, N. (2003). Cognitive behaviour therapy for PTSD. *Clinical Psychology Review*, 23, 501–522.

Harvey, A. G. and Rapee, R. M. (1995). Cognitive-behavior therapy for generalized anxiety disorder. *Psychiatric Clinics of North America*, 18, 859–870.

Hasselstrom, J., Liu-Palmgren, J. and Rasjo-Wraak, G. (2002). Prevalence of pain in general practice. *European Journal of Pain*, 6, 375–385.

Hawton, K., Salkovskis, P., Kirk, J. and Clark, D. M. (1989). *Cognitive behaviour therapy for psychiatric problems*. Oxford: Oxford University Press.

Hedman, E., Andersson, G., Andersson, E., Ljótsson, B., Rück, C., Asmundson, G. J. G. *et al.* (2011). Internet-based cognitive-behavioural therapy for severe health anxiety: Randomised controlled trial. *British Journal of Psychiatry*, 198, 230–236.

Heimberg, R. G. (1996). Social phobia, avoidant personality disorder and the multiaxial conceptualization of interpersonal anxiety. In P. Salkovskis (Ed.), *Trends in cognitive and behavioural therapies*. Chichester: Wiley.

Heimberg, R. G., Liebowitz, M. R., Hope, D. A. and Schneier, F. R. (1995). *Social phobia: Diagnosis, assessment and treatment*. New York: Guilford Press.

Heimberg, R. *et al.* (1998). Cognitive behavior group therapy vs phenelzine therapy for social phobia. *Archives of General Psychiatry*, 55, 1133–1141.

Hellstrom, K. and Ost, L. G. (1995). One-session therapist directed exposure in the treatment of spider phobia. *Behaviour Research and Therapy*, 33, 959–965.

Herbert, J., Lilienfeld, S., Lohr, J., Montgomery, R., O'Donohue, W., Rosen, G. and Tolin, D. (2000). Science and pseudo-science in the development of EMDR. *Clinical Psychology Review*, 20, 945–971.

Hibbert, G. A. (1984). Ideational components of anxiety: Their origin and content. *British Journal of Psychiatry*, 144, 618–624.

Hirsch, C. and Clark, D. M. (2004). Information processing bias in social phobia. *Clinical Psychology Review*, 24, 799–825.

Hirsch, C., Clark, D. M. and Mathews, A. (2006). Imagery and interpretations in social phobia: Support for the combined cognitive biases hypothesis. *Behavior Therapy*, 37, 223–236.

Hirsch, C., Clark, D. M., Mathews, A. and Williams, R., (2003). Self-images play a causal role in social phobia. *Behaviour Research and Therapy*, 41, 909–922.

Hofmann, S. (2000). Self-focused attention before and after treatment of social phobia. *Behaviour Research and Therapy*, 38, 717–726.

Hofmann, S. and Barlow, D. (2002). Social phobia. In D. Barlow (Ed.), *Anxiety and its disorders*. New York: Guilford Press.

Hofmann, S. *et al.* (2004). Changes in self-perception during treatment of social phobia. *Journal of Consulting Clinical Psychology*, 72, 588–596.

Hollander, E. and Leibowitz, M. R. (1990). Treatment of depersonalization with serotonin reuptake blockers. *Journal of Clinical Psychopharmacology*, 10, 200–203.

Holmes, E. and Mathews, A. (2010). Mental imagery in emotion and emotional disorders. *Clinical Psychology Review*, 30, 349–362.

Hood, H., Antony, M., Koerner, N. and Monson, C. (2010). Effects of safety behaviours on fear reduction during exposure. *Behaviour Research and Therapy*, 48, 1161–1169.

Horowitz, M. (1975). Intrusive and repetitive thoughts after experimental stress. *Archives of General Psychiatry*, 32, 1457–1463.

Horwath, E., Lish, J. D., Johnson, J., Hornig, C. D. and Weismann, M. M. (1993). Agoraphobia without panic: Clinical reappraisal of an epidemiologic finding. *American Journal of Psychiatry*, 150, 1496–1501.

Ingram, R. E. (1990). Self-focused attention in clinical disorders: Review and a conceptual model. *Psychological Bulletin*, 107, 156–176.

Insel, T. R. (1988). Obsessive-compulsive disorder: A neuroethological perspective. *Psychopharmacology Bulletin*, 24, 365–369.

Insel, T. R. (1991). Has OCD research gone to the dogs? *Neuropsychopharmacology*, 5, 13–17.

Insel, T. R. and Winslow, J. T. (1992). Neurobiology of obsessive compulsive disorder. *Psychiatric Clinics of North America*, 15, 813–824.

Janis, J. L. (1951). *Air war and emotional stress*. New York: McGraw-Hill.

Jenike, M. A., Baer, L. and Greist, J. H. (1990). Clomipramine versus fluvoxetine in obsessive-compulsive disorder: A retrospective comparison of side-effects and efficacy. *Journal of Clinical Psychopharmacology*, 10, 122–124.

Jenkins, R. (2002). *Churchill: A biography*. London: Penguin Books.

Johnston, M. (1980). Anxiety in surgical patients. *Psychological Medicine*, 10, 145–152.

Jones, E. (1954). *Sigmund Freud: Life and works, Vol. I*. London: Hogarth Press.

Jones, M. C. (1924). A laboratory study of fear. *Pedagogical Seminars*, 31, 308–315.

Juster, H. R. and Heimberg, R. G. (1995). Social phobia. Longitudinal course and long-term outcome of cognitive-behavioral treatment. *Psychiatric Clinics of North America*, 18, 821–842.

Kafka, F. ([1925] 1977). *The trial* (English ed.). London: Pan Books.

Kahneman, D. and Treisman, A. (1983). The cost of visual filtering. *Journal of Experimental Psychology: Human Perception and Performance*, 9, 497–509.

Kahneman, D., Treisman, A. and Burkell, J. (1983). The cost of visual filtering.

Journal of Experimental Psychology: Human Perception and Performance, 9, 510–522.

Kessler, R. C., Chiu, W. T., Demler, O. and Walters, E. E. (2006). Prevalence, severity, and comorbidity of 12-month DSM-IV disorders in the national comorbidity survey replication. *Archives of General Psychiatry*, 62, 617–627.

Kincey, J., Statham, S. and McFarlane, T. (1991). Women undergoing colposcopy: Their satisfaction with communication, health knowledge and level of anxiety. *Health Education Journal*, 50, 70–72.

Kirk, S. A. and Kutchins, H. (1992). *The selling of DSM: The rhetoric of science in psychiatry*. New York: Aldine de Gruyther.

Kirkpatrick, D. R. (1984). Age, gender, and patterns of common intense fears among adults. *Behaviour Research and Therapy*, 22, 141–150.

Klein, D. (1987). Anxiety reconceptualized. In D. Klein (Ed.), *Anxiety*. Basel: Karger.

Klein, D. (1993). False suffocation alarms, spontaneous panics, and related conditions: An integrative hypothesis. *Archives of General Psychiatry*, 50, 306–317.

Klein, D. (1996). A reply. [Reply following the article, 'Panic attacks: Klein's false suffocation alarm, Taylor and Rachman's data, and Ley's dyspneic fear theory']. *Archives of General Psychiatry*, 52, 83–84.

Klein, D. and Klein, H. (1989). The nosology of anxiety disorders: A critical review of hypothesis testing about spontaneous panic. In P. Tyrer (Ed.), *Psychopharmacology of anxiety*. Oxford: Oxford University Press.

Klein, D. F., Zitrin, C. M. and Woerner, M. G. (1977). Imipramine and phobia [proceedings]. *Psychopharmacology Bulletin*, 13, 24–27.

Klerman, G. L. (1985). Diagnosis of psychiatric disorders in epidemiological field studies. *Archives of General Psychiatry*, 42, 723–724.

Krijn, M. *et al.* (2004). Virtual reality treatment of anxiety disorders: A review. *Clinical Psychology Review*, 24, 259–281.

Lader, M. (1994). Treatment of anxiety. *British Medical Journal*, 309, 321–324.

Ladouceur, R. *et al.* (2000). Efficacy of cognitive behavioral therapy for GAD. *Journal of Consulting and Clinical Psychology*, 68, 957–964.

Lang, P. (1970). Stimulus control, response control and desensitization of fear. In D. Levis (Ed.), *Learning approaches to therapeutic behaviour change*. Chicago, IL: Aldine Press.

Lang, P. (1977). Imagery in therapy: An information processing analysis of fear. *Behavior Therapy*, 8, 862–886.

Lang, P. (1985). The cognitive psychophysiology of emotion: Fear and anxiety. In A. Tuma and J. Maser (Eds), *Anxiety and the anxiety disorders*. Hillsdale, NJ: Erlbaum.

Lang, P., Melamed, B. and Hart, J. (1970). A psychophysiological analysis of fear modification using an automated desensitization technique. *Journal of Abnormal Psychology*, 76, 220–234.

Lang, P. J., Levin, D. N., Miller, G. A. and Kozak, M. J. (1983). Fear behavior, fear imagery, and the psychophysiology of emotion: The problem of affective response integration. *Journal of Abnormal Psychology*, 92, 276–306.

Last, C. G. (1987). Simple phobias. In L. Michelson and M. Ascher (Eds), *Anxiety and stress disorders*. New York: Guilford Press.

Lautch, H. (1971). Dental phobia. *British Journal of Psychiatry*, 119, 151–158.

Leon, A. C., Marzuk, P. M. and Portera, L. (1995). More reliable outcome measures can reduce sample size requirements. *Archives of General Psychiatry*, 52, 867–871.

Lewis, A. (1942). Incidence of neurosis in England under war conditions. *The Lancet*, 2, 175–183.

Lewis, A. (1980). Problems presented by the ambiguous word 'anxiety' as used in psychopathology. In G. D. Burrows and B. Davies (Eds), *Handbook of studies on anxiety*. Amsterdam: Elsevier / North-Holland.

Ley, R. (1994). The 'suffocation alarm' theory of panic attacks: A critical commentary. *Journal of Behavior Therapy and Experimental Psychiatry*, 25, 269–273.

Lohr, J., Tolin, D. and Lilienfeld, S. (1999). Eye movement desensitization and reprocessing. *Journal of Anxiety Disorders*, 13, 185–207.

McClure, E. B. and Lilienfeld, S. O. (2001). Personality traits and health anxiety. In G. Asmundson, S. Taylor and B. J. Cox (Eds), *Health anxiety: Clinical and research perspectives on hypochondriasis and related conditions*. Chichester and New York: Wiley, pp. 65–94.

McEwan, K. L. and Devins, G. M. (1983). Is increased arousal in social anxiety noticed by others? *Journal of Abnormal Psychology*, 92, 417–421.

McGuire, P. K. (1995). The brain in obsessive-compulsive disorder. *Journal of Neurology, Neurosurgery and Psychiatry*, 59, 457–459.

Mackintosh, N. J. (1983). *Conditioning and associative learning*. New York: Oxford University Press.

MacLeod, C. and Cohen, I. L. (1993). Anxiety and the interpretation of ambiguity: A text comprehension study. *Journal of Abnormal Psychology*, 102, 238–247.

McManus, F., Sacadura, C. and Clark, D. M. (2008). Why social phobia persists: An experimental test of the role of safety behaviour. *Journal of Behavior Therapy and Experimental Psychiatry*, 39, 147–161.

McMillan, T. M. and Rachman, S. (1988). Fearlessness and courage in paratroopers undergoing training.

Personality and Individual Differences, 9, 373–378.

McNally, R. (1995). Cognitive biases in the anxiety disorders. *Nebraska Symposium on Motivation*, 43, 211–250.

McNally, R. (1999). Research on EMDR as a treatment for PTSD. *PTSD Research Quarterly*, 10, 1–7.

McNally, R. J. (1987). Preparedness and phobias: A review. *Psychological Bulletin*, 101, 283–303.

McNally, R. J. (1994). *Panic disorder: A critical analysis*. New York: Guilford Press.

McNally, R. J. (2003). Progress and controversy in the study of PTSD. Annual Review of Psychology, 54, 229–252.

McNally, R., Bryant, P. and Ehlers, A. (2003) Does early psychological intervention promote recovery from PTSD? *Psychological Science*, 4, 45–79.

McNally, R. J., Hornig, C. D. and Donnell, C. D. (1995). Clinical versus nonclinical panic: A test of suffocation false alarm theory. *Behaviour Research and Therapy*, 33, 127–132.

McNally, R. J., Lasko, N. B., Macklin, M. L. and Pitman, R. K. (1995). Autobiographical memory disturbance in combat-related post traumatic stress disorder. *Behaviour Research and Therapy*, 33, 619–630.

Mannuzza, S., Schneier, F. R., Chapman, T. F., Liebowitz, M. R. *et al.* (1995). Generalized social phobia: Reliability and validity. *Archives of General Psychiatry*, 52, 230–237.

Mäntyselkä, P., Kumpusalo, E., Ahonen, R., Kumpusalo, A., Kauhanen, J., Viinamäki, H. *et al.* (2001). Pain as a reason to visit the doctor: A study in Finnish primary health care. *Pain*, 89, 175–180.

Marcus, D. K., Gurley, J. R., Marchi, M. M. and Bauer, C. (2007). Cognitive and perceptual variables in hypochondriasis and health anxiety: A systematic review. *Clinical Psychology Review*, 27, 127–139.

Margraf, J. (1993). Hyperventilation and panic disorder: A psychophysiological connection. *Advances in Behavior Research and Therapy*, 15, 49–74.

Margraf, J., Ehlers, A. and Roth, W. (1986). Panic attacks: Theoretical models and empirical evidence. In I. Hand and H. Wittchen (Eds), *Panic and phobia*. Berlin: Springer.

Margraf, J., Barlow, D. H., Clark, D. M. and Telch, M. J. (1993). Psychological treatment of panic: Work in progress on outcome, active ingredients, and follow-up. *Behaviour Research and Therapy*, 31, 1–8.

Marino-Carper, T. L., Negy, C., Burns, G. and Lunt, R. A. (2010). The effects of psychoeducation on thought-action fusion, thought suppression, and responsibility. *Journal of Behavior Therapy and Experimental Psychiatry*, 41, 289–296.

Marks, I. (1987). *Fears, phobias, and rituals*. Oxford: Oxford University Press.

Marks, I., Lovell, K., Noshirvani, H. and Livanou, M. (1998). Treatment of PTSD by exposure and / or cognitive restructuring. *Archives of General Psychiatry*, 55, 317–325.

Marks, I. M. (1969). *Fears and phobias*. London: Heinemann.

Marks, M. (2003). Cognitive treatment for OCD. In R. Menzies and P. de Silva (Eds), *Obsessive compulsive disorders*. Chichester: Wiley.

Marks, M. P., Basoglu, M., Alkubaisy, T., Sengun, S. and Marks, I. M. (1991). Are anxiety symptoms and catastrophic cognitions directly related? *Journal of Anxiety Disorders*, 5, 247–254.

Masters, W. H. and Johnson, V. E. (1970). *Human sexual inadequacy*. Boston, MA: Little, Brown.

Mathews, A., Gelder, M. G. and Johnston, D. W. (1981). *Agoraphobia: Nature and treatment*. New York: Guilford Press.

Mathews, A., MacLeod, C. and Tata, P. R. (1987). An information-processing approach to anxiety. *Journal of Cognitive Psychotherapy*, 1, 105–115.

Mathews, A., Mogg, K., May, J. and Eysenck, M. (1989). Implicit and explicit memory bias in anxiety. *Journal of Abnormal Psychology*, 98, 236–240.

Mattick, R., Peters, L. and Clarke, J. (1990). Exposure and cognitive restructuring for social phobia: A controlled study. *Behavior Therapy*, 20, 3–23.

Mavissakalian, M. (1983). Antidepressants in the treatment of agoraphobia and obsessive-compulsive disorder. *Comprehensive Psychiatry*, 24, 278–284.

Mayou, R., Ehlers, A. and Hobbs, M. (2000). Psychological debriefing for road traffic accident victims. *British Journal of Psychiatry*, 176, 589–593.

Merckelbach, H., de Jong, P., Muris, P. and van den Hout, M. (1996). The etiology of specific phobias: A review. *Clinical Psychology Review*, 16, 337–361.

Miller, N. E. (1960). Learning resistance to pain and fear. *Journal of Experimental Psychology*, 60, 137–142.

Milosevic, I. and Radomsky, A. S. (2008). Safety behaviour does not necessarily interfere with exposure therapy. *Behaviour Research and Therapy*, 46, 1111–1118.

Mineka, S. (1985). Animal models of anxiety-based disorders. In A. Tuma and J. Maser (Eds), *Anxiety and the anxiety disorders*. Hillsdale, NJ: Erlbaum, pp. 199–244.

Mitte, K. (2005). Meta-analysis of cognitive behavior therapy for GAD: A comparison with pharmacotherapy. *Psychological Bulletin*, 131, 785–795.

Mortberg, R., Clark, D., Sundin, C. and Wistedt, A. (2007). Intensive group cognitive therapy and individual therapy versus treatment as usual in social phobia. *Acta Psychiatrica Scandinavica*, 115, 142–154.

Mowrer, O. H. (1939). Stimulus response theory of anxiety. *Psychological Review*, 46, 553–565.

Mowrer, O. H. (1960). *Learning theory and behavior*. New York: Wiley.

Muris, P., Bodden, D., Merckelbach, H., Ollendick, T. and King, N. (2003). Fear of the beast. *Behaviour Research and Therapy*, 41, 195–208.

Muse, K., McManus, F., Hackmann, A. and Williams, M. (2010). Intrusive imagery in severe health anxiety. *Behaviour Research and Therapy*, 48, 792–798.

Nakao, M., Shinozaki, Y., Ahern, D. and Barsky, A. (2011). Anxiety as a predictor of improvements in somatic symptoms and health anxiety associated with CBT in hypochondriasis. *Psychotherapy and Psychosomatics*, 80, 151–158.

Newth, S. and Rachman, S. (2001). The concealment of obsessions. *Behaviour Research and Therapy*, 39, 457–464.

Nisbett, R. and Wilson, T. (1977). Telling more than we can know: Verbal reports on mental processes. *Psychological Review*, 84, 231–259.

Norton, R. and Price, E. (2007). A meta-analytic review of adult CBT outcome across the anxiety disorders. *Journal of Nervous and Mental Disease*, 195, 521–531.

Norton, R., Cox, B., Asmundson, G. and Maser, J. (1995). The growth of research on anxiety disorders during the 1980s. *Journal of Anxiety Disorders*, 9, 75–85.

Noyes, R. (1999). The relationship of hypochondriasis to anxiety disorders. *General Hospital Psychiatry*, 21, 8–17.

Noyes, R. (2001). Hypochondriasis: Boundaries and comorbidities. In G. Asmundson, S. Taylor and B. J. Cox (Eds), *Health anxiety: Clinical and research perspectives*. New York: Wiley.

OED (1971). *Compact edition of the Oxford English dictionary*. Oxford: Oxford University Press.

Ohman, A. (1987). Evolution, learning and phobias. In D. Magnusson and A. Ohman (Eds), *Psychopathology*. New York: Academic Press.

Ohman, A., Erixon, G. and Lofberg, I. (1975). Phobias and preparedness: Phobic versus neutral pictures as continued stimuli for human autonomic responses. *Journal of Abnormal Psychology*, 84, 41–45.

Olatunji, B. O., Deacon, B. J. and Abramowitz, J. S. (2009). Is hypochondriasis an anxiety disorder? *British Journal of Psychiatry*, 194, 481–482.

Olatunji, B., Etzel, E., Tomarken, A., Cieselski, B. and Deacon, B. (2011). The effects of safety behaviour on health anxiety: An experiment investigation. *Behaviour Research and Therapy*, 49, 719–728.

Ollendick, T. and King, N. (1991). Origins of children's fears. *Behaviour Research and Therapy*, 29, 117–123.

Ost, L. G. (1985). Ways of acquiring phobias and outcome of behavioural treatments. *Behaviour Research and Therapy*, 23, 683–689.

Ost, L. G. (1987). Age of onset in different phobias. *Journal of Abnormal Psychology*, 96, 223–229.

Ost, L. G. (1989). One-session treatment for specific phobias. *Behaviour Research and Therapy*, 27, 1–8.

Ost, L. G. (1996). One-session group therapy for spider phobia. *Behaviour Research and Therapy*, 34, 707–715.

Ost, L. G. (1997). One-session group therapy of spider phobia: Direct vs. indirect treatments. *Behaviour Research and Therapy*, 35, 721–732.

Ost, L. G. and Hugdahl, K. (1983). Acquisition of agoraphobia, mode of onset and anxiety response patterns. *Behaviour Research and Therapy*, 21, 623–631.

Ost, L. G. and Westling, B. (1995). Applied relaxation vs. cognitive behavioural therapy in the treatment of panic disorder. *Behaviour Research and Therapy*, 33, 145–158.

Ost, L., Svenson, L., Hellstrom, K. and Lindwall, R. (2001). One-session treatment of specific phobias in youths: A randomized control trial. *Journal of Consulting and Clinical Psychology*, 69, 814–824.

Otto, M. W., Gould, R. A. and McLean, R. Y. S. (1996). The effectiveness of cognitive-behavior therapy for panic disorder without concurrent medication treatment: A reply to Power and Sharp. *Journal of Psychopharmacology*, 10, 254–256.

Otto, M., Pollack, S. and Sabatino, S. (1996). Maintenance of remission following CBT for panic disorder: Possible deleterious effects of concurrent medication treatment. *Behavior Therapy*, 27, 473–482.

Otto, M. W., Pollack, M. H., Meltzer-Brody, S. and Rosenbaum, J. F. (1992). Cognitive-behavior therapy for benzodiazepine discontinuation in panic disorder patients. *Psychopharmacology Bulletin*, 28, 123–130.

Palace, E. E. and Gorzalka, M. M. (1990). The enhancing effects of anxiety on arousal in sexually dysfunctional and functional women. *Journal of Abnormal Psychology*, 99, 403–411.

Papini, M. and Bitterman, M. (1990). The role of contingency in classical conditioning. *Psychological Review*, 97, 396–403.

Parkinson, L. and Rachman, S. (1980). Speed of recovery from an uncontrived stress. In S. Rachman (Ed.), *Unwanted intrusive cognitions*. Oxford: Pergamon Press.

Parrish, C. L. and Radomsky, A. S. (2010). Why do people seek reassurance and check repeatedly? An investigation of factors involved in compulsive behavior in OCD and depression. *Journal of Anxiety Disorders*, 24, 211–222.

Parrish, C. L., Radomsky, A. S. and Dugas, M. J. (2008). Anxiety-control strategies: Is there room for neutralization in successful exposure treatment? *Clinical Psychology Review*, 28, 1400–1412.

Paul, G. (1966). *Insight versus desensitization in psychotherapy*. Stanford, CA: Stanford University Press.

Pavlov, I. P. (1941). *Conditioned reflexes and psychiatry* (Trans. W. H. Gantt). New York: International Publishers.

Pennebaker, J. W. (1982). *The psychology of physical symptoms*. New York and Berlin: Springer-Verlag.

Peterson, R. A. and Reiss, S. (1987). *Test manual for the Anxiety Sensitivity Index*. Orland Park, IL: International Diagnostic Systems.

Philips, C. and Rachman, S. (1996). *The psychological management of chronic pain*. New York: Springer.

Philips, C. and Samson, D. (2012). The rescripting of pain images. *Behavioural and Cognitive Psychotherapy*, 40, 558–576.

Philips, H. C. (2011). Imagery and pain: The prevalence, characteristics and potency of imagery associated with pain. *Behavioural and Cognitive Psychotherapy*, 39, 523–540.

Pigott, T. M., Myers, K. R. and Williams, D. A. (1996). Obsessive-compulsive disorder: A neuropsychiatric perspective. In R. Rapee (Ed.), *Current controversies in anxiety disorders*. New York: Guilford Press.

Pollard, C. A. and Henderson, J. G. (1988). Four types of social phobia in a community sample. *Journal of Nervous and Mental Disease*, 176, 440–445.

Ponniah, K. and Hollon, S. (2008). Empirically supported psychological interventions for social phobia in adults. *Psychological Medicine*, 38, 3–14.

Poulton, R. and Menzies, R. (2002). Non-associative fear acquisition: A review of the evidence from retrospective and longitudinal research. *Behaviour Research and Therapy*, 40, 127–150.

Powers, M. and Emmelkamp, P. (2008a). Virtual reality exposure treatment for anxiety disorders: A meta-analysis. *Journal of Anxiety Disorders*, 22, 561–569.

Powers, M. and Emmelkamp, P. (2008b). A meta-analytic review of psychological treatments for social anxiety disorders. *International Journal of Cognitive Therapy*, 1, 94–113.

Powers, M. and Emmelkamp, P. (2010). A meta-analytic review of prolonged exposure for PTSD. *Clinical Psychology Review*, 30, 636–664.

Powers, M. B., Smits, J. A. and Telch, M. J. (2004). Disentangling the effects of safety-behavior utilization and safety-behavior availability during exposure-based treatment: A placebo-controlled trial. *Journal of Consulting and Clinical Psychology*, 72, 448–454.

Price, M. and Anderson, P. (2011). The impact of CBT on post-event processing among those with social anxiety disorders. *Behaviour Research and Therapy*, 49, 132–137.

Prigatano, G. and Johnson, H. (1974). Autonomic nervous system changes associated with a spider phobic reaction. *Journal of Abnormal Psychology*, 83, 169–177.

Proust, M. (1981). *Remembrance of things past, Vol. III* (Transl. by C. Moncrieff and T. Kilmartin). London: Penguin Books.

Rachman, S. (1974). Primary obsessional slowness. *Behaviour Research and Therapy*, 12, 9–18.

Rachman, S. (1978). *Fear and courage*. New York: W.H. Freeman.

Rachman, S. (1980). Emotional processing. *Behaviour Research and Therapy*, 18, 51–60.

Rachman, S. (1984). Agoraphobia: A safety signal perspective. *Behaviour Research and Therapy*, 22, 59–70.

Rachman, S. (1985). The treatment of anxiety disorders: A critique of the implications for psychopathology. In A. Tuma and J. Maser (Eds), *Anxiety and the anxiety disorders*. Hillsdale, NJ: Erlbaum, pp. 453–461.

Rachman, S. (1990). *Fear and courage* (2nd ed.). New York: Freeman.

Rachman, S. (1991). Neo-conditioning and the classical theory of fear acquisition. *Clinical Psychology Review*, 11, 155–173.

Rachman, S. (1996). The evolution of cognitive behaviour therapy. In D. M. Clark and C. Fairburn (Eds), *Science and practice of cognitive behaviour therapy*. Oxford: Oxford University Press.

Rachman, S. (1997). A cognitive theory of obsessions. *Behaviour Research and Therapy*, 35, 793–803.

Rachman, S. (2001). Emotional processing, with special reference to PTSD. *International Review of Psychiatry*, 13, 164–171.

Rachman, S. (2002). A cognitive theory of compulsive checking. *Behaviour Research and Therapy*, 40, 625–640.

Rachman, S. (2003). *The treatment of obsessions*. Oxford: Oxford University Press.

Rachman, S. (2004). Fear of contamination. *Behaviour Research and Therapy*, 42, 1227–1256.

Rachman, S. (2006). *Fear of contamination*. Oxford: Oxford University Press.

Rachman, S. (2007). Unwanted intrusive images in obsessive compulsive disorders. *Journal of Behavior Therapy and Experimental Psychiatry*, 38, 402–410.

Rachman, S. (2009). Psychological treatment of anxiety: The evolution of behavior therapy and cognitive behavior therapy. *Annual Review of Clinical Psychology*, 5, 97–119.

Rachman, S. (2010). Betrayal: A psychological analysis. *Behaviour Research and Therapy*, 48, 304–311.

Rachman, S. (2012). Health anxiety disorders: A cognitive construal. *Behaviour Research and Therapy*, 50, 502–512.

Rachman, S. and Hodgson, R. (1980). *Obsessions and compulsions*. Englewood Cliffs, NJ: Prentice Hall.

Rachman, S. and Wilson, G. T. (1980). *The effects of psychological therapy* (2nd ed.). Oxford: Pergamon Press.

Rachman, S. and Lopatka, C. (1986). Do fears summate? *Behaviour Research and Therapy*, 24, 653–660.

Rachman, S. and Bichard, S. (1988). The overprediction of fear. *Clinical Psychology Review*, 8, 303–312.

Rachman, S. and Whittal, M. L. (1989). Fast, slow and sudden reductions in fear. *Behaviour Research and Therapy*, 27, 613–620.

Rachman, S. and Cuk, M. (1992). Fearful distortions. *Behaviour Research and Therapy*, 30, 583–589.

Rachman, S. and Taylor, S. (1993). Analyses of claustrophobia. *Journal of Anxiety Disorders*, 7, 281–291.

Rachman, S. and de Silva, P. (2009). *Obsessive–compulsive disorder: The facts* (4th ed.). Oxford: Oxford University Press.

Rachman, S. and de Silva, P. (2010). *Panic disorder: The facts* (3rd ed.). Oxford: Oxford University Press.

Rachman, S., Levitt, K. and Lopatka, C. (1987). Panic – 1. The links between cognitions and bodily symptoms. *Behaviour Research and Therapy*, 25, 411–423.

Rachman, S., Gruter-Andrew, C. and Shafran, R. (2000). Post-event processing in social anxiety. *Behaviour Research and Therapy*, 38, 611–617.

Rachman, S., Hammond, D. and Radomsky, A. S. (2000). The use of safety gear in exposure therapy. Unpublished data.

Rachman, S., Radomsky, A. and Shafran, R. (2008). Safety behaviour: A reconsideration. *Behaviour Research and Therapy*, 46, 163–173.

Rachman, S., Craske, M., Tallman, K. and Solyom, C. (1986). Does safety behavior strengthen agoraphobic avoidance? A replication. *Behavior Therapy*, 17, 366–384.

Rachman, S., Elliott, C., Radomsky, A. and Shafran, R. (2009). Separating hoarding from OCD. *Behaviour Research and Therapy*, 47, 520–522.

Rachman, S., Shafran, R., Radomsky, A. and Zysk, E. (2011). Reducing contamination by exposure plus safety behaviour. *Journal of Behavior Therapy and Experimental Psychiatry*, 42, 397–404.

Rachman, S., Cobb, C., Grey, S., McDonald, B. and Sartory, G. (1979). Behavioural treatments of obsessive-compulsive disorder with and without clomipramine. *Behaviour Research and Therapy*, 17, 467–478.

Radomsky, A. and Rachman, S. (1999). Memory bias in OCD. *Behaviour Research and Therapy*, 37, 605–618.

Radomsky, A., Rachman, S. and Hammond, D. (2001). Memory bias, confidence and responsibility in compulsive checking. *Behaviour Research and Therapy*, 39, 813–822.

Radomsky, A., Gilchrist, P. and Dussault, D (2006). Repeated checking really does cause memory distrust. *Behaviour Research and Therapy*, 44, 305–317.

Radomsky, A., Shafran, R., Coughtrey, A. and Rachman, S. (2010). Cognitive behaviour therapy for compulsive checking in obsessive compulsive disorders. *Cognitive and Behavioral Practice*, 17, 119–131.

Rapee, R. (1995). Psychological factors influencing the affective response to biological challenge procedures in panic disorder. *Journal of Anxiety Disorders*, 9, 291–300.

Rapee, R. and Heimberg, R. (1997). A cognitive behaviour model of social phobia. *Behaviour Research and Therapy*, 35, 741–756.

Rapee, R. and Spence, S. (2004). The etiology of social phobia: Empirical evidence and an initial model. *Clinical Psychology Review*, 24, 737–767.

Rapee, R., Sanderson, W. C., McCauley, P. A. and di Nardo, P. A. (1992). Differences in reported symptom profile between panic disorder and other DSM-III-R anxiety disorders. *Behaviour Research and Therapy*, 30, 45–52.

Rapoport, J. (Ed.) (1989). *Obsessive-compulsive disorder in children and adolescents*. Washington, DC: American Psychiatric Press.

Rapoport, J. and Wise, S. P. (1988). Obsessive-compulsive disorder: Evidence for a basal ganglia dysfunction. *Psychopharmacology Bulletin*, 24, 380–384.

Rassin, E. (2005). *Thought suppression*. Oxford: Elsevier.

Rasmussen, S. and Eisen, J. (1992). The epidemiology and clinical features of OCD. *Psychiatric Clinics of North America*, 15, 743–758.

Reiss, S. (1987). Theoretical perspectives on the fear of anxiety. *Clinical Psychology Review*, 7, 585–596.

Reiss, S. (1991). Expectancy model of fear, anxiety and panic. *Clinical Psychology Review*, 11, 141–153.

Reiss, S. and McNally, R. J. (1985). Expectancy model of fear. In S. Reiss and R. R. Bootzin (Eds), *Theoretical issues in behavior therapy*. New York: Academic Press.

Reiss, S., Peterson, R. A., Gursky, D. M. and McNally, R. J. (1986). Anxiety sensitivity, anxiety frequency, and the prediction of fearfulness. *Behaviour Research and Therapy*, 24, 1–8.

Rescorla, R. A. (1980). *Pavlovian second-order conditioning*. Hillsdale, NJ: Erlbaum.

Rescorla, R. A. (1988). Pavlovian conditioning: It's not what you think it is. *American Psychologist*, 43, 151–160.

Resick, P. (2001). *Stress and trauma*. Hove: Psychology Press.

Revusky, S. (1979). More about appropriate controls for taste aversion learning: A reply to Riley. *Animal Learning and Behavior*, 79, 562–563.

Ritter, M. (1969). The use of contact desensitization demonstration-plus-participation in the treatment of acrophobia. *Behaviour Research and Therapy*, 7, 164–175.

Rode, H. *et al.* (2006). Health anxiety levels in chronic pain attenders. *Journal of Psychosomatic Research*, 60, 155–161.

Ruhe, H., Dekker, J., Peen, J., Holman, R. and de Jonghe, F. (2005). Clinical use of the Hamilton Depression Rating Scale: Is increased efficiency possible? A post-hoc comparison of HDRS, Maier and Beck subscales, Symptom Checklist and Clinical Global Impression. *Comprehensive Psychiatry*, 46, 417–427.

Saigh, P. A. (1984). Pre- and post-invasion anxiety in Lebanon. *Behavior Therapy*, 15, 185–190.

Saigh, P. A. (1988). Anxiety, depression and assertion across alternating intervals of stress. *Journal of Abnormal Psychology*, 97, 338–341.

Salkovskis, P. (1985). Obsessional-compulsive problems: A cognitive behavioural analysis. *Behaviour Research and Therapy*, 23, 571–583.

Salkovskis, P. (1996a). The cognitive approach to anxiety. In P. Salkovskis (Ed.), *The frontiers of cognitive therapy*. New York: Guilford Press, pp. 48–74.

Salkovskis, P. (1996b). Cognitive-behavioral approaches to the understanding of obsessional problems. In R. Rapee (Ed.), *Current controversies in anxiety disorders*. New York: Guilford Press, pp. 103–133.

Salkovskis, P. (1996c). Reply to Pigott *et al.* and to Enright. Understanding of obsessive-compulsive disorder is not improved by redefining it as something else. In R. Rapee (Ed.), *Current controversies in anxiety disorders*. New York: Guilford Press, pp. 191–200.

Salkovskis, P. and Warwick, H. (1986). Morbid preoccupations, health anxiety and reassurance: A cognitive behavioral approach to hypochondriasis. *Behaviour Research and Therapy*, 24, 597–602.

Salkovskis, P. and Warwick, H. (2001). Making sense of hypochondriasis: A cognitive theory of health anxiety. In G. Asmundson, S. Taylor and B. J. Cox (Eds), *Health anxiety: Clinical and research perspectives*. New York: Wiley.

Salkovskis, P. M., Rimes, K. A., Warwick, H. M. C. and Clark, D. M. (2002). The Health Anxiety Inventory: Development and validation of scales for the measurement of health anxiety and hypochondriasis. *Psychological Medicine*, 32, 843–853.

Salkovskis, P. *et al.* (1998). The cognitive behavioural approach to understanding obsessional thinking. *British Journal of Psychiatry*, 173, Supplement 35, 53–63.

Samuels, C. *et al.* (2008). Prevalence and correlates of hoarding behavior. *Behaviour Research and Therapy*, 46, 836–841.

Sanderson, R., Laverty, S. and Campbell, D. (1963). Traumatically conditioned responses acquired during respiratory paralysis. *Nature*, 196, 1235–1236.

Sanderson, W., Rapee, R. and Barlow, D. (1989). The influence of an illusion of control on panic attacks. *Archives of General Psychiatry*, 46, 157–162.

Sarason, I. G. (Ed.) (1980). *Test anxiety*. Hillsdale, NJ: Erlbaum.

Sartory, G. (1989). Obsessional-compulsive disorder. In G. Turpin (Ed.), *Handbook of clinical psychophysiology*. Chichester: Wiley, pp. 329–356.

Sartory, G., Rachman, S. and Grey, S. (1977). An investigation of the relation between reported fear and heart rate. *Behaviour Research and Therapy*, 15, 435–437.

Sbrocco, T. and Barlow, D. (1996). Conceptualizing the cognitive component of sexual arousal. In P. Salkovskis (Ed.), *The frontiers of cognitive therapy*. New York: Guilford Press.

Schmidt, A. (2004). Bottlenecks in the diagnosis of hypochondriasis. *Comprehensive Psychiatry*, 35, 306–315.

Schmidt, N. B., Telch, M. J. and Jaimez, T. L. (1996). Biological challenge manipulation of PCO levels: A test of Klein's suffocation alarm theory of panic. *Journal of Abnormal Psychology*, 105, 446–454.

Schneier, F. R. and Johnson, J. (1992). Social phobia: Comorbidity and morbidity in an epidemiological sample. *Archives of General Psychiatry*, 49, 282–288.

Seligman, M. (1970). On the generality of the laws of learning. *Psychological Review*, 77, 406–418.

Seligman, M. (1971). Phobias and preparedness. *Behavior Therapy*, 2, 307–320.

Seligman, M. (1988). Competing theories of panic. In S. Rachman and J. Maser (Eds), *Panic: Psychological perspectives*. Hillsdale, NJ: Erlbaum, pp. 321–330.

Seligman, M. and Hager, J. (Eds) (1972). *Biological boundaries of learning*. New York: Appleton Century Crofts.

Seligman, M. and Johnston, J. (1973). A cognitive theory of avoidance learning. In J. McGuigan and B. Lumsden (Eds), *Contemporary approaches to conditioning and learning*. New York: Wiley.

Seligman, M., Railton, P., Baumeister, R. and Sripanda, C. (2012). Navigating into the future or driven by the past: Prospection as an organizing principle of mind. In M. Seligman (Ed.), *Perspectives on psychological science*.

Shafran, R. and Rachman, S. (2004). Thought-action-fusion: A review. *Journal of Behavior Therapy and Experimental Psychiatry*, 35, 87–107.

Shafran, R., Thordarson, D. and Rachman, S. (1996). Thought action fusion in obsessive compulsive disorders. *Journal of Anxiety Disorders*, 10, 379–391.

Shapiro, F. (1995). *Eye-movement desensitization and reprocessing*. New York: Guilford Press.

Shapiro, L. E., Pollard, C. A. and Carmin, C. N. (1993). Treatment of agoraphobia. In T. R. Giles (Ed.), *Handbook of effective psychotherapy*. New York: Plenum Press.

Sher, K. J., Mann, B. and Frost, R. O. (1984). Cognitive dysfunction in compulsive checkers: Further explorations. *Behaviour Research and Therapy*, 22, 493–502.

Sherman, S. J., Cialdini, R. B., Schwartzman, D. F. and Reynolds, K. D. (1985). Imagining can heighten or lower the perceived likelihood of contracting a disease: The mediating effect of ease of imagery. *Personality and Social Psychology Bulletin*, 11, 118–127.

Sorensen, P., Birket-Smith, M., Wattar, U., Buemann, I. and Salkovskis, P. (2011). A randomized clinical trial of cognitive behavioural therapy versus short-term psychodynamic psychotherapy versus no intervention for patients with hypochondriasis. *Psychological Medicine*, 41, 431–444.

Sperling, M. (1971). Spider phobias and spider fantasies. *Journal of the American Psychoanalytic Association*, 19, 472–498.

Spielberger, C. D. (Ed.) (1966). *Anxiety and behavior*. New York: Academic Press.

Spielberger, C. D. (1983). *Manual for state–trait anxiety inventory*. California: Consulting Psych-Press.

Spitzer, R. L. (1991). An outsider-insider's views about revising the DSMs. *Journal of Abnormal Psychology*, 100, 294–296.

Spurr, J. and Stopa, L. (2002). Self-focused attention in social phobia and social anxiety. *Clinical Psychology Review*, 22, 947–976.

Stangier, U. *et al.* (2011). Cognitive therapy versus interpersonal therapy in social anxiety disorders. *Archives of General Psychiatry*, 68, 692–700.

Stanley, M. A. and Turner, S. M. (1995). Current status of pharmacological and behavioral treatment of obsessive-compulsive disorder. *Behavior Therapy*, 26, 163–186.

Stein, M. and Stein, D. (2008). Social anxiety disorders. *The Lancet*, 371, 1115–1125.

Steketee, G. and Frost, R. (2003). Compulsive hoarding: Current status of the research. *Clinical Psychology Review*, 23, 905–927.

Sternberger, R. T., Turner, S. M., Beidel, D. C. and Calhoun, K. S. (1995). Social phobia: An analysis of possible developmental factors. *Journal of Abnormal Psychology*, 104, 526–531.

Stouffer, S., Lumsdaine, A., Williams, R., Smith, M., Janis, I., Star, S. and Cottrell, L. (1949). *The American soldier: Combat and its aftermath*. Princeton, NJ: Princeton University Press.

Suedfeld, P. and Eich, E. (1995). Autobiographical memory under conditions of reduced environmental stimulation. *Journal of Environmental Psychology*, 15, 321–326.

Sutherland, G., Newman, B. and Rachman, S. (1982). Experimental investigations of the relations between mood and intrusive unwanted cognitions. *British Journal of Medical Psychology*, 55, 127–138.

Swinson, R., Antony, M., Rachman, S. and Richter, M. (Eds) (1998). *Obsessive compulsive disorders: Theory, research and treatment*. New York: Guilford Press.

Sy, J., Dixon, L., Lickel, J., Nelson, E. and Deacon, B. (2011). Failure to replicate the deleterious effects of safety behaviours in exposure therapy. *Behaviour Research and Therapy*, 49, 305–314.

Tang, N. K. Y., Salkovskis, P. M., Poplavskaya, E., Wright, K. J., Hanna, M. and Hester, J. (2007). Increased use of safety-seeking behaviors in chronic back pain patients with high health anxiety. *Behaviour Research and Therapy*, 45, 2821–2835.

Taylor, S. (1995). Anxiety sensitivity: Theoretical perspectives and recent findings. *Behaviour Research and Therapy*, 33, 243–258.

Taylor, S. and Rachman, S. (1994). Klein's suffocation theory of panic. *Archives of General Psychiatry*, 51, 505–506.

Taylor, S. E. and Brown, J. D. (1988). Illusion and well-being: A social psychological perspective on mental health. *Psychological Bulletin*, 103, 193–210.

Teasdale, T. (1988). Cognitive models and treatments for panic: A critical evaluation. In S. Rachman and J. Maser (Eds), *Panic: Psychological perspectives*. Hillsdale, NJ: Erlbaum, pp. 189–204.

Teasdale, J. and Barnard, P. (1993). *Affect, cognition and change*. Hove: Lawrence Erlbaum Associates Ltd.

Telch, M. (1988). Combined pharmacological and psychological treatment for panic sufferers. In S. Rachman and J. Maser (Eds), *Panic: Psychological perspectives*. Hillsdale, NJ: Erlbaum, pp. 167–188.

Thorpe, G. and Burns, L. (1983). *The agoraphobic syndrome*. Chichester: Wiley.

Thyer, B. A., Nesse, R. M., Curtis, G. C. and Cameron, O. G. (1986). Panic disorder: a test of the separation anxiety hypothesis. *Behaviour Research and Therapy*, 24, 209–211.

Tolin, D. F., Frost, R. O. and Steketee, G. (2008). Buried in treasures: Cognitive-behavioral therapy for compulsive hoarding. Paper presented at the 36th Annual Conference of the British Association for Behavioural and Cognitive Psychotherapies, July, Edinburgh, Scotland.

Treisman, A. M. (1960). Contextual cues in selective listening. *Quarterly Journal of Experimental Psychology*, 12, 242–248.

Tseng, W-S., Kan-Ming, M., Hsu, J., Li-Shuen, W., Li-Wah, R., Gui-Qian, C.

and Da-Wei, W. (1988). A sociocultural study of koro epidemics in Guangdong, China. *American Journal of Psychiatry*, 145, 1538–1543.

Tulving, E. (1983). *Elements of episodic memory*. Oxford: Oxford University Press.

Tyrer, P. (1986). Classification of anxiety disorders. *Journal of Affective Disorders*, 11, 99–104.

Valentine, C. W. (1946). *The psychology of early childhood* (3rd ed.). London: Methuen.

van Balkom, A. J. and Vorst, H. (1997). A meta-analysis of the treatment of panic disorder. *Journal of Nervous and Mental Disease*, 185, 510–516.

van Balkom, A. J., van Oppen, P., Vermeulen, A., van Dyck, R., Nanta, N. and Vorst, H. (1994). A meta-analysis on the treatment of OCD. *Clinical Psychology Review*, 14, 359–382.

van den Hout, M. (2012). How does EMDR work? *Journal of Experimental Psychopathology*, 3, 724–738.

van den Hout, M. and Kindt, M. (2003). Repeated checking causes memory distrust. *Behaviour Research and Therapy*, 41, 301–316.

van den Hout, M. and Engelhard, I. (2010). Counting during recall: Taxing of working memory and reduced vividness and emotionality of negative memories. *Applied Cognitive Psychology*, 24, 1–9.

van den Hout, M. and Engelhard, I. (2011). EMDR: Eye movements superior to beeps in taxing working memory and reducing vividness of recollections. *Behaviour Research and Therapy*, 49, 92–98.

van den Hout, M., Engelhard, I., Toffolo, M. and Uijen, S. (2011). Exposure plus response prevention vs exposure plus safety behaviour in reducing feelings of contamination, fear, danger and disgust: An extended replication. *Journal of Behavior Therapy and Experimental Psychiatry*, 42, 364–370.

Visser, S. and Bouman, T. K. (2001). The treatment of hypochondriasis: Exposure plus response prevention vs. cognitive therapy. *Behaviour Research and Therapy*, 39, 423–442.

Voncken, M., Bogels, S. and de Vries, K. (2003). Interpersonal and judgemental biases in social phobia. *Behaviour Research and Therapy*, 41, 1481–1488.

Wakefield, J. C. (1992). Disorder as harmful dysfunction: A conceptual critique of DSM-III-R's definition of mental disorder. *Psychological Review*, 99, 232–247.

Warwick, H. M. C. and Salkovskis, P. M. (1990). Hypochondriasis. *Behaviour Research and Therapy*, 28, 105–117.

Warwick, H. M. C., Clark, D. M., Cobb, A. M. and Salkovskis, P. M. (1996). A controlled trial of cognitive-behavioural treatment of hypochondriasis. *British Journal of Psychiatry*, 169, 189–195.

Watson, D. and Pennebaker, J. (1989). Health complaints and distress. *Psychological Review*, 96, 234–254.

Watson, J. and Rayner, R. (1920). Conditioned emotional reactions. *Journal of Experimental Psychology*, 3, 1–22.

Weiller, E., Bisserbe, J. C., Boyer, P., Lepine, J. P. and Lecrubier, Y. (1996). Social phobia in general health care. An unrecognised undertreated disabling disorder. *British Journal of Psychiatry*, 168, 169–174.

Weller, A. and Hener, T. (1993). Invasiveness of medical procedures and state anxiety in women. *Behavioral Medicine*, 19, 60–65.

Wells, A. and Hackmann, A. (1993). Imagery and core beliefs in health anxiety: Contents and origins. *Behavioural and Cognitive Psychotherapy*, 21, 265–273.

Wheaton, M., Abramovitz, J., Fabricant, L., Berman, N. and Franklin, J. (2011). Is hoarding a symptom of OCD? *International Journal of Cognitive Psychotherapy*, 4, 225–238.

Whittal, M., Woody, S., McLean, P., Rachman, S. and Robichaud, M. (2010). The treatment of obsessions: A randomized controlled trial. *Behaviour Research and Therapy*, 48, 295–303.

Wild, J., Hackmann, A. and Clark, D. M. (2008). Rescripting early memories linked to negative images in social phobia. *Behavior Therapy*, 39, 47–56.

Williams J., Watts, F., Macleod, C. and Mathews, A. (1988). *Cognitive psychology and emotional disorders*. Chichester: Wiley.

Williams, P. G. (2004). The psychopathology of self-assessed health: A cognitive approach to health anxiety and hypochondriasis. *Cognitive Therapy and Research*, 28, 629–644.

Wilner, A., Reich, T., Robins, I., Fishman, R. and van Doren, T. (1976). Obsessive-compulsive neurosis. *Comprehensive Psychiatry*, 17, 527–539.

Wilson, G. T. (1988). Alcohol and anxiety. *Behaviour Research and Therapy*, 26, 369–381.

Wilson, J. and Rapee, R. (2005). The interpretation of negative social events in social phobia. *Behaviour Research and Therapy*, 43, 373–389.

Wine, J. (1971). Test anxiety and direction of attention. *Psychological Bulletin*, 76, 92–104.

Wise, T. and Birket-Smith, M. (2002). The somatiform disorders for DSM-V: The need for changes in process and content. *Psychosomatics*, 43, 437–440.

Wittchen, H. and Fehm, L. (2003). Epidemiology and natural course of social fears and social phobias. *Acta Psychiatrica Scandinavica*, 108 (Supplement 417), 4–18.

Wolpe, J. (1958). *Psychotherapy by reciprocal inhibition*. Stanford, CA: Stanford University Press.

Wolpe, J. and Rachman, S. (1960). Psychoanalytic evidence: A critique based on Freud's case of Little Hans. *Journal of Nervous and Mental Diseases*, 131, 135–145.

Wolpe, J. and Rowan, V. (1988). Panic disorder: A product of classical conditioning. *Behaviour Research and Therapy*, 26, 441–450.

Woody, S. and Rachman, S. (1994). Generalized anxiety disorder (GAD) as an unsuccessful search for safety. *Clinical Psychology Review*, 14, 743–753.

Yule, W. (Ed.) (1999). *Post-traumatic stress disorders*. New York: Wiley.

Zajonc, R. (1980). Feeling and thinking. *American Psychologist*, 35, 151–175.

Zimmerman, M. (2011). A critique of the proposed prototype rating system for personality disorders in DSM 5. *Journal of Personality Disorders*, 25, 206–221.

Zitrin, C. (1986). New perspectives on the treatment of panic and phobic disorders. In B. Shaw and K. Dobson (Eds), *Anxiety disorders*. New York: Plenum.

Zohar, J., Insel, T. and Rasmussen, S. (Eds) (1991). *The psychobiology of obsessive-compulsive disorder*. New York: Springer.

Zucker, B., Craske, M., Barrios, V. and Holguin, M. (2002). Thought-action fusion: Can it be corrected? *Behaviour Research and Therapy*, 40, 653–664.

Index

Abraham, K. 70
Abramovitz, J. 142, 143
Abramowitz, J. S. 151, 155, 163, 164, 196
accessible memories 53
Acierno, R. 203
Acierno, R. E. 107
acrophobia 73, 92, 161, 162
affect 57–9
agoraphobia 20, 21, 25, 121–6; conditioned fear 122–3; ERP 161; panic and 99–100, 101, 103, 106; as prototypical neurosis 121–4; sense of safety 124; treatment 125
agoraphobic avoidance 18, 123, 125, 126
Agras, S. 20
Ahern, D. 167, 168
Ahonen, R. 155
AIDS, fear of 35, 36, 48, 132–3
Akhtar, S. 130
Alberts, N. 163, 164
alcohol/alcoholism 2; conditioned aversion to 83; conditioned nausea and 80; social phobia and 172–3
Allan, T. 189
alprazolam 117
Anastasiades, P. 103, 107, 108, 110, 111, 115, 117, 152, 164, 167, 168
Anderson, P. 177, 181
Andersson, E. 166

Andersson, G. 166
anger 7
'angst' 7
anguish 7
animals; conditioning 78, 89–90; fear of 21, 22, 23, 27, 90; fear induction in 81
anti-depressants 74, 100
anticipation of pain 17
anticipatory anxiety 172
Antony, M. 147, 161
anxiety and fear 4–8
anxiety defined 3–8
anxiety disorders 57; concept of 25–7
anxiety program 175
anxiety sensitivity 33, 81
Anxiety Sensitivity Index (ASI) 32, 33–4, 111
anxiety states 32
apprehensive hypervigilance 47
aquaphobia 21, 73, 92
Argyris, N. 85
Arntz, A. 157, 159, 201
arousal, elevated 7
Arrindell, W. 21
Asmundson, G. 1, 155
Asmundson, G. J. G. 151, 166
attention 37–8, 50
attentional capacity 45
attentional selectivity 42–3
Austin, D. 69, 116
automatic cognitive processing 58

aversion therapy 80, 83, 92
Avia, M. D. 167
avoidance behaviour 27, 39, 122;
    emotional processing and 56;
    fear, anxiety and 13–27;
    persistence of 14–15
avoidant personality disorder 173
Aylward, E. H. 75

Baer, L. 74
Bailey, E. D. 168
Bak, R. M. 79, 80, 83, 89
Baker, T. B. 80
Ballenger, J. 99
Bancroft, J. 47, 48
Bandura, A. 84, 91, 124, 161, 197
Barlow, D. H. 1, 2, 7, 15, 43, 44, 47,
    48, 61, 67, 68, 75, 90, 93, 95, 103,
    106, 107, 109, 110, 114, 115, 116,
    117, 146, 147, 172, 173, 175, 179,
    181, 184, 185, 186, 189, 192, 201,
    203
Barnard, P. 58, 59
Barrios, V. 159
Barsky, A. J. 151, 167, 168
Barta, P. E. 75
Bauer, C. 151, 169
Baumeister, R. 15
Beck, A. T. 2, 31, 37, 38, 43, 58, 61,
    67, 68,75, 90, 103, 107, 110, 112,
    113, 114, 116, 117, 125, 130, 146,
    147, 158, 175, 179, 181, 184, 189
Beck Depression Inventory (BDI)
    164, 165
Beech, H. R. 138
behaviour therapy 14, 64; in panic
    117
behavioural avoidance test 9
behavioural rehearsals 47–8
Beidel, D. C. 172
Bennett-Levy, J. 157, 201
benzodiazepines, panic and 101,
    103, 117–18
Berman, N. 142, 143
Bichard, S. 17, 160
biological theories of anxiety 73–6
biological value of anxiety 59
Birket-Smith, M. 151, 152, 164, 166,
    167
Bisserbe, J. C. 172

Bisson, J. 201
Bitterman, M. 84, 87
blocking of stimulus 88
blood, fear of 36, 55
Bodden, D. 85
bodily sensations: health anxiety
    150, 162; panic and 107–10, 113,
    116; social anxiety and 173
Bogels, S. 179, 181
Booth, R. 91, 115
Boring, E. G. 72
Bouman, T. K. 167
boundaries of fear 23–5
Bourgault-Fagnou, M. D. 153, 164
Bower, G. H. 54
Boyer, P. 172
Bradley, B. P. 52
Bredarts, R. 51, 52
Bregman, E. 80
Brewin, C. 7, 31, 33, 53, 67, 107,
    109, 157, 186, 192, 193, 195, 198,
    199, 201
Broadbent, D. E. 58
Brown, J. D. 156, 170
Brown, T. 151
Brozovich, F. 177, 179
Bryant, P. 201
Bryant, R. 27, 193, 201
Buemann, I. 152, 164, 166, 167
Bujold, A. 142, 146, 147
Bunyan, J. 134
Burgess, N. 157
Burish, T. G. 79
Burkell, J. 37
Burns, G. 159
Burns, L. 122, 123
Burstow, B. 27
Butler, G. 189

Cahill, S. 203
Cairns, E. 83
Calhoun, K. S. 172
Calvo, M. G. 31, 43, 58, 186
Cameron, O. G. 104
Campbell, D. 81, 104
Cannon, D. S. 80
Carey, M. P. 79
Carmin, C. N. 125
Carson, R. 17, 109, 124
Carter, M. M. 17, 109, 124

castration anxiety 70
catastrophic cognitions 33
catastrophic misinterpretation 113;
    about health 153
Cella, D. F. 79
Ceschi, G. 51, 52
Chambless, D. 51, 189
Chapman, T. F. 172
checking compulsions 131–2, 138,
    139; health anxiety and 160
children, fear induction in 81
Chiu, W. T. 93, 94
Cialdini, R. B. 159, 169
Cieselski, B. 160
Claparède, M. 52–3
Clark, D. 181
Clark, D. A. 31, 38, 43, 58, 61, 68,
    75, 90, 103, 107, 110, 112, 113,
    114, 116, 117, 125, 130, 146, 147,
    175, 179, 181, 184, 189
Clark, D. M. vii, 2, 31, 33, 38, 43,
    45, 58, 61, 68, 69, 73, 83, 102,
    103, 106–7, 108, 109, 110, 111,
    114, 115, 116, 117, 125, 146, 150,
    152, 157, 162, 163, 164, 165, 167,
    168, 172, 174, 175, 176, 177, 178,
    179, 180, 181, 189, 192, 199–202
Clarke, J. 125
claustrophobia 27, 161; panic and
    91, 105, 109
cleaning compulsions 131, 132–5
Clinical Global Impression (CGI)
    scale 166
Cloitre, M. 51
clompramine 118
Cobb, A. M. 152, 164, 165. 167, 168
Cobb, C. 116, 118, 147
cognitions about health 152
cognitive analyses of anxiety 67–9
cognitive analyses of panic 68
cognitive appraisal in anxiety 33
cognitive aspects of anxiety
    proneness 34
cognitive behavioural therapy 91;
    fear and 9; health anxiety 159,
    166, 167–8; panic and 103, 107,
    113, 115, 116–17, 118; social
    anxiety and 181
cognitive model: of obsessions 142;
    of OCD 150; of panic 150

cognitive panic 114
cognitive theory of health anxiety
    150, 167–70
cognitive theory of panic 2, 106–16,
    174; critique 112–16
cognitive theory of PTSD 195,
    199–202
cognitive theory of social anxiety
    174–7; evidence for 179–80
cognitive therapy 91
cognitive vulnerability 34
Coles, M. 51
combat fatigue 78
compulsions 68
compulsive behaviour 146, 147;
    characteristics 127–8, 129;
    hoarding 142–5; types 130–1
concentration 38
conditioned anxiety responses
    63–4
conditioned fear 77–8
conditioned nausea reactions 78
conditioned stimulus (CS) 87–8
conditioning 61, 68, 87–90
conditioning theory of fear 14,
    77–82; arguments against 82–5,
    92; evidence for 78–82, 92
congenital hypoventilation
    syndrome 104–5
consequences of anxiety 39
Constans, J. I. 51
contact contamination 132–5,
    136–7
Cook, E. W. 80
Costello, C. G. 21
Cottrell, L. 20
Coughtrey, A. 137, 139, 146, 160
courage 11–12
Covin, R. 189
Cox, B. J. 1, 21, 151
Craske, M. 15, 16, 17, 43, 93, 107,
    110, 112, 113, 114, 116, 159,
    161
Creed, F. 151
Crespo, M. 167
Crews, F. C. 71
Cuk, M. 46
Curtis, G. C. 104
Curtis, R. C. 176
Cuthbert, B. N. 80

Dalgleish, T. 51
Dannahy, L. 177, 179
dark, fear of 21
Darwin, Charles 85
Davey, G. 83, 90
Davies, S. 42, 102
Da-Wei, W. 85
de Jong, P. 87
de Jonghe, F. 166
 de Silva, P. 16, 93, 130, 140, 141,
     146, 161, 162, 163
de Vries, K. 179
de Vries, S. 91
Deacon, B. 160, 161
Deacon, B. J. 151, 164
Deffenbacher, J. L. 44
definition of anxiety 3–8
Dekker, J. 166
Demler, O. 93, 94
dental phobia 79, 83
depression 26; memory in 52; in
     obsessive-compulsive disorder
     147; panic and 103
Derakshan, N. 31, 43, 58, 186
desensitization 53, 90
Devilly, G. 203
Devins, G. M. 175
di Nardo, P. A. 51, 79, 80, 83, 89
Diagnostic and Statistical Manual
     of Mental Disorders (DSM) 1, 2,
     25, 26–7, 73, 96, 151, 183, 193
dichotic listening 31
Dickinson, A. 88
discomfort, fear of 48
distortions of perception 45
distribution of fears 83–4
Dixon, L. 161
Dixon, N. F. 58
dogs, fear of 79, 83, 89
driving phobia 22, 45–6
drug abuse 2
dual representation theory 195,
     198–9
Dugas, M. 161, 185, 189
Dugger, D. 74, 118
Dunker, D. 51, 52
Durham, R. C. 189
Dussault, D 138, 139, 160
dysfunctional beliefs 175
dysthymia 81

Edelmann, R. J. 48, 51
Ehlers, A. 38, 42, 83, 93, 102, 108,
     116, 179, 181, 192, 199–202
Ehlers-Clark cognitive theory 195,
     199–202
Eich, E. 54
Eisen, J. 133
Elliott, C. 142, 145
Emery, G. 2, 31, 37, 38, 61
Emmelkamp, P. 91, 181, 197
emotional processing 56, 198, 202
Engelhard, I. 152, 161, 203, 204
epidemics, fear of 155
Epstein, S. 10
equipotentiality premise 83
Erixon, G. 66
escape behaviour 39
Etzel, E. 160
ex consequentia reasoning 161
expectant dread 69
exposure and response prevention
     (ERP): in compulsive behavior
     146; health anxiety 161
exposure treatment method 125
extinction 91
eye-movement desensitization and
     reprocessing (EMDR) 202–4
Eysenck, H. J. 27, 31, 53, 61, 62–4,
     72, 73, 76, 77, 78, 81, 94, 122, 195
Eysenck, M. W. 31, 35, 42, 43, 50,
     51, 52, 58, 59, 157, 185, 186, 196

Fabricant, L. 142, 143
facial expressions, fear and 8–9
failure to acquire fear 82–3
failure, fear of 48
Fairburn, C. 107, 125
fatigue 38, 56
fear: conditioned 77–8;
     components 8–12, 27;
     conditioning theory of 14; of
     failure 48; nature of 8–12;
     subjective 8; varieties of 20–5;
     vs. anxiety 3, 5, 6–7
fear incubation 81
fear of fear 99
fear reduction techniques 47, 49, 62
fear signals 83
Fear Survey Schedule 21
fearful distortions 46

Fehm, L. 172
Fennell, M. 165, 181, 189, 201
Fenton, G. 189
Fenz, W. 10
Fergus, T. A. 151, 163
Field, A. 85
First, M. B. 27
Fishman, R. 130
Flanagan, J. 78
Foa, E. B. 51, 74, 118, 197
Follette, W. C. 27
food aversions 89
Frances, A. 27
Franklin, J. 142, 143
Franklin, M. E. 51
free-floating anxiety 6, 69
Freeston, M. 142, 146, 147, 185
Freud, S. 13, 69–71, 72, 85, 195, 196
Friedman, A. F. 27
Friedman, M. 192, 193, 201
Frost, R. O. 51, 142, 143, 145
Fulton, J. J. 153, 164, 168
Fyer, A. J. 91

Gagnon, F. 142, 146, 147, 185
Gelder, M. G. 16, 103, 107, 108, 110, 111, 115, 117, 152, 164, 167, 168, 189
generalized anxiety disorder (GAD) 6, 26, 27, 51, 183–90; boundary problems 184–6; lifetime prevalence 184; nature of 183–4; safety signals 186–9; treatment 189–90
Gerull, F. 84
Gilbert, D. 192
Gilchrist, P. 138, 139, 160
Gillespie, K. 201
Gillis, M. 189
Gino, A. 80
golden rule 16–17
Gorman, J. 102
Gorman, J. M. 117
Gorzalka, M. M. 48
Gould, R. A. 118
Gray, J. A. 54–5, 61, 64–6, 72, 73, 76, 187
Gregory, J. 157
Greist, J. H. 74

Grey, N. 181, 201
Grey, S. 80, 116, 118, 147
Grinker, R. 54
Grunbaum, A. 72
Gruter-Andrew, C. 157, 177
Gui-Qian, C. 85
Guisado, A. B. 167
Gurley, J. R. 151, 169
Gursky, D. M. 33, 81, 111
Guzy, L. T. 79, 80, 83, 89

habituation 91, 169
Hackmann, A. 103, 107, 108, 110, 111, 115, 117, 151, 152, 157, 158, 163, 164, 165, 167, 168, 169, 172, 177, 178, 181, 201
Hadjistavropoulos, H. D. 153, 155, 164
Hadjistavropolous, T. 168, 169
Hager, J. 65, 66
Hall, G. S. 69–70, 85
Hallam, R. S. 123
Halligan, S. 201
Hammersley, D. 80
Hammond, D. 131, 139, 160, 161
Hanna, M. 156, 170
Harlow, H. 15
Harris, G. J. 75
Hart, J. 10, 64, 80
Hartl, M. 142, 145
Harvey, A. G. 27, 189, 201
Hasselstrom, J. 155
Hawton, K. 110, 117, 125
health anxiety see hypochondriasis
health anxiety disorders (HAD) 149–70; assessment 163–4; cognitive biases 159–60; cognitive construal 151–2; cognitive theory 150, 167–70; OCD and 162–3; pain and 155–6; panic disorder and 162; pathways to fear 153–4; persistence 156; safety behaviour 160–1; threatening images 157–9; treatment 165–7
Health Anxiety Inventory (HAI) 163–4, 166
Health Cognitions Questionnaire 164, 168
Hedman, E. 166

heights, fear of 20, 21, 27, 86
Heimberg, R. G. 51, 116, 173, 177, 179, 181
Henderson, J. G. 172
Hener, T. 33, 42
Herbert, C. 201
Herbert, J. 203
Hersen, M. 107
Hester, J. 156, 170
Hibbert, G. A. 107
Hirsch, C. 174, 177, 179, 181
hoarding, compulsive 142–5
Hobbs, M. 201
Hodgson, R. 137, 163
Hoehn-Saric, R. 75
Hofmann, S. 175, 179, 181
Holguin, M. 159
Holland, J. C. 79
Hollander, E. 74
Hollon, S. D. 17, 109, 124, 181
Holman, R. 166
Holmes, E. 157, 195, 198, 201
Holt, C. S. 51
Hood, H. 161
Hope, D. A. 51, 181
Hornig, C. D. 100
Horowitz, M. 140
horses, fear of 71
Horwath, E. 100
Houts, A. C. 27
Hsu, J. 85
Hugdahl, K. 122
humiliation, fear of 48
hypersensitive alarms 104
hyperventilation 111–12
hypervigilance 29–31, 35, 37, 186; health anxiety 157, 159, 161
hypervigilant monitoring 43
hypochondriasis 68, 151, 155; see also health anxiety disorders (HAD)

illness/disease, fear of 21, 27, 36, 90
image-action-fusion 159
images, unwanted 157, 163
imipramine: obsessive-compulsive disorder and 74; panic and 100, 101, 103, 117, 118
implicit memory 31, 58

Improved Access to Psychological Therapies (IAPT) 118
impulsivity 64
in vivo exposures 91
inattentiveness 38
Ingram, R. E. 44, 45, 175
injury, fear of 21, 27, 83, 90
innate fear stimuli 65
insects, fear of 21, 22
Insel, T. R. 74, 75, 76, 147
interpretation of information 38
intolerance for uncertainty in generalized anxiety disorder 185–6
introversion, vulnerability and 31, 78
intrusive thoughts 139–41
Irrational Health Beliefs Scale 164, 168

Jaimez, T. L. 106
Janis, I. 20
Janis, J. L. 82
Janzen, J. A. 153, 164
Jeffery, R. 161
Jenike, M. A. 74
Jenkins, R. 20
Johnson, H. 80
Johnson, J. 100, 172
Johnson, V. E. 48
Johnston, D. W. 16, 117
Johnston, J. 15, 65
Johnston, M. 33
Jones, E. 193, 195, 196
Jones, M. C. 61
Juster, H. R. 181

Kahneman, D. 37
Kan-Ming, M. 85
Kauhanen, J. 155
Keane, T. 192, 201
Kehler, M. 163, 164
Kehler, M. D. 153, 164
Kessler, R. C. 93, 94
Kincey, J. 33, 42
Kindt, M. 139, 160
King, N. 85
Kirk, J. 110, 117, 125
Kirk, S. A. 27
Kirkpatrick, D. R. 21

Klein, D. 69, 73, 94, 95, 100, 101–6, 108, 112, 122, 123
Klein, D. F. 93
Klein, H. 100, 101, 108, 112
Klerman, G. L. 99
Knowles, K. 85
Koerner, N. 161
koro 85
Kozak, M. J. 8, 74, 118, 197
Krijn, M. 91
Kumpusalo, A. 155
Kumpusalo, E. 155
Kutchins, H. 27
Kwee, M. 21

Lader, M. 117, 118
Ladouceur, R. 142, 146, 147, 185, 189
Lang, P. J. 8, 10, 11, 21, 56, 64, 80
Last, C. G. 91
Lautch, H. 79, 83
Laverty, S. 81, 104
learned anxiety 53, 61–7
learned fears 67
learning theory 61
Leclerc, J. A. 153, 164
Lecrubier, Y. 172
Lee, M. 137
Leibowitz, M. R. 74
Leon, A. C. 2
Lepine, J. P. 172
Letarte, H. 142, 146, 147
Levin, D. N. 8
Levitt, K. 114
Lewis, A. 7, 22
Ley, R. 106
Li-Shuen, W. 85
Li-Wah, R. 85
Lickel, J. 161
Liebowitz, M. R. 51, 172, 181
Lilienfeld, S. 203
Lilienfeld, S. O. 164
Lipton, M. 157
Lish, J. D. 100
Liu, E. B. 168
Liu-Palmgren, J. 155
Livanou, M. 201
Ljótsson, B. 166
Lofberg, I. 66
Lohr, J. 203

Lopatka, C. 24, 114
loss of control, fear of 48, 154–5
Lovell, K. 201
Ludgate, J. 165
Lumsdaine, A. 20
Lunt, R. A. 159

Machlin, S. R. 75
Mackintosh, N. J. 88, 90
Macleod, C. 50, 51, 52
Mann, B. 51
Mannuzza, S. 172
Mansell, W. 181
Mäntyselkä, P. 155
Marchi, M. M. 151, 169
Marcus, D. K. 151, 153, 164, 168, 169
Margraf, J. 42, 93, 102, 107, 110, 111, 112, 114, 115, 117
Marino-Carper, T. L. 159
Marks, I. 90, 103, 117, 118, 146, 201
Marks, I. M. 84
Marks, M. 146
Marzuk, P. M. 2
Maser, J. 1
Masters, W. H. 48
Mathews, A. 16, 50, 51, 52, 117, 177, 179, 181, 201
Mathews, R. 201
Mattick, R. 125
Mavissakalian, M. 74
May, J. 52
Mayou, R. 201
McCarthy, P. R. 74, 118
McCauley, P. A. 51
McClure, E. B. 164
McDonald, B. 116, 118, 147
McDonald, S. 99
McEwan, K. L. 175
McFarlane, T. 33, 42
McGuire, P. K. 75
McLean, P. 142, 146, 147, 197, 201
McLean, R. Y. S. 118
McManus, F. 157–8, 163, 169,172, 174, 177, 178, 179, 181, 201
McMillan, T. M. 6, 18
McNally, R. J. 32, 33, 34, 43, 58, 66, 69, 80, 81, 84, 94, 106, 107, 110, 111, 112, 193, 201, 203
McNeil, D. W. 80

Melamed, B. G. 10, 64, 80
Meltzer-Brody, S. 119
memory 50–6, 59; confidence in
139; depression and 52; implicit
31, 58; in obsessive-compulsive
disorder 55; in post-traumatic
stress disorder 53; repression of
70
mental contamination 133–4, 135,
136–7
mental illness, fear of 154, 163
mental pollution 134
Menzies, R. 72, 83, 86, 87
Merckelbach, H. 85, 87
Merkey, T. 153, 164, 168
Middleton, H. 103, 107, 108, 110,
111, 115, 117, 152, 164, 167, 168
Miller, G. A. 8
Miller, K. 176
Miller, N. E. 89
Milosevic, I. 161
Mineka, S. 66, 84
misinterpretation of information
38
Mitte, K. 189
model of anxiety 29–39
Mogg, K. 52
Monson, C. 161
Montgomery, R. 203
Moore, E. L. 151, 155, 163, 196
Mortberg, R. 181
Mowrer, O. H. 13, 15, 39, 53, 61,
63–5, 122, 137, 138, 157
Mulsbosch, L. 91
Muris, P. 85, 87
Murphy, T. 189
Muse, K. 157–8, 163, 169
Myers, K. R. 74

Nakao, M. 167
Nanta, N. 146
Negy, C. 159
Nelson, E. 161
neo-conditioning 87–90
Nesse, R. M. 104
neurotic anxiety 69
neurotic paradox 157
neuroticism, vulnerability and
31
Newman, B. 141

Newth, S. 163
Nisbett, R.58, 174
non-associative fears 85–7
non-cognitive panics 114
non-conscious memorial processes
54
non-reward, behavioural effects of
65
Norton, R. 1, 189
Noshirvani, H. 201
Noyes, R. 99, 163

O'Donohue, W. 203
objective anxiety 69
obsessions 68; characteristics
127–8, 129; cognitive theory of
142
obsessive-compulsive disorder
(OCD) 26, 27, 36, 43, 51; affect
and 57; age of onset 130; anxiety
and 145–6; biological theories of
73–6; definition 127; gender and
130; health anxiety and 158,
162–3; hoarding and 142–5;
memory in 55;
misinterpretation 43; panic in
93; persistence 135–9;
prevalence 129–30; reducing
hypervigilance 37; self-focused
attention 43; serotonin theory of
74–6; treatment 146–7; see also
compulsive behaviour;
obsessions
OED 151, 165
Oedipus complex 70–1
off-duty/on-duty contrast 37
Ohman, A. 65, 66, 80
Olatunji, B. O. 151, 160, 164
Olivares, M. E. 167
Oliveau, D. 20
Ollendick, T. 85
Ondine's curse 104–5
onset of fear 84
ordinary memory system 198
Ost, L. G. 70, 72, 80, 84, 90, 91, 115,
122
Otto, M. W. 118, 119, 147
over-prediction: of fear 16, 17–20;
of panic 19
Owens, M. 155

pain: fear of 48; health anxiety and 155–6
Palace, E. E. 48
panic 5; bodily sensations, misinterpretation of 107–10, 113, 116; cognitive analyses of 68; cognitive theory of 2, 106–16, 174; definition 93; duration 97; experience of 97–9; incidence 99–100; induction 101–2, 103, 110, 113; nocturnal 112, 113–14; psychological induction 103–4; risk of relapse 117–18, 119; sensations/feelings 93, 94–7; spontaneous 100, 101, 103; suffocation alarm theory 103–6; treatment, 115, 116–19; vulnerability 111–12
panic attack 93, 104, 107, 123
panic disorder 25, 27, 37, 51, 68, 94; avoidance behaviour 14–15; biological theories of 73; distinctiveness of 100–1; health anxiety and 162; misinterpretation 43; revised theory of (Klein) 103–6; safety signs 38; selective attention 42; self-focused attention 43; theory of (Klein) 100–3
panic episode 93
Papini, M. 84, 87
parachuting, anticipation of fear in 10, 18
parental anxiety 41–2
Parkinson, L. 41, 140
Parrish, C. L. 161
Paul, G. 9–10
Pavlov, I. P. 13, 195
Pavlovian conditioning 89
Pearlson, P. D. 75
Peekna, H. M. 168
Peen, J. 166
Pennebaker, J. W. 156, 167
perception 45–7
perceptual defence 31
perceptual distortions 45
Perroud, A. 51, 52
Pershad, D. 130
personality models: Eysenck 62–4, 76; Gray 64–7, 76

personality theory 61
Peters, L. 125
Peterson, R. A. 33, 81, 111
phenelzine 181
Philips, H. C. 19, 156, 157, 159, 178
phobias 4, 69; definition 3, 62; see also under types
Pigott, T. M. 74
Pillay, S. 201
Pincus, H. A. 27
Pollack, M. H. 119
Pollack, S. 118, 119, 147
Pollard, C. A. 125, 172
Ponniah, K. 181
Pontillo, D. 17
Poplavskaya, E. 156, 170
Portera, L. 2
post-event processing 161, 176–7, 179
post-mortem ruminations, social anxiety and 177, 179
post-traumatic stress disorder (PTSD) 26, 27, 51, 78–9, 83, 191–204; concept of 192–3; cognitive theory 199–202; delayed-onset 193, 200; dual representation theory 198–9; emotional processing of traumatic events 195–7; explanations 194–5; eye-movement desensitization and reprocessing (EMDR) 202–4; features 191–2; memory in 53; origins 191; precipitating event, evidence of 194; reminiscences of events 195; signs and symptoms 192
Poulton, R. 72, 83, 86, 87
Powers, M. 91, 181, 197
Powers, M. B. 161
Pratt, A. 79
prediction of panic 19
preoccupying thoughts 145
prepared fears/phobias 54, 66–7, 69, 80
Price, E. 189
Price, M. 177, 181
Prigatano, G. 80
primal threat mode 68

Proust, M. 131
psychoanalytical explanations
    69–73
psychophysiological theory (Gray)
    64–7, 76
psychosexual problems 48–9
public space phobia 10, 16
public speaking anxiety 6, 10, 172
public transport phobia 10, 16
punishment, behavioural effects of
    65

Rachman, S. 6, 9, 11, 16, 17, 18, 19,
    20, 24, 37, 39, 41, 46, 51, 52, 53,
    55, 56, 61, 62, 63, 64, 67, 68, 71,
    72, 78, 80, 82, 83, 84, 85, 86, 87,
    90, 91, 93, 103, 104, 105, 108,
    114, 115, 116, 117, 118, 124,
    130, 131, 132, 133, 135, 137,
    138, 139, 140, 141, 142, 145,
    146, 147, 152, 153, 157, 158, 159,
    160, 161, 162, 163, 164, 176, 177,
    186, 187, 188, 193, 195, 196, 197,
    201
Radomsky, A. 51, 52, 55, 131, 138,
    139, 142, 145, 146, 152, 160,, 161,
    176
rage 12
Railton, P. 15
random control of stimulus 88
Rapee, R. 7, 51, 84, 109, 172, 173,
    179
Rapee, R. M. 189
Rapoport, J. 74, 75
Rasjo-Wraak, G. 155
Rasmussen, S. 74, 133, 147
Rassin, E. 158
Rauner, M. 159
Rayner, R. 61, 80
reciprocal inhibition 64, 91
Reich, T. 130
Reiss, S. 32, 33, 81, 111
relaxation 49
repression of memory 70
repugnance 12
Rescorla, R. A. 88, 89, 90
Resick, P. 191, 192, 193, 201
Resick, P.A. 26, 201
Revusky, S. 89
Reynolds, K. D. 159, 169

Rheaume, J. 142, 146, 147
Richard, K. 189
Richards, D. 201
Richards, J. 69, 116
Richter, M. 147
Rickels, K. 99
Rimes, K. A. 63
Ritter, M. 161
Robichaud, M. 142, 146, 147, 185,
    189, 197, 201
Robins, I. 130
Robson, P. 189
Rode, H. 155
Rosen, G. 203
Rosenbaum, J. F. 119
Roth, W. 42, 93, 102
Rowan, V. 108, 112, 113, 114
Rück, C. 166
Ruhe, H. 166
Ruiz, M. A. 167
Rush, A. J. 67

Sabatino, S. 118, 119, 147
Sacadura, C. 179, 181
safety behaviour in health anxiety
    160–1
safety signal hypothesis 17, 38, 65,
    186–9
Saigh, P. A. 83
Saintfort, R. 168
Salkovskis, P. M. 2, 58, 61, 68, 74,
    103, 107, 108, 110, 111, 115, 117,
    125, 138, 139, 140, 141, 146, 149,
    150, 151, 152, 156, 159, 161, 162,
    163, 164, 165, 166, 167, 168,
    170
Samson, D. 159, 178
Samuels, C. 143
Sanchez, A. 167
Sanderson, R. 81, 104
Sanderson, W. 109
Sanderson, W. C. 15, 51
Santos, R. 31, 43, 58, 186
Sarason, I. G. 43, 49, 50
Sartory, G. 80, 116, 118, 147
Sbrocco, T. 48
Schmidt, A. 151
Schmidt, N. B. 106
Schneier, F. R. 172, 181
Schuemle, M. 91

Schwartzman, D. F. 159, 169
scoline 81
selective attention 42–3, 58;
    memory and 54
selective perception 45
selective serotonin reuptake
    inhibitors (SSRIs) 74, 75
self-contamination 134
self-focused attention 43–5, 48, 59
Seligman, M. 15, 54–5, 65, 66, 70,
    72, 80, 83, 87, 100, 112, 113, 114
separation, fears of 21
serotonin theory of
    obsessive-compulsive disorder
    74–6
sexual anxiety 6, 21, 43, 47–9
Shafran, R. 137, 139, 140, 142, 145,
    146, 152, 157, 159, 160, 161, 176,
    177
Shapiro, F. 202, 203
Shapiro, L. E. 125
Sharpe, D. 153, 163, 164
Shear, M. K. 117
Shelton, R. C. 17, 109, 124
Sher, K. J. 51
Sherman, S. J. 159, 169
Shinozaki, Y. 167
short-term psychodynamic
    therapy (SSTP) 166
situational anxiety 172
situational memories 53
situationally accessible memory
    (SAM) system 198
Smeets, M. 203
Smith, M. 20
Smits, J. A. 161
snakes, fear of 3, 4, 6, 9, 20, 22–4,
    46, 66, 69, 70, 84, 86, 90, 161
social anxiety (social phobia) 6, 26,
    27, 43, 44, 47, 51, 68, 90, 171–82;
    cognitive theory of 174–7;
    definition 171–4, 182; multiple
    problems in 173–4; negative
    images 177–8; panic in 93;
    self-focused attention 43;
    treatment 180–1; within anxiety
    framework 180
social fears 21, 27
social phobia see social anxiety
Solyom, C. 16, 161

Sorensen, P. 152, 164, 166, 167
specific phobias 90–1; see also under
    types
Spence, S. 179,. 203
Sperling, M. 70
spiders, fear of 4, 21, 22, 23, 24.26.
    46, 70, 84, 161
Spiegel, J. 54
Spielberger, C. D. 32
Spitzer, R. L. 27
spontaneous decay of anxiety 138
spontaneous remission 63
Spurr, J. 179
Sripanda, C. 15
Stangier, U. 181
Stanley, M. A.146, 147
Star, S. 20
state anxiety 32, 33
State-Trait Anxiety Inventory
    (STAI) 32, 33
Statham, S. 33, 42
Stein, D. 172
Stein, M. 172
Steketee, G. 143
Steketee, G. S. 74, 118
Sternberger, R. T. 172
Stopa, L. 177, 179
Storch, E. 143
Stouffer, S. 20
stress management training (SMT)
    165–6
subliminal perceptions 58
Suedfeld, P. 54
suffocation alarm 130–6
summation of fears 24–5
Sundin, C. 181
Surawy, C. 172
Sussman, N. 99
Sutherland, G. 141
Swinson, R. 147
Sy, J. 161
Sylvester, D. 20
systematic desensitization 47, 49,
    64, 158

tachistoscope presentations 31
Tallman, K. 16, 161
Tang, N. K. Y. 156, 170
Tarrier, N. 201
Taylor, S. 32, 33, 34, 104, 105, 151

Taylor, S. E. 156, 170
Teasdale, J. 58
Teasdale, T. 112, 113
Telch, M. 15
Telch, M. J. 106, 107, 110, 114, 115, 117, 161
test anxiety 43–4, 47, 48; self-focused attention 43
Thematic Apperpercetion Test (TAT) 73
therapeutic modelling 91
Thibodeau, N. 142, 146, 147
Thordarson, D. 159
Thorpe, G. 122, 123
thought action fusion 140, 159
thoughts: intrusive 139–41; preoccupying 145
Thyer, B. A. 104
Tiffany, S. T. 80
Toffolo, M. 152, 161
Tolin, D. F. 143, 203
Tomarken, A. 160
trait anxiety 32, 33, 34
traumatic conditioning 195
Treisman, A. 37
Treisman, A. M. 58
Treliving, L. 189
Tseng, W-S. 85
Tulving, E. 58
tunnels, fear of 21
Turner, S. M. 146, 147, 172
two-dimensional model of personality (Eysenck) 62–4, 76
two-stage theory of anxiety (Mowrer) 13, 15, 137
Tyrer, P. 103

Uijen, S. 152, 161
unconditioned stimulus (US) 13, 63, 84, 87–8, 195
unconscious anxiety 6
under-predictions: of fear 18; of panic 19
unemployment 2

Valentine, C. W. 80
Valentiner, D. P. 151, 163
van Balkom, A. J. 125, 146
van den Hout, M. 87, 139, 152, 159, 160, 161, 203, 204

van der Ende, J. 21
van der Linden, M. 51, 52
van Doren, T. 130
van Dyck, R. 146
Van Hasselt, V. B. 107
van Oppen, P. 146
verbal information, transmission of fear by 85
verbally inaccessible memory (VAM) system 198
Verma, N. 130
Verma, S. K. 130
Vermeulen, A. 146
vicarious acquisition of fears 84
Viinamäki, H. 155
Visser, S. 167
Voncken, M. 179
Vorst, H. 125, 146
vulnerability 31–4; introversion and 31, 78; panic and 111–12

Waddington, L. 181, 201
Wakefield, J. A. Jr. 27
Wakefield, J. C. 27
Walters, E. E. 93, 94
Warwick, H. M. C. 107, 149, 150, 151, 152, 161, 162, 163, 164, 165, 167, 168
washing compulsions 132–5
water, fear of 21; see also aquaphobia
Watson, D. 167
Watson, J. 61, 80
Wattar, U. 152, 164, 166, 167
Watts, F. 50, 51, 52
Weiller, E. 172
Weismann, M. M. 100
Weller, A. 33, 42
Wells, A. 45, 151, 157, 158, 165, 174, 175, 176, 180
Westling, B. 115
Wheaton, M. 142, 143
Whittal, M. 91, 115, 142, 146, 147, 197, 201
Wig, N. 130
Wild, J. 178, 181, 201
Williams J. 50, 51, 52
Williams, D. A. 74
Williams, M. 157–8, 163, 169
Williams, P. G. 164

Williams, R. 20, 52, 177
Wilner, A. 130
Wilson, G. T. 117, 172
Wilson, R. 83
Wilson, T. 58, 174
Wine, J. 49
Winslow, J. T. 74, 75, 147
Wise, S. P. 75
Wise, T. 151
Wistedt, A. 181
Wittchen, H. 172
Woerner, M. G. 93
Wolpe, J. 47, 53, 61, 62, 64, 71,
   72, 76, 78, 90, 94, 108, 112,
   113, 114, 122, 164, 178, 195,
   203
Woods, S. 99
Woods, S. W. 117
Woody, S. 142, 146, 147, 187, 188,
   197, 201

World War II, overprediction of
   panic 19–20, 22, 82
worriers, chronic see generalized
   anxiety disorder
Wright, C. 161
Wright, K. J. 156, 170

Yale–Brown Obsessive
   Compulsive
   Scale–Hypochondriasis
   (YBOCS–HC) 165
Yule, W. 192

Zajonc, R. 57, 58
Zimmerman, M. 27
Zitrin, C. 103
Zitrin, C. M. 93
Zohar, J. 74, 147
Zucker, B. 159
Zysk, E. 152, 161